ST NEOTS
AND THE
GREAT WAR

Kenneth Ward

ST NEOTS
AND THE
GREAT WAR

KENNETH WOOD

FOREWORD BY SUE JARRETT

THE CHAIRMAN OF THE EATONS COMMUNITY ASSOCIATION

First published 2010

The History Press
The Mill, Brimscombe Port
Stroud, Gloucestershire, GL5 2QG
www.thehistorypress.co.uk

British Library Cataloguing in Publication Data.
A catalogue record for this book is available from the British Library.

ISBN 978 0 7524 5588 4

Typesetting and origination by The History Press
Printed in Great Britain
Manufacturing managed by Jellyfish Print Solutions Ltd

CONTENTS

FOREWORD

This book is clearly the result of years of painstaking local and national research and displays an extensive knowledge of the Great War and its impact on the local area.

The town of St Neots, which includes the three parishes of St Neots, Eynesbury and Eaton Socon, is fortunate that Kenneth has written this book which details the events of the Great War in chronological order and puts the lives and deaths of local men in their context within the war. More than 180 men from the three parishes lost their lives, together with almost thirty from the outlying villages, and Kenneth has been able to add snippets of life which continued within the local area while the men fought in the battle zones of Europe and beyond.

We should all be grateful that Kenneth has shared his wealth of knowledge of the Great War with us, providing a deeper understanding of the effect that the war had on the families living within the town of St Neots and its surrounding villages and farms.

Kenneth has been a resident of the town for several years, and his in-depth knowledge and his willingness to share it was a great help when we wrote our own book (*To the Glorious Memory*) on the men of Eaton Socon who gave their lives in the war. This new book will be a most welcome addition to the history of the town of St Neots and the local area.

Sue Jarrett, 2010
Local Historian and Chairman of the Eatons Community Association

Kenneth Wood explaining the significance of the Lochnagar Crater on the Somme to a group of 'battlefield tourists'.

ACKNOWLEDGEMENTS

For almost seventeen years, as I drove to work to teach in Biggleswade, I passed the War Memorial on the Green at Eaton Socon, often thinking about the men whose names were inscribed there, and wondering what their stories were. As I grew to know the St Neots area more, I sought out the War Memorial in Church Walk in the town where the same thoughts came to mind – who were these people and what happened to them?

My first book, *Biggleswade and the Great War*, took me almost five years to compile and taught me valuable lessons in how to research and write, and when it was finished I felt that I would like to write the same kind of book about the place I had lived in since 1991. The History Press was kind enough to commission this second book and its completion has been helped considerably by the following people, whom I should like to thank: David Bushby, St Neots Local History Society President, for his help and support; Dave and Sue Jarrett, Eaton Socon Community Association, for permission to use many of the Eaton Socon photographs in this book, and their considerable help with the first names of many of the soldiers from the area; the *St Neots Advertiser*, which was a main source for the writing of this book, and news of soldiers in its pages usually only saw the use of surname and initial; Bob Murdoch, Norris Museum, St Ives for permission to use the Great War archive there, and for the photograph of the St Neots Defence Volunteers; Karen Usher, Nigel Cutts, Sarah Carrington, Faith Back, Christine Rhoden, Hazel Presland, Brian George, Jim Hawkins, Colin Pope, David Payne, Michael Clenshaw, Terry Reynolds, Angela Fisher, Graham Usher, Alex Lees, Neil Haynes, Cat Lougher, John Cotton, Sarah Hicks, Paul Blake and Clive Gilbert for allowing me to use photographs of relatives, soldiers or headstones featured in the book; Rodney Todman for permission to use the photographs of the Hunts Cyclists in St Neots Market Square, taken by Horace Clarabut in 1914; Billy Doey for his help in improving the quality of some of the older photographs; Mark Thody for his help with photographs and maps; Graham Crust for his help with photographs; Jane Hunter for proof reading the book; The History Press, especially Nicola Guy, my commissioning editor and Jenny Briancourt, the editorial assistant, for their continued support and hard work in helping bring about the publication of this book; the staff of St Neots Library; Steve Fuller of the Bedfordshire Regiment website for his help and support; and my dear wife, Shirley, for all of her help, support and not least, patience. Quite how she endures my addiction to the Great War is sometimes beyond my comprehension!

St Neots and the surrounding villages saw over 200 men lose their lives during the Great War. Their generation was the first to experience a World War and, as I researched this book and read so many of the letters that they and other soldiers sent home, my admiration for them grew. It is hard to imagine what they and their families went through. I hope that this is a fitting tribute to them.

INTRODUCTION

The Great War has now passed from living memory within Britain, as Harry Patch and Henry Allingham, the last two surviving men to have fought, have both reached the end of their extraordinary lives; their demise has severed any remaining actual link with the monumental events of 1914-1918. Harry Patch was the last man alive to have experienced trench warfare, having been conscripted and then wounded during the Third Battle of Ypres in 1917. Henry Allingham's war was varied to say the least, for this volunteer saw action at the Battle of Jutland with the Royal Naval Air Service, and then with the newly-formed Royal Air Force. However, with the deaths of these two remarkable men, it seems highly unlikely that there will be a falling away of interest in the Great War. Indeed their passing may well spark even greater interest in a war that continues to hold the public's attention.

So where does this fascination with the Great War come from? Clearly the growing popularity of researching family history, and the impact of television programmes such as *Who Do You Think You Are?*, have had a profound effect. The Internet, with its ease as a tool for research, has also had a significant impact upon this continuing interest in the Great War. The subject remains very newsworthy, and both television and newspapers continue to broadcast and report stories relating to the First World War. Archaeological finds, such as the recent one at Fromelles, attract television coverage from across the world, and the recent discovery of Red Cross records in Switzerland may even enable us to locate the actual burial places of many soldiers who are presently commemorated on the memorials of the Western Front. Both Henry Allingham's and Harry Patch's funerals received extended national television coverage. The Commonwealth War Graves Commission and the Western Front Association have dedicated education sections on their websites to help families find out more about ancestors who fought or died during the four and a half years of conflict.

Anyone who has travelled through Northern France and Belgium, and has seen the many Commonwealth War Graves cemeteries, cannot have failed to be touched by the sheer number of white headstones. Martin Middlebrook, the renowned historian, began his writing career after visiting the Somme in 1967 where he was deeply moved by the experience. For him it was a life-changing event and, without any literary background, he decided to interview remaining survivors and tell their story in *The First Day on the Somme*. Visitors to the battlefields continue to be so moved. Memorials such as those at Thiepval, Menin Gate and Tyn Cot have become popular tourist venues, and those who visit rarely fail to find their own surname among those inscribed on these 'Silent Cities'. Indeed a whole industry of battlefield tourism has grown and concentrates upon remembrance and the Great War.

Different schools of historians continue to put forward their views regarding the justification – or not – of the Great War, and its presence in the National Curriculum provides another outlet for its continued study. Very few families fail to find a link with the First World War and research often reveals long-lost great uncles. My own was killed on the Somme in 1916 and I have been able to locate and visit his grave in France, as well as finding exact details of his service record. During my career as a teacher, I was fortunate to teach the Great War to A-Level students and to lead visits to the battlefields of the Western Front. Every student who accompanied me was visibly moved by what they saw and experienced.

My first book, *Biggleswade and the Great War*, allowed me to tell the story of how that conflict affected the town where I taught for seventeen years. Now, the time has come to try to do the same for the town I have lived in since 1991, and the following pages attempt to show how the First World War impacted upon the soldiers from the town and those they left behind.

Kenneth Wood, 2010

ONE

~1914~
A CALL TO ARMS

For a small market town such as St Neots, the annual regatta was an important occasion and hopes were high that the 1914 event would attract a good number of competitors, together with healthy numbers of spectators for the Bank Holiday, Monday 3 August. Teams from London and the Midlands were usually present and the list of entrants was not disappointing, including crews from Britannia Rowing Club, Clapton Warwick, Mildmay, and Spartan Rowing Club. As the day progressed, the weather turned from sunshine to heavy showers to more sunshine, and then back to showers. The record-breaking turnout of crews entertained spectators from 10 a.m. to 8 p.m., with many of the races seeing very close finishes. By the end of the regatta, the thoughts of competitors and spectators alike would have been moving towards events in Europe and the increasing possibility of war. On the previous day, Germany had issued an ultimatum to Belgium demanding that its troops should be allowed to pass through their country. The Belgians refused and began to prepare to defend themselves as German troops crossed the border. Britain was about to be drawn in, for she was committed to the defence of Belgium by the Treaty of London, signed some seventy-five years earlier, and on the following day the Cabinet delivered its own ultimatum to Germany. Prime Minister Asquith addressed the House of Commons as follows:

> We have repeated the request made last week to the German Government that they should give us the same assurance in regard to Belgian neutrality that was given to us and Belgium by France last week. We have asked that it should be given before midnight.

Events had been put in motion just over a month earlier with the assassination of Franz Ferdinand on 28 June in Sarajevo. It was true that the archduke's murder caused shock and outrage, but Europe had survived earlier crises during the first fourteen years of the century and the move towards war did not seem immediate, for it was summer and the harvest had more importance for most countries. However, throughout July the international crisis grew. The people of Britain were very well informed, for all of the popular national newspapers were reporting what was unfolding in the capital cities of the Great Powers: Vienna, Belgrade, Berlin, Paris, London and Moscow. Even local newspapers such as the *St Neots Advertiser* and the *Hunts Post* kept their readers well abreast of the momentous events taking place in Europe. The smell of war was in the air, and any ensuing conflict would provide the opportunity for Germany to be put in its place – a view that was welcomed by a considerable majority of the British people, who felt that Germany was intent upon challenging Britain's position as a Great

Power and, more importantly, threatening the Empire. The battleship building programme that Germany had embarked upon in the first decade of the century had provoked a fierce response in Britain, and was seen as an outright challenge to British sea power. It is easy to see, therefore, why the popular press supported the British Government's issue of an ultimatum to Germany, and every national newspaper's editorial column, apart from the *Daily Herald*'s, spoke in favour of fighting. Encouraged by the popular press, many felt strongly that Belgian neutrality should be guaranteed and certainly was worth fighting for. The British ultimatum ran out at 11 p.m. BST on Monday 3rd and when no response was received, Britain, for the first time in almost a century, prepared to take part in a European war.

In St Neots, as well as the regatta another event had taken place over the Bank Holiday weekend, and this was the ominously labelled 'Hospital Parade', where a collection was made for the Hunts County Hospital. The parade was the culmination of a week of house-to-house collecting in both the town and the surrounding villages and, on Sunday, it made its way through the town for a service in the parish church. Here Canon Hodgson spoke at length and with great feeling, saying that many of the congregation would already be aware of how close to war Britain might be, and asking them to pray 'very seriously and earnestly to their Father in Heaven to avert this awful catastrophe'.

If the mood in the parish church was reflective with a sense of impending tragedy, then the events taking place in London on the evening of 3 August were very different, for an estimated crowd of 100,000 had gathered before Buckingham Palace to show their support for both King and Country. The royal family appeared twice on the balcony of the palace and was greeted with wild enthusiasm at 8 p.m., and again after 11 p.m., following no German response to the British ultimatum. The National Anthem rang out from the assembled multitude, followed by clapping and cheering as the King, Queen and Prince of Wales emerged. There was no lack of fervour for war here.

In St Neots, the thirst for information about the war was strong and crowds waited at the railway station for the delivery of the national papers from London. Indeed the war seemed to be the focus of all interest in the town, with the *St Neots Advertiser* reporting that the progress of events had been watched with the keenest anxiety, but that it was felt by all classes that the government's action was the only one consistent with the honour of the country. Also arriving in St Neots by telegraph were mobilisation orders, which were quickly delivered on Tuesday evening. Those called up were 'Reservists', men with army experience who had served for seven years and had then gone 'onto reserve' for a further five years. The majority of these Reservists were with the Bedfordshire Regiment but other men also were called up. These were Territorials, men with full-time jobs who had joined the Territorial Army and had received training at weekends and once a year at camp. The vast majority of the Territorials from St Neots belonged to the recently formed, 500 strong, Hunts Cyclist Battalion. These men, together with the 5th Bedfordshire Territorial Battalion, received their mobilisation orders on Tuesday evening and left the town by special train on Thursday 6 August. The Hunts Cyclists were dispatched to Grimsby, where they would be employed guarding the East Coast against possible German attack or invasion. Lastly, call-up papers were received by men of the Beds Imperial Yeomanry, a mounted Territorial force whose orders were to prepare for departure.

If the Hunts Cyclist Battalion was to guard against possible Germanic incursion in Lincolnshire, then St Neots itself was about to encounter a group of Germany's allies, when surprisingly, an Austrian band arrived in the town on the Thursday morning. These musicians were on tour and they seemed quite unconcerned by international events, performing a number of musical pieces in the Market Square. Before the atmosphere could change, they were advised by Inspector Storey to move on and were last seen heading out of town towards Cambridge. These unfortunate musicians were in a dilemma, for they had no money to return to Austria, and were unwelcome in England. They turned up later that day in Huntingdon where they

Above and below: Hunts Cyclists leaving St Neots Market Square for the railway station – August 1914.

Hunts Cyclists leaving St Neots Market Square for the railway station. (Horace Clarabut)

received a hostile reception and were soon sent packing, with only a few coppers from the more generous members of the audience. The *Hunts Post* newspaper mistakenly reported that they had been 'mobbed' out of St Neots, and had made their way to Godmanchester and thence on to Huntingdon.

The local population quickly experienced the country going to a war footing, with shortages and price rises coming into effect. The impact of the war was also seen, as petrol doubled in price and became almost unobtainable in the first few days of the conflict. Those with cars or motorcycles now had to pay 3*s* or 4*s* a gallon, if they could find a retailer willing to sell to the public. As well as petrol, there was a significant increase in the price of bread, with a 2lb loaf rising a farthing to 3*d*. £1 and £10 notes were also issued and the public were advised to accept and use them instead of gold. Local interests were furthermore made quite clear when grocers in the town announced that they would continue to supply their regular customers and refuse to supply large quantities of groceries to wealthy people, who generally bought from London stores.

On 7 August the *St Neots Advertiser*, in its column 'The War', advised its readers not to panic: 'Englishmen and Englishwomen should not lose their heads but take things quietly and calmly, and not make things worse for their poorer neighbours by hoarding gold or provisions.' The same edition also urged local men to respond to the call for volunteers from the Prime Minister, Herbert Asquith, and encouraged its male readers with the following words:

> More men are urgently wanted for our Army. Surely there are many young men in this district who will esteem it a privilege to join the ranks of the defenders of their homeland. We must not be behind the rest of the country.

On Wednesday 10 August, Downing Street announced that the Prime Minister was giving up his post as Secretary of State for War because of the pressure of his other duties as leader of the country. He was replaced by Lord Kitchener, who realised that the British Army was too small to fight a major Continental war and quickly put in place the famous recruitment drive with its equally celebrated poster 'Your country needs you'.

If the Kitchener poster pointed out what the country needed, then the first few weeks of August also revealed what the country thought it didn't need; there were spy scares galore, which the press eagerly reported. Those reading both the local and the national press would have believed that Britain was a hotbed of German espionage, for spy stories abounded. Some were real, for Germany had set up a spy network in Britain before the war, but its existence had been discovered by British Intelligence and these spies were rounded up quickly and placed in prison. At later stages of the fighting, another eleven German spies were landed in Britain but they were not well trained and were promptly arrested. They were imprisoned, put on trial, found guilty, executed by firing squad in the Tower of London and then buried in East London at Plaistow.

Spy stories made people nervous and there were examples of this locally. Ernest Edmund Hunt who lived in Ermine Street, Huntingdon was employed by one of the local motor works and he was very indignant when he was accused of being a German. The *Hunts Post* newspaper possibly aggravated the situation when it included the following paragraph in its 'Local War News' section on 14 August:

DO YOU KNOW A GERMAN?
Notice has been issued by the Chief Constable calling upon householders to immediately inform the police if they have anybody of German employ resident with them. Useful service can also be given by supplying the names and addresses of any German who may be known to reside in the county.

Locally there was suspicious activity. In Huntingdon it was reported that a stranger had been noticed making notes near the town bridge, and then later the same kind of report came from Little Stukeley. As it happened this turned out to be a false alarm, for the man in question was a journalist making notes in relation to a story he was about to write. The situation did not stop rumours spreading and many believed that a German spy had been caught. In Warboys, panic bells started to ring after it was discovered that a wire on the railway had been deliberately cut, and another wire showed marks of having been interfered with. After investigation by the police and the military authorities, though, it was decided that this was not the work of spies but that 'the damage had been perpetuated in a spirit of bravado'.

Two weeks later, the whole spy scare took on almost comic proportions when Frank Heathcote, a dealer from Brampton, appeared before the Huntingdon Divisional Magistrates' Bench. He had challenged a Scottish Territorial, George Duthie, accusing him of being a German even though the soldier was in uniform. Frank Heathcote had even raised his shotgun. Under oath, Private Duthie said that the accused had said to him: 'I am afraid that you are a German and I will shoot you.' When cross-examined, Frank Heathcote explained: 'He had a very funny accent and I took him for a German!'

Not far away, in St Ives, a local man found himself challenged as he tried to enter a building that was under military control. When he was evasive with his answers the police were called, but the arriving officer recognised the man and conducted him away. This individual was lucky that he was not fired upon but the incident shows just how nervous people were, as the *St Neots Advertiser* of 14 August reported. In Southall, a railway engine cleaner was on his way to work at the locomotive yard when he was challenged by a sentry. He failed to hear the challenge and the sentry fired, wounding the man in the left arm. Emotions were running high and, 25 miles to the north of St Neots, riots broke out in Peterborough where German-owned shops were wrecked, and a public house was stoned after the licence holder was supposed to have made disparaging remarks about the local Territorials. Order was not restored for a day.

In St Neots, representatives of the War Office arrived during the second week of August and began assessing what could be used for the war effort. For three years the War Office had been preparing for the possibility of war and had compiled the War Book, a comprehensive document that included details of how the rail network was to be taken over, how workhorses and vehicles were to be commissioned, and how Reservists were to be recalled. The War Book also included details of counter-espionage, trade with enemy states, censorship, and the guarding of key points. The War Office commissioners who arrived in St Neots were instructed to assess the suitability of both horses and vehicles for service at home and abroad, and, if they reached the required standard, they were purchased. One St Neots business saw ten of its fifteen vehicles commissioned and Howard Lynn's only motor lorry was commandeered for use by the army. The horses that were commissioned were destined for either haulage work or possibly as mounts for army officers. One of the commissioners, Mr A. Jordan, described the attitude of the people of St Neots to this enforced purchase of their animals as 'splendid', telling how horses had been given up willingly, and how the owners had never questioned the price, except to say that they hoped he wouldn't pay them too much.

Whilst this was occurring in many towns such as St Neots, the opening moves of the war were taking place in Europe, as both Germany and France moved their armies into the field. The German High Command was acutely aware that these first few weeks of fighting were crucial if victory was to be achieved. Geographically Germany was at a disadvantage, for two of her main enemies were on her eastern and western borders, with another just across the North Sea. In reality this could mean having to fight a major war on each of those fronts which would stretch her resources greatly, especially if the British Navy blockaded her ports. Germany had realised that such a situation was parlous, and as early as 1899 had come up with a solution to this via the Schlieffen Plan. Mobility and speed were the key components of this plan by which Germany would attack and defeat France before Russia was ready to move. For this to work, though, German troops would have to go through neutral Belgium, and so bypass the heavily fortified frontier with France. Quite understandably, the Belgians were unhappy with the thought of thousands of German soldiers passing through their country and denied them access.

The French themselves were still smarting following their defeat at German hands just over forty years earlier during the Franco-Prussian War when they had lost Alsace and Lorraine. By Plan XVII they intended to recover these provinces, vanquish Germany and remove the national shame of the debacle of the Franco-Prussian War. The French felt that this could best be achieved through out-and-out attack, but their hopes for victory had failed to take into consideration just how warfare had developed since 1871. Germany had quickly invested in the machine-gun and artillery, and these two deadly components of a modern industrialised war reaped a terrible harvest of the attacking French, so distinctive in their blue tunics and red trousers. Casualties for the French were huge; not least among their officers who were expected to set an example and lead from the front. Ten per cent of the officer corps of the French Army was killed as Plan XVII was carried out without success, with over 200,000 casualties suffered in the first four weeks of fighting.

As German troops crossed the border, the small Belgian Army resisted fiercely what, after all, was an invasion of their country by a foreign power. In addition to the Belgian Army, there was also the obstacle of a series of fortified towns that the invading Germans had to overcome; such delays would prove costly, and the chances of a quick knockout blow against the French diminished. If the Schlieffen Plan failed, then Germany would have to fight the two-front war she so desperately wanted to avoid, and the chances of ultimate victory would be reduced considerably.

Many in Britain held the opinion that the British Navy would perhaps play the leading role as far as this country was involved, and that view was endorsed to an extent by the small army that crossed the Channel safely, without loss, on 9 August. This army, the British Expeditionary Force, consisted of one cavalry and four infantry divisions, amounting to around 100,000 men. This paled into insignificance in contrast with the millions of conscripted men that both the Germans and the French had. However, the BEF was both well trained and professional and it has been said that this was the best army that ever left Britain to fight overseas. The soldiers, in their distinctive khaki uniforms, disembarked at Le Havre, Boulogne and further inland at Rouen by river. The French authorities had wanted the BEF to arrive sooner but the logistics of moving the men across the Channel meant that 9 August was the earliest this could be achieved. British Regulars and Reservists were greeted by cheering crowds as they disembarked, and made their way towards the enemy. The French railway wagons allocated to these troops, labelled '8 chevaux, 40 hommes', had previously been used for other purposes, mainly as cattle and sheep trucks, and what was thought of the 'baaing' noises that some of the BEF jokingly made as the trains left for the front is anybody's guess.

The BEF was commanded by Sir John French and the four infantry divisions were split into two corps, 1st and 2nd, led by Sir Douglas Haig and Sir Horace Smith-Dorrien respectively. As the BEF moved forward on the French Army's left flank, they collided headlong with the advancing German 1st Army at Mons on 23 August. Much has been written about this battle, about how well the BEF acquitted itself, and the supposed comment made by the Kaiser in calling the BEF a 'contemptible little army'. The battle took place with the odds much favouring the Germans, for the BEF was outnumbered by over two to one, with 70,000 British troops facing 160,000 Germans. Infantry and artillery of both sides were involved, with the Germans holding the aces again, with 600 to 300 artillery pieces. Fighting took place in the open as the two armies met, and the BEF won the grudging respect of their grey-clad opponents with their accurate and deadly rifle fire which the Germans mistakenly believed was machine-gun fire. All those hours of practice it took to achieve the marksman's crossed rifles badge were put to good use at Mons by the soldiers of the BEF. A marksman's badge brought increased pay that often paid for the beer that quenched the thirst of many a soldier, but it also showed that a typical BEF marksman could fire up to fifteen aimed rounds a minute. Critics of the BEF's tactics during the Great War point the finger at Generals who ordered men to advance in large numbers towards well-defended positions. However, at Mons the renowned German Army attacked using these very tactics and this made an attractive target for the proficient marksmen of the BEF. German casualties in the face of such precise rifle fire were heavy and Von Kluck, the commander of the German 1st Army, had to rely upon his artillery to make a serious dent in the British ranks. Shelling destroyed many of the houses from which the BEF were firing, as well as inflicting casualties.

By the end of the day, the fighting around the canal in front of Mons resulted in 1,600 British casualties, whilst the Germans suffered over 5,000 killed or wounded. A captured German summed up the impact Mons had made, saying, 'The Russians can't shoot at all, the French are not good shots, but the English shoot and kill.' The BEF had halted the German advance but, late in the evening, started to withdraw from Mons in a south-westerly direction towards Le Cateau and Landrecies as more and more German troops appeared. The retreat was an orderly one though, carried out professionally, but it would prove to be extended and exhausting.

Regular soldiers and Reservists from St Neots and the surrounding villages were amongst the men of the BEF who were blooded at Mons and during the ensuing retreat. Private Frank Cousins of Eaton Ford was one such soldier who experienced this fighting and was left with a scar to prove it. He had been a regular with the Bedfordshire Regiment, spending four years abroad, mainly in Gibraltar and Bermuda, and after completing his seven years in 1913 was placed on reserve and went back to Eaton Ford to live with his parents. Until the outbreak of war he worked for Jordan & Addington, both in their seed stores and their ginger beer plant, but he had been recalled immediately to the 1st Battalion, the Bedfordshire Regiment and went straight over to France. The 1st Bedfords went into action on 23 August and quickly came under German attack and then artillery fire, suffering casualties on that day and on the following as they withdrew. As the Bedfords pulled back, Frank Cousins was wounded on day three of the retreat, when a bullet broke a bone above the elbow in his right arm. He and another Eaton Socon soldier, Albert Norman, were using a machine-gun with about 2,000 yards of open space in front of them and were exposed to German fire. In this unprotected position, Frank Cousins was hit as they started to retire from their shallow trench, the German bullet striking him on the back of his right arm and exiting at the front. Both entry and exit holes were quite small, no more than three quarters of an inch across, but the damage to his arm was considerable for the bone was shattered. With Frank wounded the two of them could not save or carry the machine-gun, so Albert Norman removed the bolt and managed to get away uninjured. When war broke out, Albert Norman was working in Sheffield as the manager of a boot shop and, following his call-up as a Reservist, he travelled to Belfast to join his regiment before embarking for France and fighting in all of the initial engagements of the Great War. In fact he survived the war, although he was wounded in the left arm, below the elbow, two months later at Ypres. Frank Cousins was not so fortunate, for he had a date with destiny less than a year later.

Mr and Mrs Harry Murphy of Avenue Road, St Neots had a son, Harry, serving with the 4th Battalion, the Duke of Cambridge's Own, Middlesex Regiment, and as the BEF engaged the Germans at Mons he was killed in action. Harry Murphy's regiment had a distinguished past, having the memorable nickname 'The Diehards', which they had earned during the Peninsular War in 1811. As the Germans attacked at Mons they were the first in line, and their accurate and rapid rifle fire killed many of the enemy. As the battle progressed and the BEF started to withdraw, the 4th Battalion began to be surrounded. In the desperate fighting, men from the 'Diehards' fell as German shells rained down, and their rifles began to jam with sand as they ran low on ammunition. During this struggle, Private Harry Murphy was killed. The Germans buried him in a specially-built cemetery at St Symphorien Military, Mons. Here they buried friend and foe alike, and even erected a memorial to the Middlesex Regiment.

Readers of the *St Neots Advertiser* were given a first-hand account of the fighting at Mons and after, when the paper published a letter from Private Len Goodwin of the 2nd Battalion, Grenadier Guards who came from Great Barford. The letter was sent to both the *Advertiser* and the *Biggleswade Chronicle*, where it appeared in an abridged form. In the *Advertiser* the whole letter was published, giving substantial information about what the men of BEF were facing. Goodwin wrote:

We marched 190 miles in eight days. We were marching day and night, and when we did get a stop we had to entrench ourselves and lie with bayonets fixed and ten rounds of ammunition loaded, so you see that there was no chance of getting any rest. I was in three battles; in the last of which I was wounded. I have seen some awful sights. The first fight at Mons was terrible. We did cut the Germans up there, and our Battalion never lost a man. The next fight was at Landrecies. I was in a big house in the middle of the town, and we knocked the windows out and made holes in the brickwork to fire through; and the Germans again lost heavily there. We were fighting in a wood when I got shot. We were the rear guard, covering the Division's retirement. There were about 600 of us – all my Company, and some Coldstreams and Irish. We thought that there were only a few hundred of the enemy, but in reality they were a few thousands, and they didn't half cut us up. We killed a great many of them, as we couldn't help hitting them; they were so thick. They got all the way round us, so we had no choice of getting away. I received a shot wound in the left leg, the bullet going through my knee-cap and coming out inside my leg, half way up; I had another straight through my nose, and whilst

I was lying down I had one go through the back of my jacket, but that never touched me. I think I was lucky to come out of it with my life.

Private Goodwin was captured by the advancing Germans and went on to tell:

We were prisoners for ten days and were wondering what the Germans would do with us. Four army doctors were captured with us and they dressed our wounds. On the tenth day the French made an attack, took some of our captors prisoner, and released us. You can guess we were glad.

He went on to say that some of the captured British soldiers were not so fortunate, for they had been taken back with the Germans as they retreated from the French, and there must have been casualties among them as French artillery shelled the retiring Germans. Private Goodwin was taken by train to a hospital behind the front, and was surprised to find that he would be receiving royal visitors when the King and Queen called to meet the wounded men. He ended his letter: 'My leg is getting much better, and my nose has healed up well, and is nearly all right. I shall get a furlough when I am well enough, and I shall come and have a look at you all.'

News of another St Neots man injured in these first engagements of the Great War came when it was revealed that Lieutenant George Fydell-Rowley had been hospitalised after he was wounded in the foot during the fight at Landrecies. Writing home, he told how the struggle at Landrecies had been intensely fierce and that the slaughter had been terrific, saying that the Germans had lost many more than the BEF. He went on to say that the streets of Landrecies were choked with German corpses and the enemy had to clamber over their comrades' dead bodies just to shoot at the British.

If news from France was shocking then the people of St Neots were to be distressed even more by a tragic event that occurred on 31 August. Territorial soldiers, 1st Highland Brigade, the Royal Field Artillery were encamped at St Neots, and on that fateful Monday some of

Scottish Territorials marching into St Neots in 1914. (Cambridgeshire collection)

these Scottish soldiers went along to the bathing sheds at Eynesbury to swim. On arrival they discovered that the day was designated a ladies' bathing day, so they decided to just sit and relax on the banks of the river in the field known as Coneygear. Meanwhile three local girls, Maud Andrew, Alice Mead, and Flossie Peacock, had arrived; Alice entered the water, swimming out across the river. As she did so she called back for Flossie and Maud to join her, which they did. However, as they swam out Flossie started to feel faint and giddy, and went under. Maud tried to help and grabbed hold of Flossie, but it was clear that the two of them were in difficulties. The watching soldiers were not sure at first if the girls were joking but then they quickly realised that the girls were in trouble. Walter Taylor did not hesitate and, taking off only his tunic, he dived into the water, swimming out to the two girls, trying his best to support them whilst treading water. Meanwhile, William Carr had stripped off all of his uniform and dived in, reaching Flossie and bringing her back to the riverbank. In the river, Maud was clinging on to Walter Taylor with her arms around his neck but he could not keep afloat and the two of them went under. Other soldiers had got hold of a leaky punt and were making their way out across the river when they saw Walter and Maud go under. Using the pole of the punt they helped Maud back to the surface, but Walter went under a second time and did not reappear. Maud was taken to the river's bank and the soldiers restored her breathing by artificial respiration, whilst Alice Mead was helped to reach dry land by one of the other soldiers who had got hold of a pole with a sling at its end. For between fifteen minutes and half an hour the soldiers searched for Walter Taylor – until his body was spotted, tangled in weeds, and then brought to the riverbank. Artificial respiration was used on seventeen-year-old Walter Taylor but to no avail, and Captain Squair of the Royal Army Medical Corps declared him dead. The inquest into the death of Walter Taylor found fault with the safety provision for bathers, especially with the lifebuoys that proved to be so ineffective, and recorded a verdict of accidental death. Walter Taylor had shown remarkable bravery that day and the courage of this young man and his friends saved the lives of Maud and Flossie.

The people of St Neots were quick to honour Walter Taylor and a committee was set up to ensure that he was not laid to rest in an unmarked grave. People felt that he had lost his life as bravely as if he had fallen on the field of battle and, together with his comrades, they raised £23 5s 6d to mark his grave with a memorial, appropriately made of Aberdeen granite, his place of birth. He was buried in St Neots Cemetery and the great respect for him continues to this day. In 2004, after repairs, the memorial was rededicated – ninety years to the day on which this brave young man lost his life. Rodney Todman, Geoff Marchant and Ian Webb were those behind this rededication, and when the work was completed a week before the service, they went to look at the restored memorial. As they were leaving the cemetery they looked back and saw an elderly lady standing at the memorial, so they walked back to speak to her and discovered she was Rosemary, the daughter of Maud Andrew. Each year, until she died in 1948, Maud

MEMORIAL OF A BRAVE DEED

Grave of trumpeter Walter Taylor.

had returned to St Neots from London, and then Hastings, to visit Walter Taylor's grave, and now the tradition is carried on by her daughter even though she lives far away in Southampton.

Within the town, the Corn Exchange was the scene for an enthusiastic recruiting meeting in the first week of September and many local dignitaries spoke to try to encourage local men to enlist. Something more sobering was discovered written outside on a recruitment poster – 'Cheer up, you'll soon be dead!' Recruits, though, did come forward and by the middle of the month, seventy-one men from St Neots had taken the King's Shilling. A recruitment office was set up in New Street, where Mr Alfred Johnson, the recruiting officer, enlisted men. It was hoped that this would make it easier for volunteers to come forward, rather than having to travel over to Bedford to join up. The parish of Eaton Socon had committed around seventy men and they were serving as Reservists, Yeomanry, Territorials and even Instructors. The latest recruits from the Eatons included William Hemmings, Frederick Humphrey, Sidney Cross, Tom Bruce, Percy Usher, Arthur Usher and George Nicholls, who was an old soldier.

Across the Channel, the BEF was tested sorely as the retreat from Mons continued, with soldiers weary, dusty and pressed by the enemy. The war diary of the 1st Bedfords for late August confirms that men were 'tired and footsore', and that the troops were 'absolutely tired out and hungry after marching day and night'. However, the BEF in retreat continued to prove to the following Germans that they were still a force to be reckoned with, and their pursuers' losses persisted. At Le Cateau on 26 August, the British retreat came to a halt and a decisive rearguard action took place, with accurate rifle and artillery fire again hitting the Germans hard. This rearguard action by II Corps was very costly, for the British lost over 7,800 men, but it did allow the retreat to continue in good order. Once again the 1st Bedfords were in action and their war diary reveals how well-organised this rearguard stand was, and how they covered the withdrawal of the British artillery. Private William Webb of the 1st Bedfords wrote home to Croxton telling of these testing days:

> After the battle of Mons, that big fight, we had an order to retire; not that we were beaten back, but to draw the Germans on to a larger force which was waiting for them, and I am pleased to say that the boys in khaki soon checked their little game and killed a great number of them. I was in the firing line with my regiment and I never saw a finer lot of men that stood up to the Germans that numbered five to one … We had rather a hard time of marching, as the enemy were after us, but when they ran into our army that was waiting for them they soon turned their back on us and showed a clean pair of heels. That gave us a chance for a little rest. I admit that I was beaten in the long march, but I put my heart and soul into it and came on with the remainder when we halted and had a good meal and a wash and a shave, which was very nice after so long without one.

The Bedfords were part of II Corps, commanded by Sir Horace Smith-Dorrien, and their action at Le Cateau did achieve the objective of allowing the retreat to carry on in an orderly fashion, and the BEF were untroubled by the Germans for five days. Douglas Haig commanded the other British Corps, I Corps, and he had a narrow escape in the retreat, for his driver took a wrong turn and almost ran into advancing German troops who fired on Haig's car. Quite how the war would have progressed if Haig had been captured or killed here is an intriguing question.

Also in action at Mons was Private Herbert Townsend from Jubilee Terrace, Eaton Ford who had been called up as a Reservist in those hectic days of early August. He quickly found himself at the front with his battalion, the 1st Lincolns, as they were blooded in battle at Mons. As the BEF withdrew, Private Townsend and his colleagues were told to cut their packs off their backs as this would make it easier for them to run. Over the next thirteen days the Lincolns often fought rearguard actions to cover other British soldiers who were falling back. Writing home, Herbert Townsend told how they had thrown away their greatcoats during the retreat and that these were sorely missed as night time temperatures fell. Without their backpacks, and not receiving supplies, the men had to resort to scrumping apples for food as they slogged towards Paris.

In Lincolnshire, the Hunts Cyclist Battalion continued its work in patrolling the coastline and watching for any possible German incursions. By the beginning of September the nights were pulling in and the temperature was dropping, with the men warmly appreciating the blankets and clothing they had received from home. Colour Sergeant Taylor of 'D' Company wrote:

> Dear Sir, I thank you on behalf of the NCOs and men of this Company for your kindness in soliciting gifts of warm garments for the men … It is very cold here at night and during the early hours of the morning. Our men are doing their trying work very cheerfully … I should like some of the St Neots people to see our men parading at 6.30 in the evening to take up their night duties, with cycle and arms and ammunition, blanket and waterproof sheet, and then see them start off their various beats along the cliffs, etc, and to visit them at the small hours of the morning – as I have done – with not a soul to speak to and the roar of the sea enough to deafen them. With rifle loaded, always on the alert, I say, if St Neots people could see these men when they return home at 5.30 in the morning and hear them sing and telling of their experiences of the past night, I think they would be proud of them … I should certainly like the men to have good thick shirts as they need them very badly. Of course we have had a little sickness with some of the men but nothing serious. A good many men have volunteered for the front. Again thanking you for your kindness, I remain, yours faithfully, D Taylor, Color Sergt. [*sic*]

HUNTS. CYCLIST BATTALION, "D" CO. FOOTBALL TEAM.

Left to right :
1st row—Col. Sergt. Buck (reserve), Pte. Page (reserve), Pte. Hook, Pte. Oldham, Pte. Malin, Lce. c. Brett (sec.), Pte. Jackson (reserve), Pte. Earle (referee).
2nd row—Pte. Asbury, L.c. Dighton, Pte. Levitt.
3rd row—Pte. Young, Pte. Dodson, Sergt. Davies, Sergt. Cooper, Corpl. Basson.

'D' Company Hunts Cyclists Football Team.

The men of the Hunts Cyclist Battalion were taking their work seriously. One night, in early September, two sentries close to the sea wall saw a light and then heard voices. When no response was made to their challenge they fired unknowingly on two Corporation workmen cleaning sewers and attending to dustbins. These workmen heard a bullet whizz past a few inches above their heads, and then a second bullet just missed them. They then shouted out and the two sentries came up to them at the double, asking them what they were doing at the seafront at such an hour and with a light. The workmen stated that they were carrying out their duties and hadn't heard any challenge. The soldiers replied that if they saw lights again they would have to fire. The sentries said they were sorry, but they had their orders too and had to obey them.

These two workmen avoided becoming casualties, but the people of St Neots saw at first-hand actual casualties from France and Belgium on Sunday 6 September, when an ambulance train, en route to the military hospitals at Lincoln, passed through St Neots station. The troops aboard were categorised according to their wounds; the first few carriages were used for the most serious cases of men who couldn't sit up, followed by the less seriously wounded and then those who could walk. The train contained about 120 men, the majority of whom were cheerful enough and happy to receive hot tea, cocoa, milk, soup, cake and, needless to say, cigarettes. Some men were so badly injured that they took little interest, but the faces of all of the men showed what a gruelling time they had had in battle and in retreat. The men were understandably reticent in telling what had happened to them, although they did have ready appetites and the cake they were given went down especially well.

As if to endorse the deadly nature of the fighting across the Channel, the following notice appeared in the local press, under the title 'Ambulance Men Wanted'. The notice took the form of a letter and ran as follows:

Dear Sir, The Eastern Mounted Brigade Field Ambulance, commanded by Col. Cross, having offered for service abroad (90 per cent), a Reserve Field Ambulance is being recruited at headquarters, Grove Road, Luton and at Ashburnham Road, Bedford, in accordance with War Office Letter ...

I should be obliged to you Sir, if you would give me the opportunity of appealing through your paper for recruiting for this Reserve Unit. I would especially appeal to those who have already served in this, or some Field Ambulance.
The Conditions of Service are:
Enlistment for 4 years. Men enlisting either for General or Home service may be discharged at the end of the War and the County Association are asked to waive the fine.
Enlistment for General Service, i.e. for service at home or abroad. Men joining this service will take the Imperial Service Obligations.
Enlistment for home service, 40 per cent of the strength of the Unit is required for this service.
Thanking you for the prominence you have given in the past to our Corps communications.
I remain, yours faithfully,
C.E. Kaye Sharpe, Lieut. R.A.M.C.

There was, however, some concern that Huntingdonshire men were slow in coming forward for either the Field Ambulance Unit or general enlistment and, at a recruiting meeting at Kimbolton, Lord Montagu (the Earl of Sandwich) and Lord Lovat spoke regarding this, saying that recruiting in the county had begun very badly, which could perhaps be excused by the fact that Huntingdonshire had heard very little of the war, especially in some of the smaller villages. The two lords even went on to say that they had hoped to raise a Huntingdonshire Battalion, but that would require 1,100 men, and so far only about 400 had come forward. The speakers used terms such as 'shirkers', 'a disgrace to the county' and even spoke of attaching 'white feathers' to those who hung back. Lord Montagu went as far as saying that it might be a good thing for the Germans to come over for two or three days to stir things up! Perhaps to encourage men from the county to enlist, King George V made a visit to Huntingdon during the third week of September and inspected the Highland Mounted Brigade billeted there. After the inspection, the King rode out along the road past Hinchinbrooke to Brampton Wood, where he watched field training in the form of a mock attack upon Huntingdon by 'enemy' troops, and its defence by the British Army. The King then returned to London by train.

Whether men were reluctant or not to take the King's Shilling, there could be no doubt about the commitment of the Chamberlain family from Eynesbury, for here five sons – Joseph, Edward, Robert, William and George – had all taken their place in the 5th Bedfordshire Battalion, even though their mother was a widow.

The *St Neots Advertiser* of 25 September included a lengthy letter giving an insight into army life from Walter Hopwood, who had recently left St Neots to join up. Under a heading 'My Life as a Recruit', Private Hopwood told how he had enlisted in Cambridge at the Corn Exchange, together with a friend. He had trained at Bury St Edmunds before moving to Folkestone, where he saw Lord Kitchener:

> Last Sunday was a 'red letter' day for us, as we were reviewed by our Commander in Chief, Lord Kitchener, and of course we all did our best on our parade, as we knew every movement we made was being closely watched.

The tone of his letter was very upbeat and he certainly encouraged others to follow his lead:

> Many young fellows seem to think that the life of a soldier is something dreadful and to be feared, but let them once experience it and they will then tell a different tale. Since I enlisted it has been more like a holiday than work, although the conditions are somewhat different to those of a holiday, but one is expected to rough it a little at first … I can honestly say that I do not at all regret volunteering, but feel quite proud of wearing the King's uniform, and I must say that it is the most happy and enjoyable time I have ever spent, since I volunteered, and I can well recommend a soldier's life as being one of the best 'livings' going, and I will now conclude my story and say – God Save the King.

Lord Montagu and Lord Lovat's recruitment drive showed no sign of abating and they arrived in Huntingdon to continue their campaign to encourage and chivvy men to enlist. On the third Saturday of September they spoke at a meeting in the town's Market Square, together with the Mayor of Huntingdon. Lord Montagu was last to speak and he certainly looked the part, wearing the uniform of an honorary colonel of the Hunts Cyclist Battalion, which had now reached its recruitment target, so he therefore urged men to join the New Armies of Lord Kitchener. He went on to say that recruiting in Huntingdonshire was now fairly good, but that every man was wanted, and it would be a disgrace to any man who did not at once offer his services. He said that a roll would be kept of all the men in Huntingdonshire who had enlisted or offered their services. This, he said, would be preserved and he would feel sorry for the man whose name was not on the list.

On the Continent another kind of list was growing, that of men wounded or killed as the BEF continued its withdrawal. However, the British in retreat remained a deadly and dangerous foe, as the advancing Germans found to their cost. Indeed, the mood of the khaki-clad men was one of resistance, believing that they were lulling the Germans, drawing them on, and that soon their time would come and they would turn, fight and drive their enemy back. On 6 September that faith was justified when the Allies attacked and brought any hope of the Schlieffen Plan succeeding to a crashing halt 30 miles from Paris, when the German Army suffered its first major defeat of the war and found itself in full retreat. The Battle of the

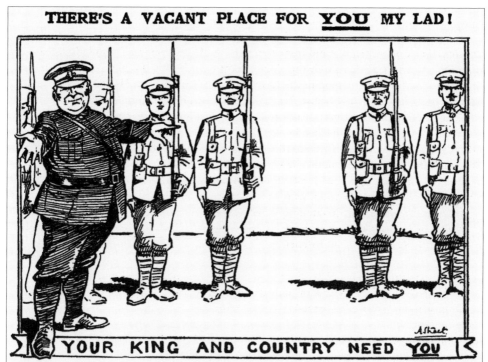

THERE'S A VACANT PLACE FOR YOU MY LAD!

YOUR KING AND COUNTRY NEED YOU

Lord Kitchener has obtained 900,000 recruits, and only 100,000 are needed to make up the first million. So take *your* place in the ranks, young man, at once, and enlist at the nearest recruiting office, for the sake of your King and Country.

Recruitment poster, September 1914.

Marne took place over a period of five days and for some time the outcome was uncertain, but eventually the arrival of 6,000 reinforcements from the Paris Garrison, who were transported to the battleground by Paris taxi cabs, tipped the balance as the German Army lost its nerve. Its commander, von Moltke, ordered his army to start to fall back – but not all the way to Germany, for although they retreated almost 60 miles, they did so until they reached ground that they could defend strongly. The British and the French followed cautiously and when the Germans reached the Aisne they dug in, and the nature of the fighting so far was to change drastically. The Marne was certainly one of the defining battles of the Great War for, following it, the notion of a war of movement came to a close. The nature of the fighting now changed, and, after the so-called 'race to the sea', the trench system, that for many is the embodiment of the Great War and which would stretch from the Belgian coast for over 400 miles to the Swiss border, came into being.

Geographically and tactically the Aisne proved to be a serious obstacle to the pursuing Allies as, on the night of 12 September, the Germans dug in at the top of steep banks on the far side of the river. At first the BEF tried frontal assaults as they attacked on the 13th, but these failed when they came under intense artillery, machine-gun and rifle fire. However, a few bridgeheads were established and on the 14th the fighting intensified. The day began with thick fog, which did not help the attacking BEF as they tried to consolidate those initial bridgeheads across the river. Amongst the battalions attacking were the Grenadier Guards, and within their ranks was Second Lieutenant John Reynolds Pickersgill-Cunliffe, the only son of Harry and Arlette Pickersgill-Cunliffe of Great Staughton Manor. As the 2nd Battalion, nicknamed the Models, advanced, the nineteen-year-old lieutenant was killed in action during this First Battle of the Aisne. Indeed, casualties for 14 September were high and the BEF lost over 3,500 killed, wounded or missing in action. Fighting continued the next day but the Allies were unable to drive the Germans from the heights above the Aisne, and this area, known locally as the Chemin des Dames, became a German stronghold that would endure for much of the war. Also killed in action in the fighting at the Aisne was twenty-seven-year-old Lance Corporal Edwin Cook, another serving with the 2nd Battalion, Grenadier Guards. His sister, Mrs J. Smith, who lived in Cambridge Street, heard the sad news that her brother had died, leaving a wife and a child, only weeks old, in Barnes, London.

Further news of the fighting on the Aisne came from Private F. 'Stub' Wagstaff, 1st Bedfords, who was a member of the Sandy Football team. He wrote to friends in St Neots telling how the Bedfords attacked after crossing the river by pontoon and raft:

> We had a proper stiff fight on the River Aisne … It made me hold me breath when the order came to fix bayonets ready to charge the German trenches … we had got through one wood and then we had to retire, and you ought to have seen us rolling down a great hill with fixed bayonets all of a heap.

At the same time that the report of Lieutenant Pickersgill-Cunliffe's death reached St Neots, so did news of the torpedoing of HMS *Aboukir*. Amongst the crew of this cruiser was Stoker William Webb, who had served for five years in the Royal Navy before going on to the Naval Reserve. Before the outbreak of war he had been working at the paper mills in St Neots and had been called up for his annual month's training on 12 July, so he was actually on board when war was declared. When the *Aboukir* was sent to patrol the North Sea, this twenty-eight-year-old from Great Paxton was amongst the crew. The *Aboukir*, HMS *Cressy* and HMS *Hogue* were spotted by the German submarine U9 early on the morning of 22 September as they patrolled the area of the North Sea known as the Broad Fourteens, around 20 miles north-west of the Hook of Holland. The cruisers were not zigzagging, the standard way to minimise attack by U-boat, and the commander of U9, Otto Weddigen, prepared to attack these inviting targets. The *Aboukir* was hit by torpedo and its skipper, Captain Drummond, at first thought that it had struck a mine and signalled the other two cruisers to come and help. Quickly realising that he was mistaken, Drummond then ordered *Cressy* and *Hogue* to pull away, but the *Hogue* was hit by torpedo as she tried to lower boats to rescue the crew of the *Aboukir*, many of whom had jumped into the sea as the ship began to sink. The *Hogue* didn't last long and also began to sink quickly. U9 now turned its attention to the *Cressy* which, although it fired at the periscope of the U-boat, was unable to avoid the fate of the two other cruisers and sank after it was hit by U9's last torpedo. Merchant ships, trawlers, Dutch patrol boats and Royal Navy destroyers steamed to help, and they started to pick the survivors up. Although just over 800 men were rescued, almost 1,500 men were killed or drowned as the submarine established itself as a deadly addition to the weapons of war.

Stoker William Webb was one of the lucky survivors, for he was picked up by a small whaling boat and was taken to Holland. On 2 October the readers of the *St Neots Advertiser* were able to learn in detail about Stoker Webb's experience aboard the *Aboukir*. The newspaper told how he had been asleep in his bunk when, at around 6.30 a.m., he was woken by a terrific crash. The ship heaved, then shook and rolled, and the crew quickly closed all watertight doors but it was to no avail, for it was obvious that the *Aboukir* was doomed. Stoker Webb told how the crew were given orders to form in line on the upper deck, which they did without the slightest confusion and with strict discipline prevailing. He then told how he only had the chance to put on a shirt and trousers before lining up. There was only one lifeboat and into this were placed three or four sick men, and one who had been injured when the torpedo struck, together with a few other hands. Stoker Webb then told how the *Aboukir*, having been hit by just one torpedo in the forward boiler, began to list at once with her guns out of action, as one side of the boat was under water, and the guns on the other faced skywards. The *Aboukir* was now starting to overturn, so Captain Drummond gave the order to abandon ship and said that every man should try to save himself. Anything that might be buoyant was thrown overboard for the men to use to try to keep afloat, and the crew began to jump into the sea. William Webb's account of how he left the ship revealed remarkable calmness, for he told how he took off his shirt and trousers and just walked off the deck into the water. It was very fortunate that there was little suction, and he managed to swim clear of the swarms of drowning and struggling sailors. At first he started to swim towards the *Hogue*, but then she was hit. Stoker Webb said that he was only a fair swimmer but he was steady, and that he was about three quarters of the distance to the *Hogue* when she was torpedoed. He told how men were struck by severe cramp and drowning in the terribly cold water. Just as it seemed he would be lost, he was picked up by a small whaling boat that was crammed with rescued sailors, some of whom were unconscious or without clothing. The whaler sat low in the water due to all of the men it had picked up, with waves continuing to break over the boat and water needing to be bailed out. When the sun rose the men warmed up and they were given food and water. William Webb was later transferred to the Lowestoft trawler, *Coriander*, and taken to Holland, where he should have been interned; however he, and the other survivors, were returned to Britain. His wife, who lived in New Street, heard of his survival about a week later and was told that he was on his way home.

In St Neots, recruiting continued to be steady if unspectacular, and drew comment in the local press. The following letter, printed in the *Advertiser* of 2 October, pulled no punches:

> Out of a population of 4,359, 450 men in Leiston, Suffolk have been accepted for foreign service and others have joined branches of the Service ... What a Suffolk village can do, St Neots and Eynesbury ought to be able to do ... The present figures for St Neots and Eynesbury are: Territorial Force – 80, Kitchener's Army 75.

For those who had enlisted, these first few weeks of training were perhaps not all they had expected, for there was a shortage of both uniform and rifles, and as the autumn nights took their hold, some men were very cold, being billeted in either huts or tents. Appeals went out for help and the people of St Neots busied themselves putting together parcels of warm clothing for the recruits. The Hunts Cyclist Battalion, St Neots 'D' Company, were the recipients of such parcels and gratefully accepted the socks, pants, scarves, vests and blankets that were dispatched to them. Support for those fighting was also seen as £27 7s was collected for the Soldiers' and Sailors' Families Association during these first two months of the conflict.

Appeals also went out for help for over a quarter of a million Belgian refugees arriving in Britain. Asquith's government could not cope with such an influx without the help of local authorities to house them, and both Huntingdonshire and Cambridgeshire responded. Belgian refugees arrived in Little Barford early in October, when five families from Aerschot were welcomed. This town in Belgium had been sacked by the Germans in late August and over 150 citizens killed, whilst others were subjected to beatings and rape as the town was pillaged. Aerschot was one of a number of Belgian towns that suffered such a fate and there was international outrage over the actions of the invading troops. The Germans offered as explanation that they had been fired upon by locals with some German troops being killed, and they had to make an example that would stop this. This excuse for their actions cut little ice with the British population and recruitment figures improved considerably, following the brutal behaviour of some of the invading German soldiers.

The five families who settled in Little Barford had fled on foot from Aerschot to Antwerp and thence to Britain. Their number increased from twenty-four to twenty-five when one of the women gave birth in a stable, lying on straw right next to a horse, and the group just managed to get away before German troops arrived. These refugees were artisan families, including weavers and a gas fitter, but quite what work the miner amongst them hoped to find in Great Barford is intriguing. More refugees continued to arrive locally as the year progressed and the *St Neots Advertiser* even started to include a regular column in its pages in Belgian for the newcomers.

Across the Channel, both sides now turned their attention northwards as the 'race to the sea' began. Axis and Allied forces both moved towards the Channel, trying to outflank each other. This 'race to the sea' saw casualties continue within the BEF as the fighting moved northwards, often crossing some of the earlier battlegrounds of August and September. Private Fred Sandever, who was serving with No. 4 Ambulance Train, RAMC wrote to his mother in Eaton Ford just before returning to Britain with wounded soldiers, and he described the fighting moving towards the Channel Coast:

> Just a few lines hoping you are quite well as it leaves me at present. I am still knocking along all right and happy, and having a good time. I am writing this because we are at a sea port and the boat is leaving tonight. I have not got any news for you; we are just knocking along in the same way, busy with the wounded, plenty of them. We have been within four miles of the big battles. It is a sight to see the shells bursting all over the place but not near us. We have passed through some old battlefields and it is a pitiful sight, being full up with graves, clothing, rifles, bayonets and packs, most of them French and German.

Wounded soldiers were treated in special Red Cross hospitals in Britain, two of which were set up in St Neots and Eaton Socon. Local people went to see and meet these wounded men as they recuperated, and, if classed fit enough, the soldiers were readied to move on back to the front. Some soldiers who were too badly injured to return were pensioned out of the army, and this gave a certain Charles Rowsell an idea how to make some money for himself. The *St Neots Advertiser* ran a story entitled 'Wounded Soldier Swindle' in which it was told that Charles Rowsell, a recruit in the West Kent Regiment, had been sentenced in Croydon to three months' hard labour for falsely representing himself as a wounded soldier from Mons, by limping about and begging for money.

By October, the 'race to the sea' was complete and the two sides faced each other over a 400-mile front that snaked its way from Nieuwpoort on the Belgian coast southwards to the Swiss border. For Germany to stand any chance of victory now, the Channel ports had to be captured, and the BEF soon found itself back in the firing line as the Germans attempted to break through and capture the ports. They felt that if they could break the BEF it would have a significant effect upon the Allies' ability to continue the war, and that defeat would lead to Britain exiting the war. As the fighting swung northwards, the BEF had found itself back in Belgium and dug in, in shallow trenches around the town of Ypres. In October this was the last Belgian town remaining in Allied hands, and the only major obstacle standing in the way of the Germans – by 1918 the name would be permanently carved into the history of the Great War.

In early October, German troops had passed through Ypres, leaving a poor impression as they wrecked the town's telegraph system and exacted a fine of 70,000 francs for the good behaviour of the town's citizens during their three-day stay. The town had a rich heritage that centred upon the imposing cathedral and cloth hall, indicating how the town had been an important centre for both trade and religion in earlier times. By 1914 that importance had declined, but the town was rightly proud of its past and these two magnificent buildings could be seen for miles around. Ypres sits in a flatland basin surrounded by higher ground, and the cathedral and the cloth hall stood out as landmarks that were easily visible from the elevated ground. Over the next four years these two buildings were gradually destroyed, together with much of the town itself, until it was said that a man on horseback could look across from one side of the town all the way over to the other, as Ypres was gradually reduced to rubble by German shelling. In October, the BEF arrived and received a very different welcome to that the Germans recently had. Scottish troops were amongst those first British troops to enter the town and they were greeted warmly by the citizens of Ypres, who were fascinated by the kilts the Scots wore. Over the next few weeks those citizens would gradually be forced to leave their homes as more and more German shells smashed into the town. By the end of the year Ypres was a town inhabited only by soldiers, as they made their way through towards the front line.

The open nature of the earlier fighting changed now, with both sides making use of their entrenching tools, and any spades they could get hold of, to dig in. The renowned trench system now started. Initially trenches were a single line, but this would change as the war progressed, and by 1916 were three lines – front, reserve and support, all connected by communication trenches. The depth and construction of these trenches also differed, depending upon where on the Western Front they were dug. The water level in France was reached at a deeper level and the Germans actually dug down between 20 and 40ft in the chalk land of the Somme, where they built deep dugouts over the next couple of years. These dugouts were almost indestructible, being only threatened by a direct hit from a high explosive shell, and they had a huge impact upon the outcome of the first day of the Battle of the Somme in 1916. In Belgium, trench construction was different, as the water level was reached at about 4ft, meaning that trenches could not be dug deep enough to give men complete protection. The solution to this situation was the construction of an altogether different kind of trench. The front and the back of the trench, the parapet and the parados, were raised by sandbags which gave soldiers some shelter from snipers' bullets and machine-gun fire. By 1917 the Germans had further strengthened their trench lines in the Ypres Salient with the construction of reinforced concrete blockhouses. Further south they had built the Hindenburg Line, a formidable series of defences that would prove to be very difficult for attacking Allied troops. However, in the autumn of 1914 these developments were still to come and the German focus was on breaking the British line at Ypres.

The First Battle of Ypres began in October and would last through to November, with the Germans coming tantalisingly close to achieving their objective. 1st Ypres, as the battle is usually referred to, also had a devastating effect upon the surviving members of the original BEF that had landed in France in August, for it was a battle that stretched the BEF almost to breaking point, as more and more of the 'Old Contemptibles' were killed or wounded. Their numbers would become so depleted that a first Territorial battalion, the London Scottish, was called upon to fight overseas. Many other Territorial battalions would follow.

Private Albert Norman of the 1st Bedfords was one of those facing the Germans at Ypres and he remained in a confident mood. He wrote home in October:

> I don't think this will last much longer as they are almost on the point of finishing. In any case I hope so. I am sure everyone is fed up with it. We are all very nicely cared for out here by the [local] people who give us half of what they have got, so they cannot do any more. It does seem a shame to see the poor people's homes blown down by the Germans. They are a fierce lot. Of course they are driven to these things by their officers, who don't seem to care what they do. I have seen as much of the places they have looted and it looks quite a shame. When you write, you might put an envelope and a sheet of paper in, as we can only get cards.

He also asked for cigarettes and cigarette papers, before finishing: 'I hope to be home with you all again very shortly.' His wish came true, but not perhaps as he might have wanted, for he was back in Eaton Ford in November after being wounded.

The fierce fighting at Ypres, and slightly to the south at La Bassée and Armentières, saw more local men enter the fray and, of course, there were casualties. News reached St Neots just before 1st Ypres began, that Private Henry George Barnes, who had been born in Eaton Socon and whose mother now lived in Russell Street, St Neots, was killed in action on 17 October when the 1st Bedfords and the Germans clashed near Givenchy. At the outbreak of the war, Henry George Barnes had been 'on reserve' but had been recalled immediately, going over to France with the Bedfords, fighting at Mons and then during the retreat. When he was killed on that Saturday morning he was twenty-nine years of age, and sadly his last resting place was lost during the continuing fighting. Today he is commemorated on Le Touret Memorial. Also in action with the Bedfords that day was Private George Childs, a regular soldier who had been in the army for two years. He was wounded in the right shoulder by a German bullet that exited through his back, and by the end of the month he was being treated in hospital in Norwich. He would be seriously wounded again in 1915 and an even worse fate awaited him in 1917.

At the same time as news of Private Barnes' death was reaching St Neots, so was information about other men from the town who had been wounded at either Ypres or in the fighting to the south. Arthur Townsend was wounded by a piece of shrapnel on 7 October and, as he was being taken back to a field hospital, he was hit again, but this time by a lump of hard clay knocked up by a shell exploding close by. After treatment he was given time to recuperate back home and he arrived in St Neots in late October with much to tell. Arthur Townsend lived in Eynesbury with his wife and had been a policeman in St Neots before the war. He had been called up at once, for he was 'on reserve', and joined his old regiment, the Coldstream Guards, with whom he had soldiered for eight years from 1904. He had sailed for France on the SS *Cawdor Castle* on 21 August and had written to family back home telling of the enthusiastic reception they received there, and how the French were so keen to exchange food for cap badges and buttons. He had first gone into action on 6 September when his battalion had captured around 120 Germans and fourteen Maxim machine-guns. As the Germans pulled back after the Marne, he narrowly avoided serious injury when the Germans blew up a bridge that the Coldstream Guards were about to cross. At this time he suffered a

Private Arthur Townsend.

bad attack of colic and was taken to hospital, where he had another lucky escape when it was shelled by German artillery. The majority of patients were wounded German prisoners, together with a few British soldiers who were being treated. The artillery bombardment led to fire breaking out which caused great panic, especially for the 280 German patients, as the flames spread quickly. Only two German and four British soldiers got out alive, and Arthur Townsend survived by crawling about 300 yards and sheltering behind a tree, from where he watched as another German shell exploded right in the mouth of a cave where Grenadier Guards and the Coldstream Guards medical officer were taking refuge. All were killed. In the stories he told about life at the front he recounted how dangerous smoking could be, with the tale of one of his friends who was so desperate for a smoke that he jumped out of the trench and ran back to a reserve area to get a match to light his cigarette. Arthur Townsend warned him not to do this but his friend took no notice, getting away with it a few times. On the last occasion, just as he was about to drop back down into the trench a German shell exploded, taking his head clean off. Arthur Townsend went on to tell that the first thing men asked for generally after being wounded was a cigarette.

Arthur Townsend clearly enjoyed speaking about his experiences and his stories brought home to many in St Neots exactly how hard life was at the front. He told how gruelling it was to spend up to five days in a front-line trench, often have to fight knee-deep in water, never being allowed to take off clothes when going to sleep. Indeed they had special orders not to take off their boots. He returned to his unit in November, but told friends and family that he did not mind going back.

Robert Chamberlain from Eynesbury was also back home after being wounded in the right arm by a German bullet on 13 October when his battalion, 1st Bedfords, came under heavy bombardment and then enfilade fire from the enemy at Givenchy. The Bedfords had been subjected to German shelling all day and, at around midday, the bombardment reached a crescendo, destroying both the shallow trenches and the houses of the village in which the Bedfords were positioned. The smoke from exploding shells and the dust from the debris of falling houses made conditions very difficult for the defending troops, severely reducing visibility as the Germans advanced. The two sides fought at close quarters and the Bedfords were forced to withdraw and dig a new trench line, about 300 yards to the rear of Givenchy. Casualties were high, with seven officers and 140 men either killed or wounded. Robert Chamberlain and his four brothers were all serving and he was the first to receive a wound stripe. He was taken to a field hospital before transferring to Wandsworth Military Hospital and then given fourteen days' leave back in St Neots. Robert Chamberlain had seen action right from Mons, about which he said, 'It was like hell'. He didn't want to describe other sights he had seen, saying that they were too terrible to talk about. When his leave was up he returned to his battalion via the regiment's base at Bedford, and thence on over to the Western Front. Robert's brother William was serving in the same battalion, the 1st Bedfords.

On 19 October, Private Herbert Townsend, a veteran of Mons, the Marne and the Aisne, attacked with the 1st Lincolns at La Bassée and his record of escaping injury came to an end. At about 10.30 in the morning he was engaged in trench-digging duties when he was hit by shrapnel, with metal from the exploding shell hitting him in the right leg, the right arm and more seriously in the right side. He was treated, then taken back through the lines to a field hospital and eventually back home to Britain, where he described his war so far. One story told how he and a sergeant were returning to their company after escorting a sick colleague to the rear. En route, they were told by an officer of the Royal Scots to take cover as the Germans were shelling the area heavily, so they sheltered in an abandoned house and lay down to try to get some 'shuteye' just by the window. As they slept, they were awoken by a shell that screamed through the top windowpane of the house and exited through the wall into the street, without exploding. Neither Herbert Townsend nor the sergeant were injured other than being showered with glass from the windowpane. A few days after Herbert Townsend was treated at La Bassée Field Hospital, his brother Harry Townsend, a Private with the 1st Bedfords, was wounded at Ypres in the right wrist. He was taken to the same field hospital as his brother, where the staff asked him if he had a brother serving with the Lincolns. When he answered in the affirmative they gave him the very same bed that his brother had occupied some days earlier. Harry Townsend underwent two operations on his wrist before he too was sent home to Britain for further treatment.

Two days later at Ypres the BEF was outnumbered and sorely pressed by the advancing Germans. Within the British ranks was thirty-year-old Private Frank Mayes, 1st Battalion, South Wales Borderers, who originally came from Great Staughton but now lived in Luke Street, Eynesbury after getting married. In August he was yet another who was on reserve, receiving his call-up papers immediately, and he was quickly drafted to France, leaving behind his pregnant wife Kate. He regularly wrote during those first few weeks of the struggle and became a father, but then the letters stopped arriving, causing his wife to fear the worst. It did not help that her letters to him were now returned unopened. For months Kate Mayes wrote to the War Office asking for news and, in reply, was told that her husband 'was still in the firing line'. In January 1915 the War Office suggested how she might get a letter to her husband but again there was no reply, and then in April a letter from the War Office arrived, telling that her husband was amongst thirty South Wales Borderers who had gone missing in action on 21 October, and that he had been killed as his battalion faced the Germans outside Ypres. His body was later recovered and lies today 2 miles to the east of Ypres in Perth Cemetery.

On 22 October, George Robert Thornhill became the third local man to be killed on the Western Front. Around 12 miles south of Ypres, the 1st Battalion East Kent Regiment, the Buffs, were in action close to Armentières when Lieutenant Thornhill received instructions which would lead to his death. In the confused close fighting at Armentières, he received the wrong orders which resulted in him leading his men forward into what was virtually an ambush. The Germans inflicted severe losses upon Thornhill's men and the lieutenant himself was badly wounded. The battalion war diary recorded that the men had been 'terribly cut up' and George Thornhill's wounds were so severe that he could not be carried or helped back as the Buffs retreated. As the fighting continued, Lieutenant Thornhill's body and final resting place were lost and today he is one of the missing of the Western Front, his name being inscribed on the Ploegsteert Memorial. Evelyn Thornhill, the father of George, received the news from the War Office that his son was missing in action at first, then that this was a mistake and that he had been wounded, and then finally in mid-November that his younger son was missing, presumed killed in action. The war was not yet done with the Thornhill family of Cross Hall Lodge and four years later Evelyn Thornhill would receive devastating news about his elder son.

Another local man, Private Arthur Robert Chandler of the 1st Bedfords, wrote home in graphic terms of the fighting at Ypres and gave his opinion of the enemy. He firstly told of the impact of artillery: 'When we look around here at night it looks like the 5th November, as there is [sic] some rather big villages in front of us and they are burning in several places.' He then went on to say that the wounds received by some of his comrades were so big he feared that the Germans were using dum-dum bullets. He also added, though, that the Germans were now treating wounded soldiers better, writing:

> I also think the Germans are getting a little more civilised, as some of our wounded were captured the other day and the German soldiers bandaged them up, got them mattresses to lay [sic] on, and shared their rations with them. When they were forced to retire they left our fellows behind, so that was how we got to hear of it. One of our fellows had five bullet wounds and he came limping along and the first thing he said was 'Who has got a Woodbine to give me'.

He concluded with this opinion: 'Most of the Germans are fighting with a bad heart. I expect they can only see defeat in front of them … I don't think I have much more to say, only that we are still on our way to Berlin.'

News of further casualties now arrived in St Neots thick and fast, with Privates Albert Norman, Arthur Johnson and George Harlott of the 1st Bedfords, and Privates Charles Chapman and Albert Durham of the 2nd Bedfords, all being wounded during October. Albert Norman had escaped unscathed at Mons but was wounded in the left arm by a German bullet at Dixmude near Ypres. In November, he arrived home in Eaton Ford Green and spent two months recuperating before heading back to France. Whilst at home, he told how the war had become one of 'artillery by day and infantry by night'. He told of seeing aerial dogfights and meeting Indian troops, of whom he spoke highly. He also revealed how he had hardly a button left on his tunic, for French girls had taken them all for souvenirs. Arthur Johnson wrote to his uncle in Eaton Ford from Chelsea:

I am in hospital with wounds received at the Front. I have a fractured thigh and two wounds in the ribs, and am now waiting to undergo an operation to take out pieces of shell out of my leg. We had a very rough time out there. I was taken prisoner by the Germans when wounded, and kept by them four days and three nights, but the village was retaken by our chaps. I saw Albert Norman when they were bringing me away on the stretcher, and spoke a few words to him. He was all right on the 18th.

George Harlott was a regular in the army, serving in South Africa at the outbreak of the war, but now was wounded in the leg by shrapnel at Ypres, seriously enough for him to be brought back from Belgium. George Harlott's family lived in Cambridge Street and heard from him as he recovered in hospital in Dublin, where he was treated for six weeks. He wrote telling them how the piece of shrapnel in his leg remained there for eight days before it was removed, and he also told how he had been waiting at the railway station in Ypres with other wounded soldiers, ready to be sent home, when the Germans started to shell the town once more. Three of the wounded soldiers were wounded again, two wounded soldiers were killed and the German bombardment only stopped when an Allied armoured train opened fire on the German guns. George Harlott had been at the front for just over three weeks and had previously escaped being injured as he made his way to the front line, when German shelling forced him to dive into a ditch. Now he was wounded, and when he returned to St Neots in January 1915 he recounted the horrors of the trenches where initially he spent eleven days without a break and, for two of these, the men were without food. He also told how the nights were the time of most activity, as men had to dig and reinforce trenches during the hours of darkness. He recalled how cold it was in the trenches and that it was impossible to get more than about two hours sleep. As the battle for Ypres raged, he told how the 2nd Bedfords had charged the Germans with bayonet and had driven them back on 18 October, suffering around twenty casualties. George Harlott was wounded when shrapnel hit him in his left leg below the kneecap, just as the charge was about to kick off, but he witnessed it first-hand from the jump-off trench where he lay after being injured.

Charles Chapman, whose father Samuel lived in Huntingdon Street, was another to suffer a leg wound from shrapnel, but his injury was not as serious and he quickly returned to duty. Albert Durham was wounded at the end of October in the right shoulder and his mother heard that he was in hospital in Liverpool. Albert Durham was another who had been in South Africa in August, but he was quickly recalled, and this Private in 'C' Company, 2nd Bedfords was amongst the many casualties during 1st Ypres. From Dublin he was given fourteen days' leave back in St Neots to assist his recovery and, whilst there, he learned that his younger brother William had answered Kitchener's call for more men.

These men were joined back home by Sergeant Percy Page, whose wound was a compound fracture of his left leg, sustained as the 2nd Bedfords defended Ypres. Percy Page was also in South Africa, near Pretoria, in 1914 and had returned, landing at Southampton in mid-September. After a quick refit the 2nd Bedfords were sent over to Zeebrugge on 7 October and then on to the front, first encountering the Germans outside of Ypres eleven days later.

The wounding of these men brought anxiety to their families but events on 31 October brought two other local families even more distressing news, when Lance Corporal George Pindred and Private William Braybrook Burns were both killed with the 2nd Bedfords at Ypres, as they were entrenched close to the Gheluvelt-Zandvoorde Road. Two platoons of 'C' Company, under the command of Captain Lemon, were ordered forward from their positions in Inverness Copse at 2.30 a.m. to a small fir wood that had been shelled heavily whilst occupied by the Lancashire Regiment the day before. As dawn broke, the Germans began shelling the wood again and started to advance in considerable numbers. When this was seen, orders were sent to Captain Lemon to withdraw, and during the fighting and retreat George Pindred and William Braybrook Burns were killed. Neither man has a known grave, and both are commemorated on the Menin Gate in Ypres. Captain Arthur Lemon was wounded and captured by the Germans. Further details about George Pindred's time in the trenches came to St Neots when his sister received a letter from Private Arthur Maydwell, who had been wounded and had been with George just days before he was killed. He wrote:

> I was wounded in the right shoulder at Ypres on October 23rd, and invalided home, where I am in hospital, and progressing nicely. George was in my trench when I got hit and helped me a little way to the dressing station. George and I slept together in the trench and fought together, and it is needless for me to add that I was deeply upset at receiving the news. I must tell you that you had a very plucky brother, and who was everything a soldier should be. He died a soldier's death, in a good cause and I promise you that when I get out there again I will endeavour to avenge his death.

More information about the deaths of George Pindred and William Braybrook Burns came from Private Harry Stapleford, who was badly wounded when his two St Neots chums were killed. Private Stapleford had been in the trenches for sixteen days, and during that time he had not had a wash or even a drink of tea, living off hard tack biscuits and turnips. When he arrived in St Neots in January 1915, he described how the Germans had been only about 75 yards away and how a shell had landed in his very trench, killing all but three of the 120 men who were with him. William Braybrook Burns was killed close by and George Pindred was just a few yards from him when he was hit. Private Stapleford was wounded when part of the shell went right through his lung, with other pieces of red-hot metal slicing off part of the first finger of his left hand as well as smashing the knuckle of the second finger. A few days earlier he had had a narrow escape when a German bullet had gone through the sleeve of his coat, his tunic and his shirt, leaving a brownish scar on his arm. At Le Cateau in August he had gone to help a wounded comrade and had picked up the man, who had put his arm around Private Stapleford's neck for support, when two bullets crashed through the wounded man's head. Private Stapleford feigned death himself from 8 a.m., the time the wounded man was shot through the brain, until 6 p.m. when it became dark and it was safe for him to move away. Later on, his narrow escapes continued when the bottom of his greatcoat was riddled with bullets but he was untouched. The wounding on 31 October was much more serious, as for some days he was unconscious before eventually waking up in hospital in Ypres. He was then transferred to hospitals back in Blighty where he underwent a number of operations. From Sheffield he wrote to his mother in Church Street:

I hope soon to be home for a holiday, but they will send me to a Convalescence Home first to get my strength back again. I had a lucky escape, one shrapnel wound is just over the heart, and I lost a finger, the top was blown off. And the best part of it when it was done I could not feel it. The shell, a big one, burst just in front of us, killing several; it knocked me down but I soon got up to see how far the Germans were away. They were only 100 yards or so, and the thought of being taken a prisoner came into my mind, so I ran for it and fell unconscious in a wood. I became conscious two days afterwards and found myself in hospital, and, my word, the comfort of a good bed after the trenches is glorious. I am being well looked after in Sheffield, plenty of everything we want. Visitors are always bringing in plenty of nice things for us. I am not out of bed yet, but am quite all right and doing fine.

Although Harry Stapleford's lung wound healed on the outside, he would feel the effect of the wound internally for many years. The damage to his left hand would be a visible reminder of that fateful day for the rest of his life. When back in St Neots, Private Stapleford was very reticent about what he had seen but eventually opened up and revealed how he himself had killed at least nine Germans.

More news of St Neots men came via a letter from Belfast's Victoria Barracks Hospital, where Private Robert Ayres of the 2nd Bedfords was recovering from wounds also incurred on 31 October. He wrote to his mother:

Just a line hoping you are all well, as it leaves me going on steady. It has been pretty rough where I have been. I have been fighting in Belgium against the Germans. The first Sunday morning we went into firing line we were shelled awful and lost 6 officers, 2 Lieutenants and 23 men wounded. That was a start. We were only 800 yards off the big guns of the Germans. The shells mowed our men down. It was awful. When I was wounded I was sitting on top of our trenches. The Germans started throwing their 'coal boxes' – that means their big shells what they fire, and the air and the sky appeared thick with shells, when one struck me in my foot, just below the ankle, and a bit more hit me on my finger. Two of my mates carried me along on a stretcher and when they were going back to the trench they both got killed. I hope I shall soon be better and with you again in England when I will tell you all about it. Charlie Chapman (Huntingdon Street) got shot in the leg, but it was not so bad and he got better in two days. We had it a bit rough coming from France.

The 2nd Bedfords were extremely hard pressed during this part of 1st Ypres, being in front-line action for eighteen days before they were pulled back. Quite how hard the battalion was hit during this period can be seen in the fact that its usual strength was around 800 men, with about a further 200 being held in reserve. By the end of 1 November 1914, the 2nd Bedfords were down to four officers and between 350 and 400 men, having lost over half of their battalion strength in the desperate fighting to stop the Germans from capturing Ypres.

On 31 October, the Germans came very close to capturing Ypres, and it was only last ditch defence and an almost suicidal counter-attack by the 2nd Battalion, Worcestershire Regiment that prevented them breaking through at Gheluvelt. The Germans had advanced in overwhelming numbers to capture the village and break the British line, thus leaving the BEF on the point of defeat. The Worcesters could only muster around 370 troops and the charge of these men, many of whom had lost their caps and puttees, saw 187 killed or wounded, but their bravery resulted in the gap in the British line being closed and the German attack halted. The Worcesters showed incredible valour that day and the regiment proudly records the date in its battle honours as Gheluvelt Day.

News of the fighting at Ypres and Armentières reached readers of the *St Neots Advertiser*, as letters from local serving soldiers were regularly published or summarised in the pages of the paper. At the start of November, the paper printed extracts from letters from Private Thomas Jacques and Sergeant Major Hall, both serving with the 1ˢᵗ Bedfords. Thomas Jacques of 'D' Company wrote:

> We sometimes have to be in the trenches for days and nights without being able to do anything, and the weather has been simply rotten, but just lately things have been a little better as the rain has gone off, for how long I cannot say; the continual firing of so many guns helps a lot to bring down the rain. I am writing this letter in the trench our troops have dug, we have been here now for a week right off, sleep in at night, what little sleep we do get. Sometimes we are lucky enough to get a few hours in the daytime, and then we have to be on the alert at night so as not to be surprised by the enemy. It is not very pleasant to be down in the trenches and do not know when you will have one of the German's eighty-pound shells dropped into it from something like five or eight miles back, and when they do arrive, my word! They make holes in the earth quite large enough to bury a good-sized horse in, but they very rarely have the luck to hit us. The Germans are very fond of shelling villages right behind our troops in the firing line, in the hope, I suppose of some of our troops being billeted there, and also to do as much damage as they can. The places where they have been are simply ruined; and in most cases blown out of all resemblance of a village – nothing but heaps of bricks and stones. The poor old people lose their homes and all they have in a few hours. It is this kind of thing that touches one in a very tender spot, more than all the fighting we have to do, but there will be a day of reckoning soon, and woe betide those German devils – they are nothing less than that.

Sadly Thomas Jacques would not live to see that day, or even the end of 1914.

Colour Sergeant Major Charles Hall from Croxton was a regular soldier with fifteen years' service when war broke out. He had fought through Mons, the Marne and the Aisne, having some narrow escapes. During the retreat from Mons, he was running down the street of a town when a 'Jack Johnson' shell flew just over his head, bursting in the ground a few yards ahead of him and stopping him in his tracks, but he came away uninjured. A few weeks later, he was sheltering from a German bombardment when a shell took off the corner of the house he was in and totally demolished the adjoining house, killing or injuring other soldiers taking cover there. As he left the house to try to help, it too was flattened by another German shell. At Givenchy on 22 October, he was in charge of a platoon and had been ordered to advance against the enemy. As they did so they came under a hail of bullets and he commanded his men to make for a trench a few yards away. Whilst they were trying to get there, a German bullet struck Charles Hall in the right arm with so much force that it actually spun him around. He tried to use his rifle as a support but, after a short time, he lost all feeling in the arm and was forced to drop his weapon. Luckily for him though, the bullet had passed through his arm without touching bone. Three days later he was back in Britain in Newcastle for treatment, but he was back at the front later that year. The war was not done with Charles Hall, and in November 1916 he was awarded the Distinguished Conduct Medal. The official citation read:

> For conspicuous gallantry in action. He rallied the supporting troops and directed them to their objective. Later, he organised bombing and working parties, and rendered most valuable assistance in the consolidation of the position.

Whilst the battle for Ypres was raging, another altogether stranger death of a soldier took place in nearby Bedford, when Private Arthur Charker of the Cameron Highlanders was fatally stabbed by a bayonet on 12 October. These Territorials were encamped at Bedford and Arthur

Charker had gone out drinking with Private John Fraser when an argument broke out, which led to Arthur Charker being stabbed by John Fraser's bayonet as they proceeded down Union Street. John Fraser appeared before Bedford Assizes, pleading guilty to manslaughter, but saying that the stabbing was unintentional. He was given fifteen months' hard labour.

The magistrates in Bedford were busy at this time with cases concerning the military, for during the first week of November they heard the case of Private Donald Anderson and his wife Lizzie, who were charged with attempted suicide. Nineteen-year-old Donald Anderson was serving with the Gordon Highlanders and his wife, who was a year younger, had even come down to Bedford from Scotland at the start of October to be nearer her husband. When they heard that his regiment was likely to be sent over to the Western Front, the two of them came to an astonishing decision – to die together rather than be parted. On Wednesday 4 November, Donald and Lizzie Anderson went to the Picture Palace in Bedford and then went to the river embankment, where at around midnight they jumped into the Great Ouse together. Screams were heard by a local resident, who ran to see what was happening and found Donald Anderson holding up his wife in the river; she was in a collapsed state. The Town Clerk told the court that he did not wish to pursue the charge against Lizzie and, as the military authorities were willing to take Donald back, he was quite happy with that. Lizzie Anderson was discharged and Donald returned to his regiment. Donald Anderson does not appear amongst the casualties for the Gordon Highlanders during the Great War, so it seems likely that these two young lovers were happily reunited after the war.

Across the Channel, the Germans renewed their attempt to take Ypres – and once more came agonisingly close. This time the decisive action took place at Nonnesboschen on 11 November, when an intense German bombardment rained down on the BEF for hours, destroying trenches and dugouts and even felling trees. Outnumbered two to one, the BEF fought back fiercely as the elite Prussian Guards attacked on a cold, misty morning and broke through, forcing a decisive gap in the British line. The hand-to-hand fighting here was violent and uncompromising as both British and German bayonets did terrible work. Just when it seemed that disaster could not be averted, the BEF counter-attacked and drove the Germans out of Nonnesboschen Wood. If the Germans had held on to, and extended the break in, the BEF line, then Ypres would have fallen and their chance of victory on the Western Front would have increased significantly.

News of the struggle for Ypres reached St Neots via letters from Privates Arthur Davies and Arthur Rollings, who gave detailed reports as the fighting raged. Private Davies had been in Canada as war was declared, but he quickly returned and was serving with the 2nd Northamptonshire Battalion right from the start at Mons. In the last week of November he was hospitalised with rheumatic problems, three days after going into action again. He wrote from his hospital bed in Boulogne and then from Shrewsbury, telling of a fierce fight on the weekend of 15/16 November:

I went into the firing line on Saturday night, 15th. Although we had a little bit of a scrap on Saturday night it was nothing much to speak of. But we made up for it on Sunday night … The Germans, who were entrenched only about 200 yards away from us, made several charges on Sunday night and tried hard to draw us out of our trenches, but they failed and were found to fall back into their trenches. They lost a tremendous lot of men. I think they had got a lot more men than us so it was no good us getting out of the trenches and advancing. There is no fighting going on in the day time much. Only snipers on the lookout, as soon as they see anyone they snipe but don't always get a bull's eye. After being in the trenches three days I was taken sick with rheumatism owing to the damp conditions of the trenches. The fighting line now extends 300 miles and I was in the battle in which the Germans are fighting for Calais … the only way the wounded can escape is at dusk before any firing commences. There were two Germans taken prisoner, one of them threw down his rifle and said 'Thank God I am captured. I have never shot an Englishman in my life. I was born and bred in England' and turning round said 'This other b★★!!★★! is the same opinion as me only he cannot speak English.' Most of them have been waiters in London. If we shout out 'waiter' some of them bob their heads out of the trenches. The troops seem pretty lively although the trenches are very bad owing to the rain … It seems rather good sport to have a shot when we see any of their heads above the trenches.

Private Rollings was with the 3rd Battalion, the Coldstream Guards, outside of Ypres. He wrote:

> … they started shelling again. They kept getting nearer and nearer each time until we all thought one was coming in amongst us, we could hear it coming as we lay flat on the ground – which is the safest position to be in when they are shelling. Everyone was looking in the direction where this shell was coming from, was it going to burst in amongst us that was everybody's thought. But no; it burst some yards in front of us, ploughing the earth up in the air some distance. No one was hurt and we could all breathe freely once again.

Private Rollings, a Reservist prior to the war, was a regular writer and his letters frequently featured in the *St Neots Advertiser*. He looked forward to receiving the newspaper in the trenches and enjoyed reading how his fellow soldiers from the town were getting on. One such letter from him was published in the edition of 4 December, which told of witnessing an enemy aircraft being brought down by Allied fire:

> An aeroplane came along and dropped some lights along our artillery big guns so as to give the enemy some idea where our guns are situated, and as he was rather low one company of our men were told to fetch him down. They commenced to fire at this for a second or two, at last the machine burst in flames in the air. It did look a sight and the man jumped out and you can guess his fate when he reached the ground. The machine settled some distance away all in flames.

During the Great War, pilots of either side were not issued with parachutes and they had the agonising decision to make if they were hit – whether to stay in the aircraft and burn to death or jump to certain death. Many pilots kept a revolver in the cockpit, preferring to shoot themselves rather than burn or drop like a stone.

From Ypres, news of more casualties reached St Neots. More details of Private George Child's wounding revealed that he had been injured on 31 October, being hit in the right shoulder by a German bullet. He returned to Britain and was taken to Norwich Hospital where he was treated for a fortnight and the bullet was removed. In late November he was back in St Neots, with the X-ray showing just where the bullet had lodged in his shoulder. He was also able to tell how twelve stitches were needed to seal the wound after surgeons finally got the bullet out. On 7 November, Private Arthur Darrington Townsend joined the growing number of men from the area to be killed. Arthur Townsend was a Wyboston man serving with the 1st Bedfords as they returned to the front line at Ypres on 6 November, relieving the 2nd Bedfords. The following day the Germans attacked, breaking into the Bedfords' trenches, but were then driven back. The Bedfords' casualties were seven officers and 140 other ranks killed or wounded. Arthur Townsend was amongst those killed and his body was never recovered. For over seven weeks his family sought news of him, but it was not until 1915 that it was confirmed he had been killed in action.

Two days after Arthur Townsend died, another local man with the 1st Bedfords was also killed. In a daring raid upon the German front line, the Bedfords crept up to the enemy trenches

Private Will Medlock.

close to Hooge to try to recapture two machine-guns lost earlier. The raid was a success, for although only one machine-gun was discovered, the raiders also brought back a wounded Bedford soldier. Casualties were seven wounded and seventeen killed, amongst whom was thirty-four-year-old Private William Green, the son of William and Elizabeth Green from Bushmead, a single man who had enlisted at Huntingdon before going over to France during August. He was added to the list of those who have no known grave and today he is commemorated on Le Touret Memorial.

These first four months of fighting were hard on the men of the BEF, and those who survived had tales to tell. Privates Will and Ted Medlock, with the 1st Bedfords, were just two who fell into this category. Writing home from hospital in Oxford in late November, Will said:

My brother and I are Huntingdonshire men from Great Gransden, and this is the only chance we have had to send a letter suitable for publication since we left England for the Front on August 14th, 1914, and I can tell you I have had some hardships, both great and small, but I had to take all in good part from the retirement from Mons up to the time I got wounded at Ypres ... I myself have seen enough to make the strongest man's nerves break, and I am not ashamed to say have made me cry, but they are only everyday occurrences and one gets hardened to anything at the Front ... I have been in the battles of Mons, Le Cateau, Crepy, battle of the Aisne, Cha. Michael, La Bassee and Ypres, where I got bowled over by what they call a 'Jack Johnson', that is a 700lbs shell, but out at the front we give everything, which details would fill a book, but Tommy Atkins seems to take it all in good part. Out of 17 in my section at Mons I was the only one remaining until I got my present which got me home.

What Will Medlock failed to mention was that on 29 October he had shown considerable bravery when he and a comrade advanced under heavy enemy fire towards a farmhouse occupied by about fifty Germans near Festubert and set fire to it. The Germans inside withdrew, abandoning a building that had given them an appreciable tactical advantage. In June 1915, Will Medlock was awarded the Distinguished Conduct Medal for his bravery here. Ted Medlock was also wounded at Ypres and the two brothers found themselves next to each other in hospital beds back in Blighty.

The First Battle of Ypres came to a halt during the middle weeks of November as the weather worsened, making fighting difficult to say the least. Both sides accepted that the struggle here would have to wait for the New Year and better weather, with the Germans acknowledging their failure to take Ypres. In halting the Germans, the BEF lost 10,500 soldiers, and fewer than 2,000 ended up with a known grave as artillery churned up the ground and destroyed many last resting places. The idea that the war would be 'over by Christmas' proved to be wrong and both sides now realised that there would be no quick victory. On the Western Front, daily shelling and trench raids continued, but no major offensive took place until spring 1915. During one of those daily duels at the start of December, twenty-seven-year-old Private Thomas Jacques from Weald died – two days after being wounded – and was the only man in his battalion hit by enemy fire that day. His mother received a postcard from him on the morning of 7 December telling that he had been wounded, and then later on that very same day a letter was delivered that told her he had died. The letter from Chaplain Fitch read:

> Your son Pte Jakes in the Bedfordshire Regiment was brought to the ambulance here two days ago. He was badly wounded in the back. I regret to say he passed away this morning. I saw him shortly before he died, and he asked me to write to you and tell you he had been hit. He sent no special message – only his love. He died bravely, as he had lived. I buried him today at noon in the Churchyard of the Parish Church at Dranouter, about two miles N.E. of Bailleul; a little wooden cross marks his grave. May God comfort you in your great loss.

Thomas Jacques had been a Reservist before the outbreak of hostilities, working as a valet to a gentleman, and he was to be married just as war broke out. Today he rests in Dranouter Cemetery to the south of Ypres.

Four days before Christmas another local man, Private Horace Usher, with the 1st Battalion Northants Regiment, was killed close to La Bassée. Horace Usher, a regular soldier who had been born in Staploe and whose father lived in Bushmead, had been in the army for just over a year when he was killed. Initially this nineteen-year-old was reported as missing in action, but eleven months later that changed and his grieving father, Christopher, received confirmation that his eldest son had died on 21 December. Nine years later Horace Usher's identity tag, with a large jagged hole in it, was discovered by a French farmer, and when the Imperial War Graves started their work after the war, his body was amongst those that was identified and relocated to Pont du Hem Military Cemetery near La Bassée.

As the end of the year drew near, a remarkable event took place along some

Private Horace Usher.

sections of the Western Front, beginning on Christmas Eve and lasting for some days afterwards – the so-called Christmas Truce. German troops, notably those from Saxon regiments, initiated the ceasefire when they started to put up lanterns and Christmas trees decorated with candles. This was followed by carol singing on Christmas Eve, and on Christmas Day German soldiers started to climb out of their front-line trenches, calling over that they wouldn't fire if the British didn't. British Tommies climbed out of their trenches and both sides moved towards each other, and then exchanged cigarettes, alcohol and food. Officers were at first uncertain what to do – some turned a blind eye, whilst others took the opportunity to see the German lines in daylight. There was also the chance for both sides to bury the dead of No Man's Land.

Men from St Neots certainly witnessed and participated in the truce, as Private Martin Byatt of the 2nd Bedfords told when he wrote home in January 1915:

> Just a few lines hoping St Neots is looking quite as well as it was before I left on August 8th 1914. I am sorry to say we have had a lot of wet this last month. I am glad to say the troops have had quite a fine time in the trenches at Christmas time. The Germans came out of their trenches and called to the Bedfords to go one at a time half way, and they would come half way, so we stopped firing at them and went half way across to them and had some smokes together with them, so they asked us if we would have a game at football with them. We had not got a ball with us, or I think we should have had a game with them.

Private John Holyoaks, also with the 2nd Bedfords, endorsed Martin Byatt's letter, writing home:

> For four days we did not fire a shot at one another. Some of them are nice fellows, and cannot make out why they are fighting the English. The Guards played them at football on our right. We had no ball or we should have done the same.

He went on to say that he was sending home the gift from Princess Margaret that all troops in the BEF received, together with souvenirs taken from the enemy, including German money, two cigars, a German helmet badge and a medal. He explained that the badge was one of the effects exchanged during the truce in No Man's Land on Christmas Day and Boxing Day.

The truce lasted for several days in some sections of the front, until the top brass of both sides ordered it should cease. Even so, New Year's Eve was celebrated, the Germans an hour earlier than the Tommies because of Continental time, and although there was no fraternisation in No Man's Land, there was little shelling of each other's trenches.

In St Neots, there was concern that rising river levels might flood parts of the town at Christmas and indeed Cambridge Street, High Street and Huntingdon Street were seriously affected. Rain, sleet and snow had fallen heavily and the view from the town bridge was simply one stretch of water, with all of the meadows and fields on each side of the road being submerged. Some homes were under several inches of water and perhaps this gave St Neotians a degree of empathy with the soldiers on the Western Front, who daily had to stand in flooded trenches. The St Neots Workhouse escaped and the inmates enjoyed a Christmas menu of roast beef, potatoes, carrots, plum puddings, beer and mineral water, followed by apples, oranges and tobacco for the men, sweets for the women. The day ended with an impromptu concert. The water covered Eaton Ford but not Eaton Socon, where a football match between 'Married' and Single' took place that resulted in a 3–3 draw and £1 6d was raised to buy cigarettes and tobacco for the troops at the front.

By the end of 1914, trench warfare was established and the popular image of the Great War, with soldiers living a troglodyte existence, now began to take shape. These early trenches were quite basic, but they soon developed into the formidable defences faced by attacking troops in later years of the conflict. The daily routine of trench life was quickly established, as days started with 'morning hate', an artillery bombardment from both sides that was followed by a 'stand to', where troops manned the fire steps of the trench in case the enemy attacked. If this did not materialise, they would settle down to breakfast, often bacon. During the day, trench walls often had to be repaired to keep them stable, and men who were not on sentry duty would try to get some 'shuteye'. The temptation of looking over the parapet had to be resisted, for snipers practised their deadly work on the careless and the curious. Latrines were dug, usually at the end on a sap, and men had to be especially careful here, for the clouds of rising flies clearly indicated that the latrine was being used. Snipers and alert artillery observers often targeted these latrines.

Tinned food, bully beef, plum and apple jam, and Maconochies – a form of soup made from carrots and turnips – became the staple diet. Men also had a daily bread allowance and were given hard tack biscuits that had to be soaked in liquid, usually condensed milk, to make them edible. Water was brought to the front in empty petrol cans that were supposed to have been 'fired' to remove the smell of the fuel, but soldiers joked that they could tell whether a Shell or Esso can had been used. Night was when the trenches came alive, with barbed wire repairs in No Man's Land and trench raids. Sometimes the working parties in No Man's Land clashed, but also there were occasions when German and British soldiers ignored each other and just carried out necessary repairs. Such an example took place in early 1915 as Sapper Knights of the Canadian Engineers told his brother, Revd H.J. West Knights of St Neots. Sapper Knights wrote:

> We were putting up wire entanglements in front of the firing line between the English and the German trenches, and directly the Germans heard us at work they came out and started fixing their entanglements, and not a shot was fired.

Rats, lice, shelling and sniping made trench life hard, and British trenches were often inferior to German ones which were built to consolidate and keep the land they had taken so far. The British top brass did not want their men getting too comfortable in cosy trenches, as they thought this would take away their attacking edge. Men did adapt to this unfamiliar world and underground existence and, when back home on leave and even after the war, many men told of the camaraderie that developed in the trenches. Actual sightings of the enemy were rare and men could complete many tours of the front line without even seeing a single German. Death or injury, when it came, often arrived in the shape of shells sometimes fired from miles away.

One such casualty was Bombardier William Gilbert from St Neots, who was literally blown up when a German shell exploded near to him at La Bassée in late November, wounding him and causing shock and a nervous breakdown. This condition would be described as 'shellshock' later in the war. Bombardier Gilbert returned to England on Boxing Day for treatment at Alder Hey Hospital in Derby. In November, a letter from Bombardier Gilbert had appeared in the *St Neots Advertiser*, in which he had urged local men to enlist. He wrote:

> I see we have a few from St Neots on active service. I do hope that the young men of St Neots will think of their duty to their country and rally round the flag in Kitchener's Army and not let it be said that the boys of St Neots were backward. I feel sure that the men from St Neots who are out here will give a good account of themselves. I am sure Hunts can turn out men as good as any county in England … I came out with the first force and have been in all the large battles up to the present, and have been very lucky on more than one occasion. I am still in good health at present and doing well. We get plenty of good food and are well provided with warm clothes and tobacco – thanks to the British public. I wish I could tell you about the War, but as you know we are not allowed to.

William Gilbert made a quick recovery from the shock of being blown up and wrote home:

> The Sergeant of my gun detachment was wounded and I had hardly taken his place when one of their 90 pounders dropped straight into us. I was blown some yards away and received such a shock that I was taken to Hospital, it is a marvel I wasn't blown to pieces, all I saw before I went to Hospital was legs, arms and heads of our poor fellows. I was sent to St Maur Hospital, from there to Versailles, near Paris and from there to Le Havre. At Le Havre I had to have 18 teeth out. After being in hospital there a fortnight I was sent to Liverpool, and I hope to be in St Neots shortly. I am still suffering from shock but am improving greatly.

By the end of 1914, the original BEF had acquitted itself with distinction but had suffered staggering losses, with much of its pre-war strength dead or wounded. When the First Battle of Ypres ended, the total casualties for the BEF on the Western Front amounted to 3,627 officers and 86,237 other ranks, killed or wounded. The need for replacements had seen the Territorials called on from late October, but Kitchener's volunteers were still undergoing training for they were far from being ready. Their day would soon come, though perhaps before they were prepared. As 1914 came to an end, no conclusion to the hostilities was in sight. Those who had believed that this would be a short war were wrong and it dawned upon soldiers, politicians and those left at home that a modern mechanised war would likely be lengthy and costly in terms of lives and resources. Quite what 1915 would bring was anybody's guess.

TWO

⌒1915⌒
A WIDENING CONFLICT

Quite how much the original BEF had suffered was aptly summed up at the start of 1915, with the issue of another appeal from Lord Kitchener which read: 'Another 100,000 men with the least possible delay are urgently needed to complete the requirements of the Army.' Those answering the appeal were directed to the nearest military barracks or recruiting office, and to endorse the appeal many papers printed a headline that read: 'Avenge Scarborough!' which referred to the German Navy's shelling of the East Coast late in 1914. The few short lines of the article did not mince words and ran as follows:

> The wholesale murder of innocent women and children demands vengeance!
> Men of England, the innocent victims of German brutality call upon you to avenge them.
> Show the German barbarians that Britain's shores cannot be bombarded with impunity.
> ENLIST TODAY.

A first-hand account of Scarborough's shelling reached St Neots in late December 1914 when Mr Alfred Murphy wrote home to his wife. He had been on business in Scarborough, staying at the Castle Hotel, when the bombardment took place; he told his wife that the shelling started at 8 a.m. on 16 December and lasted for about twenty minutes. Mr Murphy had a lucky escape for the bedroom next to his was hit by a shell, and he told how the whole hotel shook so much that he felt it would collapse. He described how around 100 shells had been fired, with over 200 buildings being damaged. He added that business had come to a halt and many people were leaving the town. In fact Hartlepool, West Hartlepool and Whitby were also shelled, with around 1,150 shells fired, resulting in 137 people being killed and a further 592 being wounded. The raid caused outrage in Britain and the Royal Navy was criticised for its failure to prevent the attack.

In January, Huntingdon and St Neots town councils discussed the possibility of German attack, not by naval bombardment but rather by air. Dover had been bombed on Christmas Eve and the British Government was well aware of Zeppelin airship development. There was talk of Cambridge being attacked, and Huntingdon and St Neots were not so far away. Therefore precautions such as turning the gas off from the gas works were debated, as it was thought that some people might forget to turn the gas taps off in their homes, and incendiary bombs would then have a dramatic effect. It was also agreed that the fire brigade would be on standby, and that a blackout should come into force during the hours of darkness. Church bells were to ring in the event of an attack.

Private Edgar Boon.

Just ten days into 1915, a ninth local man died on the Western Front. Private Edgar Boon had been born in Great Barford where his parents still lived, but in 1914 he was living in St Neots and 'on reserve'. He was immediately called up and rejoined the 1st Bedfords. Edgar Boon fought at Mons, the Marne, La Bassée and then Ypres, but at the start of 1915 he was entrenched near Bailleul at Dranoutre and, although this was a quiet period, casualties occurred on a daily basis. In the first ten days of January, eight were killed and nine were wounded as shelling and sniping gnawed away at the resolve and morale of the men. On the 9th the Germans shelled the Bedfords using a motorised gun and on the following day, as the men worked to repair trenches, Edgar Boon was killed when a shell burst and he was hit in the head by a piece of shrapnel. The BEF suffered increasing numbers of fatalities from head wounds, as the soft caps worn by the men offered little protection. Casualty figures from this kind of wound certainly fell after soldiers were issued with steel helmets from the start of 1916. Sadly this was a year too late for Edgar Boon and the hand of tragedy did not release its grip on the Boon family; one and a half years later they would again be touched. In February his parents heard from H.V. Farnfield, chaplain of the Bedfords:

> He fought nobly and died nobly, and you will bear your loss, I feel sure, as he would have you bear it, nobly. I conducted the last rights in the Cemetery. Over his grave is erected a Cross upon which is his name, regiment, etc, 'Died from wounds received in action'. Nothing grander could be said of him. He died for God, for King and for Country.

More fortunate was Private William Webb of the 1st Bedfords, who escaped serious injury in 1914 and then again in the New Year. Writing home in January, he told:

> I have had four narrow escapes. I had a shrapnel bullet go through my cap, just catching my head, which knocked me down for a few minutes; it tore my cap half way across the top. The next one I got across the back of my hand, which just cut me, but not serious; the third one through the peak of my cap, and the fourth hit my rifle just as I was taking aim at the few Germans who were exposing themselves too much. A bullet hit my rifle not an eighth of an inch from my little finger on my left hand. If I had moved my hand a little farther down I should be minus two fingers, so I think I should thank God for sparing me from all this. I had rather a surprise a few days ago. Whilst on sentry go in [*sic*] the trenches I saw two Germans knocking their hands to keep them warm and in a few minutes I had them both. A third came up and looked across to me through a pair of glasses, and I soon had him to the ground. What surprised me was the way they stood up on top of their trenches just as if nothing was going on. I must say that some of them are very brave indeed. That is three more Germans I can add to my list.

In four months time William Webb's luck would run out.

The day before Edgar Boon was killed, thirty-five-year-old Captain Denzil Newton died of wounds, twenty-four hours after being hit. Denzil Newton's family were from Croxton and he had had a notable military career prior to the Great War, serving during the Boer War and then being the Aide de Camp to the Governor General of Canada. He had been decorated by the Emperor of Japan, receiving the Order of the Rising Sun, and was with the first Canadian troops, the Princess Patricia's Light Infantry, when they landed in France in December 1914. On 6 January they entered the Ypres Salient, and two days later, as they were entrenched at Dickebusch, they came under heavy artillery fire. Denzil Newton was Captain of

No. 4 Company. As they manned their waterlogged trenches on that Friday morning, German shells fell and two men were killed outright, whilst Captain Newton was among five who were wounded. Early next day, Denzil Onslow Cochrane Newton succumbed to his wounds and became the first Canadian officer to die during the Great War. His brother George ran the estate in Croxton which Denzil had visited just weeks earlier when attending the funeral of his mother, Lady Alice Cochrane. Today Denzil Newton rests in Dickebusch Military Cemetery in Ypres.

During January, wounded and ill soldiers became a familiar sight in Eaton Socon, as the hospital at Mrs Butler's house was now affiliated to the 1st Eastern General Hospital, Cambridge, and thirty-four wounded men had already been treated there. On the first Sunday of January, Private Arthur Smith was a surprise visitor back in his home in Eynesbury. He had left St Neots at the start of the fighting and had been at the front since 12 September, but by December he was not in good shape and was carried out of the trenches, suffering from exhaustion and rheumatism. After hospital treatment he was given leave, and back in St Neots he told of his war, having fought at La Bassée, Ypres and Dixmude; he had been in the front line for nineteen days without a break on one occasion. Arthur Smith was a veteran of the Boer War, but he thought that there was no comparison between that and the present war, describing the former as 'a fleabite'.

Bad weather meant that no new offensives could be mounted and the early months of 1915 did bring something of a respite for those in the trenches. However, it did not always follow that the front line was a peaceful place, for the artillery of both sides continued to shell enemy trenches on a regular, if not daily, basis. In a war where artillery was the chief cause of death, the early months of 1915 saw casualties and fatalities continue, with many of the BEF injured or killed by head wounds as shrapnel tore through their soft caps.

Danger from enemy shelling was ever present, as the two sides waited for the weather to improve in the spring – but men became casualties in other ways, notably in trench raids which were a regular feature of British tactics. These raids were made across No Man's Land to try to capture enemy soldiers, bring them back and get information from them, which could be invaluable in establishing the strength and morale of the enemy, or to plan attacks. Sometimes the raiders were lucky, for the capture of an enemy officer could be priceless. The Germans even sent men over dressed in British uniform, who could speak perfect English, to spy out the enemy front line. British Tommies often reported unknown officers in their trenches who asked them detailed questions. Such a ruse was reported in November 1914, when a figure dressed as a Gurkha officer approached some of the Indian Army Corps entrenched in France and told them to move out, for another Gurkha unit was coming to replace them. However, an actual officer with the Gurkhas suspected something was wrong and challenged the stranger who fled, but he only got about five yards away before the officer shot him. The stranger did indeed prove to be a German in disguise.

Raids were dangerous and officers sought volunteers carefully. Raiders armed themselves with studded clubs, cudgels, large sheath knives, grenades and pistols, camouflaging themselves by blackening faces with burnt cork and wearing balaclavas. Knives and bayonets were dulled by soot or soil on the blades so they would not reflect when crossing No Man's Land, and if Very lights were fired men were instructed to freeze to try to prevent discovery. The raiders gradually approached the enemy's trenches, listening carefully for sentries' conversation, or the tell-tale sign of a lighted cigarette. When they got close they stormed the enemy trench, fighting, killing and capturing before making a swift exit back to their own lines. The British High Command continually stressed the importance of these raids, for as well as getting information they felt that they served the purpose of keeping troops reminded that they were on the offensive. Removing German troops from both France and Belgium remained the prime aim, and these raids were an important feature of achieving that objective.

Conditions in the trenches during January 1915 remained dreadful, with waterlogging and collapse of the breastworks being common problems. The 2nd Battalion of the Royal Berkshire Regiment suffered such problems at La Bassée and, on 29 January, Private John Anderson of Eaton Socon was killed as the battalion tried to improve front-line trenches, which were often knee-deep in water and mud. The men of the 2nd Battalion spent two weeks attempting to build breastworks made from sandbags above the trench, but this was a dangerous job and thirteen men were killed carrying out this work. John Anderson was the twelfth man from the battalion killed as the Berkshires tried to complete this task. Before the war he had been a Reservist, but he was called up on 4 August, leaving his wife and two children behind in Eaton Socon. He had crossed over to France in November 1914, moving to trenches at Fauquissart which were in very low-lying ground that flooded constantly, and the men suffered terribly from trench foot. Over Christmas the Berkshires had participated in the truce, enjoying three days of peace. By the end of January that seemed an age ago and everlasting peace came to John Anderson on the 29th. Three months later, John Anderson's widow received the following letter from the British Red Cross:

Dear Mrs Anderson, In case the information has not yet reached you, I am writing to let you know that the grave of your husband, Private J Anderson, 6198, 2nd Royal Berks Regt., is at Fauquissart Lavantic near Neuve Chapelle. You may like to know that the grave is being cared for and has been marked so that later on when the War is over proper measures can be taken to preserve the memory of those who have fallen for their Country. Believe me with true sympathy, Yours faithfully, Mrs G G Buckler, for Lord Robert Cecil.

Today, James Anderson rests in Fauquissart Military Cemetery.

Also wounded on 29 January was twenty-two-year-old Rifleman Charles Drake, one of four brothers serving and a regular soldier who had been in India at the start of the war. His father lived in Leyton whilst his uncle, Walter Firmin Drake, lived in Eaton Socon, working as the postmaster. Writing in February, he told of his wounding as he served with the 3rd Battalion, Kings Royal Rifle Corps:

Dear Father, Just a few lines to let you know, if you do not know already, that I have been rather badly wounded. I was hit by shrapnel in the left shoulder, near the arm, and the right hand just in the bend of the wrist. I do not know how I am writing this letter, as I have no use whatever in my right hand, only just the fingers, and my shoulder is awfully painful, being slightly fractured. This job happened on the 29th Jan, about mid-day, and I could not be got away until dark. I had a lively time, there were 23 shells came over my end of the trench, No. 21 'put my wind up', No. 22 hit me, and the 23rd buried me and all my belongings ... Five of my fellows got hit as well as I, two in my trench and three in a trench lower down, but it was nothing to speak of, it was poor me who stopped the Jack Johnson, a left and right. Well, Dad, I have absolutely nothing now, I lost everything, new top boots, my rifle and equipment, and my valise, and all my private things in it, all pounded up and buried by Jack Johnsons, and they had to cut my clothes off me to dress my wounds. Well I must close now, as I am suffering agony in my writing. Please write to Eaton Socon for me. With best love to all, from your ever loving son.

Charles Drake recovered from his wounds to return to the front line, only for a worse fate just four months later.

Not everybody serving abroad in these first six months of the war was male; in faraway Serbia, Jennie Sibley, a qualified nurse from St Neots, was working in Skopje at Lady Leila Paget's Hospital. Miss Sibley, who had responded to the call for nurses to help the humanitarian Serbian Relief Fund, had left for the Balkans in October 1914 and by January was heavily involved in treating both Serbian and Austro-Hungarian wounded. In late January, the *Daily News* described the work of these volunteer nurses:

> There they lie in rows, suffering and maimed ... brought from a dozen different lands, speaking a dozen different tongues, Serbian and Austrian all equals and friends in common human misery, all devoted to their devoted English nurses.

The volunteer nurses continued their work at Skopje until late October 1915, when they were forced to leave as a Bulgarian invading army advanced upon the town. The nurses were evacuated to Britain.

By the start of February, the BEF had suffered an astonishing 104,000 casualties and the need for more men was evident in the increase in recruiting posters in the press. Numbers of men coming forward had slowed, possibly because of the sight of so many wounded men coming home, combined with growing casualty lists. Life in the army no longer seemed to be the great adventure that it had in the early autumn of 1914. Soldiers at the front endorsed the need for more men, as can be seen from the letter that Sapper Harold Harrison sent home. He wrote:

> The chief thing we require out here is more men, so that men can be relieved more often, as it is a sight to see troops returning from the trenches all over mud and water, and it makes you wonder how they can keep their smiling faces, and make jokes as they pass you along the road. It speaks well for an Englishman's endurance. I am glad to see that men are still enlisting in St Neots and around about, for the more men we get the sooner the war will be over.

His letter also included the following information, which showed that all German troops did not share the same enthusiasm for the fight:

> One night the troops who were in the German trenches put up a big board on which was written, 'We are Saxons in these trenches and do not wish to fight you, so do not shoot at us, and we will not shoot at you, but keep your shots for the Prussians, who are relieving us tomorrow night' – and the shooting stopped for the 24 hours which the Saxon troops remained in the trenches.

These first few weeks of 1915 were hard-going for soldiers in the trenches, especially in the Ypres Salient where freezing cold or heavy rain made life miserable. Men suffered badly from frozen feet and Private William Wadsworth was just one soldier affected. He had only been in the trenches for two stretches of forty-eight hours each and yet the cold was so bad that he was invalided home with frozen feet. It was not that Private Wadsworth was an inexperienced soldier, having served twelve years with the Leicesters, but he was called up from reserve to the Bedfords and sent over to France in early February. After being treated in hospitals in Birmingham and Coventry, he turned up at his home in Luke Street, Eynesbury in late February on leave, explaining, 'I had the bad luck to get frostbitten quick, and therefore had no exciting experiences.' He also told that he had seen Privates Bettles and Medlow from Eaton Socon as he came out of the front line, and said that they were both all right then. Indeed, George Bettles confirmed this when he wrote to both his sister and mother in March, telling them that the weather was fine during the day but that it was very cold still at night.

Many soldiers suffered from trench foot caused by days of standing in water, which at Ypres was reached at about 4ft below ground. To try to combat this, the height of the trench was increased by building above ground level, with sandbags used as breastworks to afford men more protection. Sapper Knights of the Canadian Engineers described this in his letter to his brother in St Neots in February, telling how, 'Some of the new trenches are not dug but built up on the ground, thus avoiding flooding.' He went on to say how his carelessness had almost cost him his life: 'One night I absent-mindedly struck a match to light my pipe, and whizz came a German sniper's bullet past my ear.'

Not so fortunate, in the trenches just south of Ypres, was Private Charlie Payne of the 1st Bedfords, who was killed on Saturday, 20 February, when German mortars fell, killing two men just before the Bedfords were about to be relieved and go into reserve. Charlie Payne's parents were the landlord and landlady of the Plough Inn, Wyboston and the death of their twenty-three-year-old son hit them particularly hard, for he was a single man who still lived at home. Before the war he had been on reserve and he had something of a reputation as a marksman. He had left for the front on 8 August and then had fought through Mons, the Marne, the Aisne and 1st Ypres, at one stage having been in the front line for three weeks without a break. Charlie Payne had written to his mother just five days before he died, saying that he was tired of fighting:

> I have seen enough of it and shall be glad when all is over. It is not half as rough as it was when we first joined. They tell me I am getting fat. I know that I look a lot better than I did.

Charlie Payne is buried in RE Farm Cemetery, 6 miles south of Ypres.

As the weather improved the pressure on the BEF to take the offensive increased, and this resulted in the offensive that took place at Neuve Chapelle in March. This was the first large-scale attack that the BEF undertook, after prompting from the French. Neuve Chapelle is located on a flat plain south of Lille, and the aim of the attack was to show both commitment to the Allied cause and to take the high ground known as Aubers Ridge. The offensive was to be combined with a French one to the south at Vimy Ridge, and the first target was the area of enemy line that jutted out towards the Allies at Neuve Chapelle. Such a feature was known as

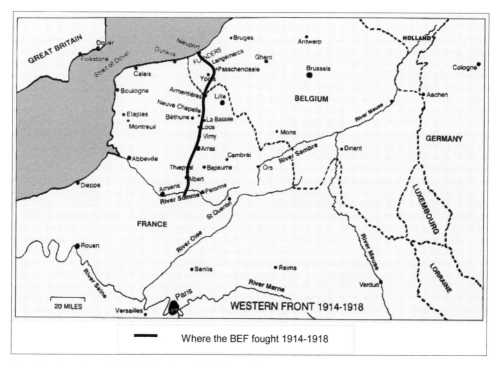

Map showing where the BEF fought on the Western Front.

a salient and it was here that the British attacked in March. The assault was carefully planned, for there was a need to ensure that shells were not wasted. Both sides had not expected trench warfare and shell production had concentrated upon shrapnel for use against troops in the open. As such, there was a real shortage of shells that were suitable for trench warfare, and these were rationed and stored for major offensives. This can clearly be seen during the First Battle of Ypres, where the British artillery was restricted to just nine rounds per day towards the end of October 1914.

On 10 March 1915, at 7.30 a.m., 342 guns of the British artillery bombarded the German lines at Neuve Chapelle, using a majority of shrapnel shells to try to cut the barbed wire in front of the enemy trenches. The advance followed as the artillery shifted beyond the German line in an attempt to stop German reinforcements from getting through. On the whole the attack went well and objectives were taken, but the problem was one that would go on to haunt both sides throughout the war – communication between attacking troops and their commanders behind. Messages usually had to be relayed by runners since telephone lines were quickly blown up and, of course, there were not the portable wireless/radio communications that we take for granted today. At Neuve Chapelle this was crucial, for although the initial objectives were taken, no orders were given to the reserves to follow on and consolidate the gains. This pause gave the Germans time to replenish their defences and the battle continued for two more days. The BEF might well have made a significant breakthrough at Neuve Chapelle, but communication problems prevented them exploiting initial success. Lessons were learned though, not least the importance of adequate shell supplies and accurate artillery fire. For the Germans, the battle made them realise that one trench line was not enough and that a second or third line was required. However, command and control of attacking troops, and the difficulty of communication, were the real lessons of Neuve Chapelle.

Men from St Neots fought at Neuve Chapelle and sadly one of them, Private Joseph Davies of 2nd Battalion, South Staffordshire Regiment, was killed. This thirty-one-year-old was the son of Joseph and Alice Davies, who used to run the Old Plough in Huntingdon Street but, in 1914, he was living in Hull although he enlisted in Wolverhampton. His war came to an abrupt end at Neuve Chapelle and his body was lost as the fighting raged, so today he is commemorated on Le Touret Memorial. First-hand accounts of the struggle at Neuve Chapelle reached St Neots via soldiers' letters. Private Walter Gale wrote:

> We came out of the trenches Saturday night after having a week in them, and going through the worst battle ever known. I must say I am very lucky to be alive for it was hellish. The Germans were dropping shells right into our trench nearly the whole of the time. One bursting against me knocked me down flat. When I got up there were dead and wounded all around me. Another time a man each side of me was hit. The Germans must have suffered terribly. There were hundreds of them came over to our trenches and gave themselves up, and we were shooting those who tried to get away. I was glad enough to get out of it and get a wash and a little rest, but I can't sleep much yet, I must be too tired. Remember me to all old friends.

Walter Gale had indeed been lucky, for BEF casualties at Neuve Chapelle were estimated at almost 12,000 killed or wounded.

News of further casualties soon arrived in St Neots. As the 2nd Bedfords attacked south of Neuve Chapelle, Private George Childs was wounded yet again, this time by gunshot wound to the face, and was in hospital once more. Then twenty-five-year-old Corporal Arthur Chandler from Spaldwick, whose letters appeared regularly in the *Advertiser*, was shot in the neck at Ypres. German snipers were a real problem for the 1st Bedfords at Ypres at this time as the battalion's war diary reveals:

7th March – Sniping very considerable, total casualties 3 killed, 1 wounded

11th March – Impossible to show a periscope for more than a few seconds without getting a bullet through it; & quite impossible to see where firing comes from as no heads (enemy's) show above their parapets & no rifles can be seen at loopholes.

16th March [the day Arthur Chandler was hit] – trench heavily bombed & sniped, casualties 3 killed and 11 wounded.

Arthur Chandler was a married man with two young children and his wife, Ida, received the following letters from 'C' Company. Corporal Green wrote:

Regarding Arthur. He died on the morning of the 16th inst. [March] at half past three. I had been talking to him about half an hour previous. It was very dark, and hearing a shot, I asked him if he was hit. He said 'I think so'. Those were the only words he spoke. I found he had been shot in the neck, and he lived only 10 minutes.

Major Allasun wrote:

A pluckier man in action I have never seen, always ready to do his duty. He was the best bomb thrower in the company and did very good work throwing bombs into the German trenches. He was killed instantly by a chance shot. His comrades asked permission to carry him right back to a chateau near Ypres, where he was buried.

Today he rests in Perth Cemetery, Ypres.

Private James Coppock, of the Northants Regiment, was another who was wounded in early March. He was brought back to hospital in Birmingham, where his thigh wound was treated. Although he had been wounded he had also been fortunate, for another German bullet had lodged in a full tobacco tin in his pocket. James Coppock and his wife were in Canada before the war, but at the outbreak of hostilities he had returned, for he had been on reserve. They initially returned to Eaton Socon to be close to his father in Eaton Ford, but they then moved into town. He was not the first in the family to be wounded, for Albert Norman was the brother of James Coppock's wife.

During the first three months of 1915, the people of St Neots tried to support the men at the front and various schemes were introduced to make their lives a little easier. One such example saw Bolnhurst School children encouraged to knit for soldiers and collect parcels for them. These parcels were forwarded to the Bedfordshire Education Committee who sent them on to the trenches, usually to the Bedfordshire Regiment. Soldiers gratefully received these gifts and often wrote back expressing their appreciation. One such soldier was Andrew Lee, who had been badly hurt by an exploding shell. He was now back in Britain at Landguard Camp near Felixstowe, training and preparing men for the front. His letter thanked Miss Whitworth from Bolnhurst School for her parcel, telling her: 'I was fighting the German Iron Army at Mons where my Regiment lost very heavily, but God took me through safely … My two chums beside me were killed.' He went on to say how bad some of the trenches were, 'standing on turnips and straw to prevent the water rising too far up our bodies', and finally telling how he had been injured on 27 October:

A big black shell found me; it smashed the gun, killed the Sergeant, and wounded ten others. Fortunately for me, after I was hit in the head, I was buried for three hours. The Germans advanced, walked over me and took me for dead. I laid [sic] until a Sergeant found me, with just my feet showing. Another 5 minutes I would have been a dead man, but a drop of rum saved me, the Germans took my eight other chums prisoner.

He thanked young Miss Whitworth for the scarf she had sent and ended up apologising: 'I am still under the doctor with concussion of the brain, so I am afraid I can't go out again and fight for you.'

Another young lady from Bolnhurst School to hear from a wounded soldier was eleven-year-old Annie Swales. Private Thomas Bartholomew, who was also recovering at Landguard but whose war was over, wrote:

> My Dear Little Friend, I have received a pair of socks from you today and I thought that I must write and thank you for them. I am very sorry to tell you that I am home wounded from the Front, and that I have lost the sight of one eye, so I don't think I shall be able to go out again and fight those nasty Germans … I hope and pray that the Allies will soon be victorious, and that we shall soon see our brave boys marching home again, and you must please remember that when you say your prayers.

Private Albert Norman, who had been wounded also in October 1914, had expected to be back in France in January 1915, but his injuries had not healed properly and he was given the job of repairing boots at Landguard Camp. Whilst he was there he was joined by another wounded soldier who had also been allocated a job as boot repairer, and as they talked it came to light that this man had received a pair of socks from Mary Flowerdew, a scholar at Eaton Socon School.

Although children were encouraged to knit for the troops, the gift that most soldiers seemed to appreciate was tobacco or cigarettes which adults sent off to them. Sometimes these did not reach the intended recipient, especially if the parcel was marked cigarettes or chocolate. Private Walter Gale even wrote home to his mother to advise of this:

> There was a small parcel for me yesterday and the Corporal brought the mails up and left it in this hut but someone must have had more rights to it than I, so he pinched it and I didn't know who it was from. I am hoping it was not from you. Parcels containing money should be registered. It is a great mistake to write 'Cigarettes' or 'Chocolate' on a parcel, as they are often taken out when they reach this end.

Private Martin Byatt also wrote home to the *Advertiser* with thanks for cigarettes and told of George Childs' wounding:

> I am writing a few lines to the people of St Neots who have been kind enough to send fags, and other things out to the Front for the men, and I am sure we are very pleased to get a fag at times when we are in the trenches … I am sorry to say that George Childs, of Cambridge Street, St Neots, has been wounded again in action. The 2nd Beds Regiment has got a very good name for the brave work they done [*sic*] in this war up to the present time, and I am very pleased to say that I belong to them.

Other wounded soldiers did not get back home if their wounds were felt not to be serious. Private Will Medlock of the 1st Bedfords was one such example and, although he had been hit in the head by a German bullet during March, the wound was only slight and he was treated at a convalescence camp in Northern France. One soldier who did get back to Blighty at the end of March was Private Arthur Rollings of Cambridge Street, although it wasn't to this address that he got permission to head for. Instead he went to Shipton in Oxfordshire on compassionate leave and, whilst at his in-laws there, his wife died, aged just thirty-five. Private Rollings was now a widower with a ten-year-old son. 1914 and 1915 had been very cruel to him for, apart from his wife, he had also lost his father and his wife's brother had been killed in action.

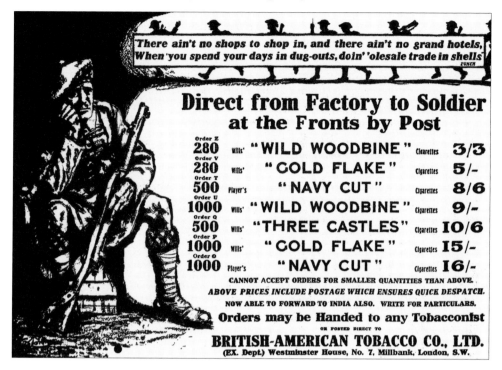

Advert for cigarettes that featured in the local press.

As a soldier, this Private with the Coldstream Guards was a realist and knew how difficult it would be to drive the Germans from the positions they occupied, and said that the only way for the Allies to win was for more men to come forward.

Private Robert Chamberlain, of the 1st Bedfords, stressed that those serving were doing their bit and he wrote home in late March telling how the Bedfords were plugging away at the Germans: 'We are trying to do it and will do it. We have answered our country's call, "Men your King and Country needs [*sic*] you!"' Robert was one of five brothers serving and he was one of the two who would not see the end of the war. This family from Eynesbury certainly gave their all for the war effort, as did the Haywards who had lived in Eaton Socon but had moved to Eynesbury before leaving the area. They had seven sons, Edwin, Ernest, Harold, Arthur, Cecil, Rupert and Frank, serving in the army, the navy and the Royal Navy Air Service.

That a great number of men had already come forward was evident, for women in many parts of Britain were carrying out work that usually had been the remit of men. In Huntingdonshire that was not quite the case by 1915, for the Earl of Sandwich, at a Hunts County Council Meeting at the end of March, stated that women were hardly employed at all except in their own homes or in shops. He went on to say that women in the county devoted a great deal of time to the solace of the military that happened to be quartered in the county. He finished by saying that he felt that, owing to the great absence of men, women might be employed to much greater advantage than at present.

On the Western Front the weather was at last improving, as Private George Berril from Eynesbury confirmed in writing to his grandparents in St Mary's Street: 'The weather out here has put on a change; it is quite warm during the day and passable through the night, although a fire is needed sometimes at night.' He went on to tell how the advance at Neuve Chapelle meant that the BEF now occupied better ground, even being able to make use of abandoned houses. 'We are in a strongly entrenched position, with houses much broken down by now with the constant shelling, which gives us a dry shelter.' George Berril was a signaller with the King's Own Regiment and his letter told of his work: 'I have my instrument here as I am on telegraph out here in the trenches.' He went on to say that he was looking forward to coming off duty to have some bacon, cheese, jam and bread, and added how important cigarettes were: 'There is one comfort here, that is cigarettes which they send from home.' Smoking was certainly more popular than it is today, and cigarettes and tobacco served another purpose as the smell of cigarette smoke, to a degree, took away the stench of decaying bodies in No Man's Land.

Cigarettes were also welcomed by men of the Hunts Cyclists 'D' Company stationed on the East Coast, and in the first week of April each man from St Neots, Eynesbury and the Eatons received a box of cigarettes. Food here was definitely better than what the average soldier received on the Western Front, and it was warm too. The following menu for the first week in April was sent to the *Advertiser* for printing, in the hope that it would encourage more young men to come forward and take the King's Shilling.

SUNDAY
6.30 am – biscuits and coffee
Breakfast – eggs and bacon, tea, bread
Dinner – roast beef, potatoes, custard and prunes
Tea – bread, butter, jam and tea
9.00 pm – bread, cheese
MONDAY
6.30 am – biscuits and cocoa
Breakfast – fried beef and bacon, tea, bread
Dinner – roast beef, potatoes, carrots,
Tea – bread, butter, marmalade
9.00 pm – bread and cold beef
TUESDAY
6.30 am – biscuits and tea
Breakfast – sausages, tea, bread
Dinner – stew, consisting of carrots, peas and onions; potatoes, rice puddings
Tea – bread, butter and jam, tea
9.00 pm – bread, cheese
WEDNESDAY
6.30 am – biscuits and coffee
Breakfast – fried steak, bread, butter, tea
Dinner – stew, consisting of carrots, peas and onions, potatoes
Tea – bread, butter, marmalade, tea
9.00 am – bread, cheese
THURSDAY
6.30 am – biscuits and cocoa
Breakfast – eggs and bacon, tea, bread
Dinner – roast beef, Yorkshire pudding, potatoes
Tea – bread, butter, jam, tea
9.00 pm – bread and cold beef
FRIDAY
6.30 am – biscuits and tea
Breakfast – fried cod chops, tea, bread
Dinner – stew, consisting of carrots, peas and onions, potatoes
Tea – bread, butter, jam, hot cross buns, tea

SATURDAY
6.30 am – biscuits and coffee
Breakfast – cold ham, bread, butter, tea
Dinner – stew, consisting of carrots, peas and onions, potatoes, haricot beans
Tea – bread, butter, marmalade, tea
9.00 am – bread, cheese

Clearly the men of 'D' Company were well looked after and, in an age where vegetarians were few and far between, the menu above must have seemed much better than they were used to at home. Whether the thought of such regular food was tempting is hard to say, for it was counter-balanced by growing casualty lists and increasing numbers of wounded local soldiers back home.

Amongst those wounded soldiers was twenty-year-old Private Robert G.M. Slaymaker of Eaton Ford, who turned up without warning at his parents' home with a frightful wound to his face. This Private with the 3rd Battalion Coldstream Guards had been wounded in early February when a German shell exploded, killing three Guards outright and wounding eight others. Private Slaymaker was over 6ft tall and the trenches were not an easy place for such tall men. Now his right ear was torn away, as his face was slashed from that ear across to his nose, and the surgeons used pioneering work to try to repair the damage by taking a piece of flesh from his right thigh and then grafting it onto his face. The operation was successful but, although the wound was healing, Private Slaymaker was scarred for life. Whilst he was back in Eaton Ford recovering, he told how the water in front-line trenches often reached soldiers' knees and sometimes their waists, and that on the day he was wounded the Guards had suffered seventy-three casualties. Three and a half years later, Robert Slaymaker was wounded again, this time in the right wrist, just hours before the Armistice came into effect.

Those fighting at the front could be quite dismissive of those they felt were slow in coming forward, and a letter from Private Will Medlock, printed in the local press in mid-April, did not hold back, calling those who had not volunteered 'shirkers'. Writing from hospital in Boulogne he said:

> So all shirkers, rally round the old Flag, don't hesitate … So boys who are Britishers and true Englishmen don't hesitate, but answer to your Country's call, for I have met several of the St Neots boys, and others from all around the outskirts.

On the Western Front casualties continued to increase and on 21 April another local man was killed, just eight months after being seriously wounded at Mons. Lance Corporal Frank Cousins had recovered and, in February, returned to the 1st Bedfords at Ypres, soon settling back into the routine of trench warfare, and writing home asking for cigarettes to be sent out. He also wrote to enquire about his twin brother, Jack, a Private with the 4th Hussars who arrived back in Eaton Ford during April, after suffering epilepsy and fits following a shocking experience when he was buried alive for an hour after a German shell exploded. When Frank Cousins' letter arrived in Eaton Socon, he was just days away from being killed; when another letter failed to arrive his parents started to worry. The next letter that arrived was not from Frank Cousins, but from his friend, Drummer George Bellamy of the same battalion, telling of the grim struggle at Hill 60 at Ypres and Frank's death. The Germans hit the Bedfords very hard on 21 April at Hill 60 with intense machine-gun fire, and shelling from artillery and mortars. The Bedfords suffered around 400 casualties that day and amongst the dead was Frank Cousins. Drummer Bellamy's letter read:

> Dear Mrs Cousins,
> I am just writing these few lines to let you know that your son Frank was killed in action on

the morning of the 21st about half past six with a bullet wound to the head. He was firing over the parapet at the Germans. He had just fired when they returned one. I was about two yards from him when he got hit and I did all [I] could for him but it was no good, no one could save him. We were in a very rough place at the time; we lost about ---- men in our regiment at the same time. I was very lucky myself to get out of it. We had been in the trenches ---- days, and we blew up the trenches which the Germans got last Saturday night, and they tried to get the trenches back again. We got relieved about half an hour after Frank got killed. I am very sorry he got killed, as he was one of the best Chums I had ever since I left school. I feel very sorry for you. He was a very nice fellow and is greatly missed by all his Company. I thought I would write and tell you because the War Office are a long time before they let you know. I think I will close now, hoping to find you all well at home.

I remain, yours sincerely,

DRUMMER G. BELLAMY

Frank Cousins was one of five brothers serving, and he and Arthur would not return. Brothers Ernest, Jack and George all survived, though the health of two of them was poor following their experiences: Jack remembering the awful episode when he was buried alive, whilst George had been hit by bronchitis during his time in France and, as a result, had been placed on home defence for the duration of the war. Ernest was captured by the enemy in 1917 and spent the rest of the war as a POW. George Bellamy died nineteen days before the war ended.

Shortly after Frank Cousins was killed at Hill 60, a new and terrifying weapon of war was introduced when the Germans used gas at Ypres. This was the second time that they had tried this new weapon – the first being on the Eastern Front, but this had failed as the gas had frozen in its canisters. Between 22 and 24 April they tried again, this time at Ypres where French, French Colonial, British and Canadian soldiers were subjected to it. Chlorine gas was used on that fateful Thursday and, as the yellow cloud drifted slowly towards them, Allied soldiers were initially puzzled, but their curiosity turned to panic as the choking gas enveloped them. French Colonial troops were affected badly, breaking in the face of this unknown weapon, which could have led to a significant breakthrough for the Germans. However, they were as uncertain as the Allies and the gas attack was not followed up. Two days later the Germans used chlorine gas again and this time it was against Canadian troops. Although a breakthrough once again was

Lance Corporal Frank Cousins, not in uniform.

close, the Canadians held their ground and 'The Brooding Soldier', a striking monument to the Canadians' resolve, can be seen today at St Julien, the very site where the Canadians stood and fought.

Amongst the Canadians at St Julien was thirty-one-year-old Private Leonard Bundy, of the 7th Battalion, Canadian Infantry, British Colombia Regiment and the son of George and Mary Bundy of Eaton Socon. Leonard had moved to Canada in 1907 and travelled for a while before starting work as an attendant in a Vancouver asylum. When war broke out, he quickly enlisted at Valcartier, Quebec in September 1914, and having previous military experience, he was welcomed into the ranks of the Canadian Expeditionary Force. After arriving in England, the 7th Battalion trained on Salisbury Plain and Leonard Bundy even managed to visit his parents in Eaton Socon before going overseas. His battalion received their baptism of fire at Ypres between 22 and 24 April, where they took a considerable pounding from the Germans. Gas was followed by artillery and mortar shelling, and then the advance of a whole German brigade. Although the Canadians suffered heavy casualties, they hung on with grim resolve, even though their Ross rifles kept jamming. Their war diary gives figures of 585 men killed, wounded or missing in action during this German attack. However, they showed considerable courage and no less invention and improvisation in soaking towels and cotton bandoliers to use as gas masks as they stood their ground. Leonard Bundy was killed as the Germans advanced and his body was lost during the battle. His letters home ceased in May and then his parents received official confirmation that he was missing in action. For over a year his death was not confirmed, and indeed his body was never recovered or identified. Today his name is amongst the 55,000 missing in the Ypres Salient remembered on the Menin Gate.

The use of gas sparked outrage from the Allies and the reporting of it in the British press simply served to confirm the brutal nature of the German Army. To try to counter the effects of this frightening new weapon, respirators were issued to the troops. This was certainly an improvement on how soldiers had tried initially to counter the effects of gas by urinating on handkerchiefs and holding them to their mouths and noses, the ammonia of the urine offsetting the chlorine within the gas.

Not everybody who was wounded was right in the front line; the Germans made a point of shelling behind the lines where troops were moving up to the front, or where command centres might be located. On 8 May, one such incident took place at Aubers Ridge when the Brigade Headquarters of the Army Cyclist Corps came under fire from gas and ordinary shells. Private Walter Gale was amongst those wounded as shells rained down. Writing home, he told:

> I must have got some gas as I was sick when I got down here and could eat nothing for four days. The Germans are using it in their shells. I was Brigade Orderly and had been up the trenches twice before I was hit. Of course I was wearing a pack over my mouth, but it was only one that I had made myself. The Brigade Headquarters was only about 150 yards from the trenches, it being what was left of an old farm house. The Germans must have known it was being used for something for they were shelling it the whole of the time and it was there that I received my souvenir. Well I was very lucky, for from the size of the piece of shell, it was high explosive; it looks as if it must have killed me. I have got the piece and will try to send it home, as I am not expecting to get home now. My wound is going on all right.

Walter Gale was mistaken, for the wound to the top of his head required medical treatment in Birmingham and Dartford, and he did get home to Cambridge Street during June.

The 1st Bedfordshires got first-hand experience of gas during 2nd Ypres at the infamous Hill 60. Any high ground around Ypres gave its occupants a significant advantage and Hill 60 was a prime example of this, even though it was only 60ft above sea level, hence the name. Local men with the Bedfords who were wounded there included Private Robert Chamberlain, who was hit in the head by a piece of shrapnel, and Private Theodore Rowlett, who wrote to his mother in Huntingdon Street: 'I was wounded in the right shoulder and wrist four days ago … I am a little better today. I was wounded in the fighting at Hill 60. Only 360 were left out of my Regiment at the end.' Theodore Rowlett was brought back to Britain, and within two days his mother received both his letter and a telegram telling that he was dangerously ill at Chislehurst Hospital in Kent. She visited him and Theodore Rowlett pulled through.

Private George Corbett was another soldier with the 1st Bedfords at Hill 60 who was a victim of poisonous gas. He had had a difficult time in 1915, suffering from frozen feet and an attack of fever. When he returned to his battalion at Hill 60 he encountered the latest development in the use of gas, for some German shells now incorporated gas which was far more effective, with no reliance upon wind direction but rather a successful explosion. At first, soldiers were confused as gas shells exploded with a 'plop' rather than a crashing detonation, and many soldiers were badly affected as they mistook the gas shells for duds. George Corbett wrote home to Eaton Ford:

> Dear Mother and Father … I have got a dose of gas poison, but I am getting over the effects of it now. The Germans shelled our trenches with poisonous gasses. It was awful. We could hardly breathe in it. I don't know how I got out. I am afraid a lot of our chaps could not escape and a lot of them died when they did not get out. It is not fighting now. We expect shot and shell, but no one can stand against that stuff.

Other local men were involved at Hill 60; Private Samuel Garner of Southoe was wounded by shrapnel from a shell, whilst Lance Corporal Fred Cox from Great Staughton was killed when he was hit in the stomach by a bullet, and although he was taken to a casualty clearing station he could not be saved. Gunner Arthur Medlow from Eaton Socon suffered a wound just above his right eye which left him without the sight in that eye. He was brought home to hospital in Eastbourne and turned up in Eaton Socon during July, but he still had not recovered vision in his eye.

Private William Webb of Croxton, whose letters featured regularly in the *Advertiser*, also encountered gas at Hill 60 as he fought with the 1st Bedfords. A letter from him in May told of gas and his view of the Germans who used it. He wrote:

> Once more I am pleased to say I have managed to scrape through this great battle of Hill 60 after 28 days in the trenches. It has been nothing less than murder. It is impossible to call it war … they sent us some asphyxiating gas to poison us. They cannot beat us with shell and rifle, so they are trying to poison us; they are a cowardly lot, they cannot fight like men … I got a little gas, but not enough to take effect, as we were told that the gas was coming, so we put our pads over our mouths to stop it a little … I am sorry to say that my brother was seriously wounded in the same trench as me, he had his arm smashed above the elbow with a shell, one piece of shell entered his shoulder, three pieces in his left thigh, and one in his right. I can tell you it is horrible to see the poor fellows dying with wounds. What a blessing it will be when this is all over. I would like to tell you more but I am not allowed.

During the fighting at Hill 60, Private Edward Warner of the 1st Battalion of the Bedfordshire Regiment won the Victoria Cross. This brave man from St Albans had been on the Western Front since August 1914 and had fought at Mons, Le Cateau, the Marne and 1st Ypres. When the Germans attacked Hill 60 on 1 May the Bedfords had been forced to withdraw from Trench 46, as many of the men were violently sick after breathing in gas. Private Warner quickly realised that the loss of this trench would be disastrous and decided to defend it single-handedly against the advancing Germans, even though he was breathing in gas. When the Germans hesitated in pressing on, he returned to his battalion, persuaded others to come back to Trench 46, and the

German attack was stopped. Edward Warner was utterly exhausted after his efforts and he died the next day as a result of the effects of the gas. Yet again, he was one of those whose grave was lost as the fighting continued and his name rests on the Menin Gate.

At the start of May, the Allies decided to attack the German line to the South of Ypres, once again near Neuve Chapelle. The BEF attacked Aubers Ridge on 9 May and suffered appalling casualties, with around 11,000 men killed or wounded within yards of their own trench lines. The British attack was a distraction for a larger French attack 15 miles further south at Vimy Ridge, but both failed. Six days later the BEF attacked again, slightly more to the south at Festubert, and this time the 2nd Bedfords were involved. Private George Bettles of Eaton Socon, with 'C' Company, was one of those who went into action and two days later, at around 2.30 a.m. on the 17th, he was wounded in the arm, the face and in both legs. Writing home he made a brave face of it, telling his parents that it wasn't too bad and that they should not worry. Indeed George Bettles was safe for a while, being transferred to hospital in Leicester and operated on later in the month, when shrapnel was removed from his arm and legs and a bullet from his head. He wrote home saying he was being looked after 'like a toff' and was being waited on 'hand and foot'. As usual for soldiers, his thoughts turned to cigarettes and he asked his mother to send him some Woodbines.

Not every soldier engaged in fighting the enemy was on the Western Front; twenty-four-year-old Private Walter Whittlesea Dighton, from Brampton, was thousands of miles away, fighting the Turks close to Basra in the Persian Gulf. He belonged to the 2nd Battalion, the Norfolk Regiment, and they had been in the area since November of the previous year, when they had been blooded in capturing Basra. Over the next twelve months the Norfolks were regularly in action against the Turks, culminating in the dreadful disaster at Kut. In May 1915, the *Advertiser* printed a detailed synopsis of Private Dighton's experiences that ran to two columns and told of desert sandstorms, Turkish attacks, marching in terrific heat and overpowering temperatures, and details of the battalion going into action on 15 April. Walter Dighton described how the Turks first shelled the Norfolks and then blasted them with volleys of bullets, some of which he thought were 'dum dums', for they made fearful holes when they hit flesh. One section of one of his letters told of how he felt when he first came under fire and makes extraordinary reading. He wrote:

> Perhaps you would like to know what it feels like when first going into action. I will try to describe my feelings. I felt just as if I would like to get up and run away anywhere. I was very nervous and felt like a man in a dream. A thousand and one thoughts flash through you, you think of home a great lot, I know I did, and kept expecting every minute to get one … but after a time the feeling gradually wears away and you suddenly pull yourself [together], and think to yourself, well I am a British soldier, and your blood boils to think you ever thought of proving yourself a coward. You seem to get fresh life and into it hammer and tongs, knowing that if you don't shoot your opponent he will you, and all fear vanishes.

Walter Whittlesea Dighton's letters gave local people a rare insight into fighting that was quite different from that across the Channel. He survived six more months of war in the Persian Gulf before he died at Kut on 22 November.

Closer to home, another fatality was driver John Harrow, an eighteen-year-old with the Highland Mountain Brigade of the Royal Field Artillery who was struck by a train at Huntingdon on 24 May. John Harrow was attempting to cross a railway line, to get to the Boat House at Huntingdon and go for a row on the river, when he was caught by the buffer of a train and hurled to the bank below. Perhaps the fact that he had been excused duties for a few days due to a sprained ankle meant that he was not quick enough to get out of the way of the oncoming train; the impact fractured his pelvis, his skull and caused internal injuries. He was taken to a military hospital but died an hour later. He was buried with full military honours at Huntingdon Cemetery.

By spring 1915, many politicians at home were starting to think about other fronts where the Germans and their allies might be seriously weakened, and a plan was hatched for an attack on Turkey that would have a real impact upon the outcome of the war. An attempt to break the deadlock of the Western Front was launched with an Allied attack in the Dardanelles at Gallipoli, hopefully leading to the capture of Constantinople. If successful, this would result in German troops being taken away from the Western Front, thus weakening them there – success at Gallipoli might even knock Turkey out of the war. In February and March 1915, the plan began with a naval bombardment of Turkish artillery on the Gallipoli peninsula that guarded the straits, but this failed, mainly because of the number of mines that the Turkish Navy had laid; three Allied battleships were sunk. It quickly became clear that the only way to negotiate the straits successfully was for Allied troops to land on the peninsula and attack and destroy the Turkish defences there, thus giving the battleships safe passage through the straits. In April the landings began, involving British, Australian, New Zealand and French troops, and that at 'W' Beach on 25 April saw the Lancashire Fusiliers famously win '6 VCs before Breakfast'. Amongst the attackers were the 1st Essex, and in their ranks was Corporal Chas Newton from St Neots. He told that enemy fire was so intense upon landing that they had to lie down for a long time just to survive. In the next few days he was hit four times by bullets, but only once was his skin broken when a bullet that had passed through his sleeve went on to strike his hand. The other times he was hit, the bullets had just about spent their force and did not penetrate his leg, his groin or his shoulder. Later, Chas Newton fell seriously ill with fever and was taken to hospital in Alexandria, before being brought back to Blighty. Further unsuccessful landings took place in May and August, with British, Australian and New Zealand divisions suffering over 100,000 casualties before the campaign drew to a close in December 1915.

Walter Billington of Eaton Socon heard of the bombardment of the Gallipoli Peninsula when he received a letter from his brother-in-law serving aboard HMS *Sapphire*. The letter arrived in May and read:

> Just finished a hard day's battle, what a day, never been heard of before in history, started five in the morning and finished seven in the evening, one long terrific cannonade, talk about Neuve Chapelle gun fire, it is nowhere near it. God help Turkey, she will soon be a heap of ruins. I saw three Turkey soldiers blown to pieces by one of our shells; we were so close to them. I have not got a scratch yet … We mean to reach Constantinople, neck or nothing, but never fear. I shall come through all right. I don't think it will last much longer. If we succeed in this job it will make a lot of difference, so cheer up.

At the beginning of June, news of more casualties abroad started to flicker through to St Neots and wounded soldiers also arrived home. Private Charles Chapman of the 2nd Bedfords returned suffering from a nervous breakdown after a shell had exploded at his feet, but the blast went downwards, causing him to fall into the crater it created. Charles Chapman also wore three wound stripes on the sleeve of his tunic after being hit by German bullets on the ankle, the calf and the knee of his right leg on three different occasions between November 1914 and May 1915. He had also been buried alive, together with Private George Bellamy from St Neots, earlier in 1915 when a German shell exploded. As Private Chapman recuperated back in town, he started to talk of his experiences, including being present at the Christmas Truce and of fighting at Ypres, La Bassée, Neuve Chapelle and Aubers Ridge. He also told how he and Private Charlie Byatt had a very close shave during 1st Ypres, when a shell blew up just yards from them, causing the ground to fall away from their feet.

June 11 1915
**PTE. MARTIN BYATT, OF ST. NEOTS,
KILLED.**

Private Martin Byatt.

Charlie Byatt's brother Martin was also with the 2nd Bedfords and news reached St Neots in those first few days of June that he was seriously ill, after being hit by a bullet at the end of May. He was taken to a military hospital in Abbeville and his father, Arthur, received a letter from the War Office saying that he could visit his son but at his own expense. In the few days that Arthur Byatt tried to make up his mind if he could afford to travel, the condition of his son worsened and, on 3 June, Martin died. The next letter that the Byatt family received told them their son was dead and that he had been buried in Abbeville. The war had been cruel to the Byatts, for Charlie had suffered a compound fracture when shrapnel shattered his thigh on 31 October 1914 at Ypres. Martin Byatt was a butcher in London before the war and had written home regularly, his letters featuring often in the *St Neots Advertiser*. On the last occasion he had commented that the improving weather made life easier in the front line: 'It is nice now to be in the trenches.' Now his face, with cigarette in mouth, gazed out from the pages of the paper under the headline 'Pte. Martin Byatt, of St Neots killed'. On the day after Mr and Mrs Byatt heard of the death of their son Martin, their spirits were lifted somewhat, for Charlie turned up at their home in Cambridge Street following seventeen weeks of treatment for his shattered thigh. The war wasn't, however, finished with them and three years later their youngest son was killed in action.

In 1915, the number of casualties continued to grow and Arthur Watson of Montagu Street, Eynesbury received the dreadful news that his son Percy was dead. Percy Watson was a twenty-three-year-old Reservist who had been called up initially to the 3rd Bedfords at Landguard. He was then sent overseas to the 2nd Bedfords at Ypres, going into action with them on 18 May at Festubert after they received instructions to advance in support of the Cameroon Highlanders, who had captured German trenches. Meanwhile, the Cameroon Highlanders had lost control of the German trenches when a counter-attack had bombed them out and forced them to pull back. Orders were sent to the Bedfords to try to consolidate the ground they had covered, but they came under heavy artillery fire. They did hold on until they were relieved the next day by the 2nd Yorkshires, but they had suffered many casualties; eleven officers being killed or wounded, forty-five other ranks being killed, sixty-eight men missing and 276 wounded, of whom four would later die. Many men fell on the battlefield as the Bedfords attacked and seven stretcher bearers were killed or wounded as they tended the fallen. Percy Watson was one of those who were wounded as the advance went ahead and he was seen falling by his platoon sergeant. Soldiers were under strict orders not to stop to help any wounded comrades during an advance, since this could reduce the chances of success. Whether or not the stretcher bearers got to Percy Watson is not known, but he was pronounced missing at first and then declared dead.

His father Arthur received two letters within two days at the start of June. The first was from the platoon sergeant who saw Percy fall and the next day the official brown envelope was delivered from the War Office, declaring him dead. Percy Watson had joined the army at sixteen and after completing his initial period of service had gone on to reserve. He had been working at Lansbury Farm for Arthur Browning before he was recalled to the Colours. His body was never recovered from the battlefield at Festubert and today he is commemorated on Le Touret Monument.

Also at Festubert, on 15 May, Edward Reynolds was advancing with the Canadians when he was hit in the head by a piece of shell fragment and was very seriously wounded. Operations left him liable to seizures and he was invalided out of the army. Although his family were wealthy landowners in Eaton Socon, Hail Weston and Little Paxton, he returned to Canada, but sadly died there in September 1918 when he suffered a brain seizure that led to a fatal accident.

These first few days of June must have been a very difficult time for the relatives of serving soldiers, for there seemed to be no end to the bad news reaching the town and the surrounding villages. In Croxton, the fiancée of William Webb, whose letters had featured regularly in the *Advertiser*, received devastating news at the beginning of the month from Sergeant Major George Bull:

Dear Miss Sewell, It is with the deepest sympathy that I write to inform you of the death of Lance Corporal Webb of my Company, who I believe was your sweetheart. I feel deeply for you, but I hope you will not take it too much to heart, as no doubt it was God's will for him to be taken while fighting for his country. He was not actually fighting when he was wounded, but it happened like this. We were just behind the firing line in dug-outs, when a shell came and burst right in the one he was in, wounding five, including your boy. I myself helped to bandage him up, and then I saw him safely away on a stretcher. But the news was brought to me last night that he was dead. I feel very sorry for he was a 'Townie' of mine, as we call anyone who comes from the same county. I come from Godmanchester, near Huntingdon. He was a good and brave soldier and one of my best Lance Corporals. All the men miss him very much, as they were so much devoted to him. Perhaps you will let his parents know of the sad affair, as I cannot write myself not knowing their address. I hardly know how to write to you as I can guess how you will feel about it. But I think it is best to let you know at once … Well, I shall have to close now, hoping you will let me know if you get this letter safely. I remain, yours in deepest sympathy Geo. Bull, Co. Sergt. Major.

Sadly this was not the end of the story, for on the same day that William Webb died, his brother Harry, also in the 1st Bedfords, was killed, and William Webb was telling Albert Norman about this when the German shell struck the dugout. Miss Sewell was unable to tell William Webb's parents about his death for both were already dead, and William had been brought up by others after he had been orphaned. Mrs Eversden of Huntingdon Street had brought William up until the age of twelve, and then he had been raised by Mrs Byatt and then Mrs Cochrane. He had joined the army and had served for seven years before going on reserve, but, together with thousands of others, had been recalled in August 1914. Having fought through Mons and Ypres, it was close to Hill 60 that he was fatally wounded on 24 May, dying the next day. Both William and Harry Webb have marked graves, William resting in Bailleul Cemetery and Harry in Poperinghe.

Also killed on 24 May at Ypres, was Private Maurice Jones, whose grandfather still lived in St Neots but whose mother had left to live in Hull. Maurice Jones had only been on the Western Front for just over a month when he was killed, and he too left behind a fiancée, Miss Hilda Stelling, who received news of his death from one of his comrades. Private Charles Lawson, who served with Maurice in 8 Platoon, 4th East Yorks, wrote:

I find it a painful duty as Maurice's chum to break the news of his passing away from us to you. Poor old chappie. He was a proper brick to the last, and thought of little else than his mother. Your Maurice was wounded seriously in the back by an explosive bullet at about two p.m. on Monday May 24th. His end came as we were transferring him from the trenches to the dressing station. Be assured he was well dressed and looked after.

Maurice Jones had lived for many years in St Neots, and before the war had worked as an engineer on an ocean liner. His grave was lost and today his name sits with almost 55,000 others on the Menin Gate Memorial in Ypres.

The fighting in late May saw soldiers yet again having to contend with mud for, although the weather had improved, rain still fell frequently, leaving trenches wet. Soldiers had no chance to wash in the front line and they found themselves plastered with mud, which often hung heavily on their tunics. Private Fred Gilbert of St Neots was one who told of this when he wrote home in June, saying how relieved he was to get away from the mud:

I am glad to say we are out of the trenches now for a bit, and in billets for a rest. It was a treat to get a good wash, after being amongst the dead and wounded. There is a canal close by where we go for a good swim every day when we have finished our drill.

He was pleased to receive the *St Neots Advertiser* through the post, commenting that he had seen the Hunts Cyclist Battalion, 'D' Company photograph, where he recognised some old friends. At the front he had only come across two other St Neotians, one of whom was in his battalion, the 1st Grenadier Guards. He ended up saying that he hoped to come across some of the Aberdeen Territorials he had met in St Neots earlier when on leave, but said he would prefer to meet them again in England!

The number of casualties suffered by the BEF was certainly high, resulting in a definite dip in numbers of volunteers coming forward, and in May 1915 the Prime Minister, Herbert Asquith, appointed Lord Derby as Director General of Recruitment. Derby's task was to find a way to fill the gaps in the ranks that Kitchener's volunteers could not, as more and more soldiers were killed or wounded. Derby was against the concept of conscription and he devised an idea that became known as the Derby Scheme, where eligible men were identified and invited to enlist, with the proviso that they could choose which regiment they wanted to join. Married men were advised that they would only have to come forward after the supply of single men was used up. It seemed more likely that conscription was not too far away and the Derby Scheme gave men the choice of which regiment to join, whereas conscription would not allow this choice. Certain men were excluded on account of their occupations, which were deemed necessary for the war effort – munitions workers being a prime example, but overall the scheme was unsuccessful for only 350,000 men came forward. Those that did were given a distinctive armband to wear that spared them a 'white feather' from members of the public, usually women, signifying their faintheartedness. One local man chose a very unusual way to try to avoid the stigma of being given a white feather. William Nicholson of Eaton Socon wrote to the local press in June asking them to print the explanation why he had not enlisted, which was that he had varicose veins.

Soldiers at the front frequently commented on the large numbers of men holding back, and were astonished to see so many not in uniform when they were home on leave. Private Joseph Shelton of the Royal Fusiliers was quite disparaging about the situation and specifically wrote to the *St Neots Advertiser* in June, making his feelings known. Part of his letter read:

I was fortunate enough a fortnight ago to obtain leave for five days in my dear old home. When I got to a certain part of Bedfordshire I was greatly surprised to see the number of young men promenading in the evenings. I had understood that practically all eligible men were in some part of His Majesty's Service and the sight of these fellows idling their time rather dismayed me.

Some young men did respond in early June when the Bedfordshires' Recruiting March reached Eaton Socon. The 3rd and 5th Bedfordshires March began in Baldock and wended its way across both Hertfordshire and Bedfordshire, seeking to recruit 100 men. It arrived in Biggleswade on Tuesday 8 June, and then moved on to Sandy and Eaton Socon, before completing its 225 mile march at Bedford on Saturday 12th. Such marches usually contained a brass and bugle band, recruitment officers, medical officers, NCOs and ordinary soldiers. This march comprised of around 150 soldiers who were no longer suitable for service overseas, and it was billeted on Eaton Socon Green where recruiting sergeants, whose caps were decorated with red, white and blue ribbons, tried to drum up support. The meeting got underway at the start of Friday evening when Captain Lathom spoke, his object being to raise men for the 3rd Bedfords, a battalion that was created to train men to fill gaps in the Bedfordshire Battalions at the front. Captain Lathom was very well informed, for his documents advised him that there were twenty-five eligible young men who had not come forward so far from the Eatons and he urged these single and married men to enlist, both to defend Britain and to prevent the possibility of a German invasion. Perhaps the most controversial part of his talk was when he spoke of Rolls of Honour that featured in many church porches. These were lists of men who had already volunteered and showed which regiment they were with. Captain Lathom said that there should be two of these rolls, one of 'Honour' and one of 'Dishonour', with the latter giving the names of all single men who had not joined up. The talk had the desired effect in that thirteen men did come forward and nine were signed up, the other four failing to meet the criteria. Those accepted were Thomas Usher, William Payne, Fred Thornton, Frank Oakley, Albert Vincent Medlow, Ernest Evernden, Bert Hand, Fred Mardlin, Albert John Dimmock and Sam Darrington, who signed up later in the week. Those rejected were William Barringer and Robert Humphrey, who were under age, Fred Barringer, who was not tall enough, and William Nicholson, who was not fit for service. The Recruiting March left Eaton Socon early on Saturday morning, calling in at Roxton, Great Barford and Goldington en route to Bedford. That Saturday evening there was a Smoking Concert in Bedford in the Corn Exchange, but it was not a great success for only fifteen men volunteered and three of these were rejected.

As the Recruiting March was leaving Eaton Socon, unwelcome news reached Little Paxton concerning Private Samuel Irons, 'A' Company, King's Royal Rifles who had been at the front for some months and had written home regularly. He was an experienced soldier, having fought during the Boer War in his seven years with the Colours, and had been awarded the King's Medal for service there. When war broke out he was working at the St Neots Paper Mills, his period of being on reserve having expired, but that did not stop him from volunteering and he was sent over to France in February 1915. Sam Irons had been brought up in Eynesbury and still had strong connections with St Neots. Initially thirty-one-year-old Sam was lucky, for during the fighting at Hill 60 he had been sitting in a trench when a German shell exploded close by and shrapnel hit him in the stomach, but its force was almost spent as it did not penetrate and bounced off him, dropping into the mug of tea he was drinking. On 31 May that luck deserted him, when he was killed in action close to La Bassée. Although the Battle of Festubert had ended, German artillery continued its daily 'hate' and shelled British positions, killing Sam Irons. His wife, Lillian, heard of her husband's death when she received a letter from his friend, Rifleman Arthur Withey. It read:

Dear Mrs Irons, I am sorry to inform you that I was present at the time of your husband's death, if you have not heard from the War Office that he was killed in action on 31st May.

I am glad to say that he died a true and brave death and did not suffer any pain. I send all his comrades deepest sympathy as he was very much liked in his Company … I was requested by Sam if anything should happen to him to let you know.

Two and a half years later, Arthur Withey was killed at Ypres and he has no known grave, but his friend Sam Irons is buried in Woburn Abbey Cemetery, Cuinchy, Northern France.

It was not only men from St Neots that the local populace had concerns about, for many had become fond of soldiers billeted with them during 1914 and 1915. Many Scottish Territorials had been accommodated in the town and they kept in touch with the families they had stayed with. Staff Sergeant Whitburn Bailey of the 1st Highland Artillery wrote to Mr Hayler, who he had stayed with, telling how the war had devastated the landscape: 'We put up for eight days in a village which was totally divested of inhabitants, save a stray dog, cat or pigeon or two. All the houses were blown either down, or to skeleton form, by shell fire.' Another member of the 1st Brigade, Highland Artillery, Private Donald Kennedy, had lodged with Mrs Pindred of Prospect Row, and the news about him was not welcome, for he had been killed by a bomb on 16 June, close to La Bassée.

Better news concerned two injured soldiers arriving back in St Neots for leave and recuperation. Private Theodore Rowlett of the 1st Bedfords returned after being wounded at Hill 60 and had much to tell. He had been hit by a German bullet in the right shoulder and the bullet had continued its journey, ending up in his chest where it still remained. This was not the first time he had flirted with danger, for after an enemy shell exploded he was buried, and the shell caused the back of his greatcoat to be scorched by a corrosive substance emanating from the shell, and it was only his collar being turned up that saved him from being burned. His head showed a scar from a German bullet and there was another on his right wrist, whilst the top of the finger of his left hand was missing, again as a result of a German bullet. Later he was fortunate again, when another soldier called to him and, as he turned his head, a bullet grazed the side of his face. Lastly he told how he had been carrying tea along a trench when a shell exploded and blew away half the head of the man next to him. Not surprisingly, he felt that he was deserving of more than a week's leave after all he had been through.

Walter Gale arrived at his home in Cambridge Street, during the third week of June, for a few days before he was due back with the Army Cyclist Corps. He was able to tell of being entrenched only 50 yards from the enemy, on occasions where both sides constantly shouted comments to each other that were not particularly complimentary. He also recounted with sadness how, whilst on sentry duty at Estairee, he had chanced to meet Private Martin Byatt before his death and told how the two of them had managed to spend an evening together, probably at an estaminet. Walter Gale was typical of soldiers who fought during the Great War in being disinclined to talk much about his experiences, and what he had seen had to be teased from him. For years after the conflict, many of those who had survived were of a similar disposition and most kept their ordeal to themselves. Indeed Harry Patch, the last Tommy, only spoke about this during the final few years of his life, after the turning on and off of a light by staff opposite his room at his care home sparked memories of shellfire.

Some soldiers considered themselves quite lucky not to be in the front line, and even though they were within range of German guns, they were happy to be behind the lines. Edgar Chapman had joined the Royal Engineers Signals, and his experience as the telegraphist at St Neots Post Office had been put to good use. In June he wrote that his war so far was hardly like soldiering, explaining:

I'm working 8 hours on and 8 hours off, and shut up in a signals office all the time. It doesn't seem like soldiering. We are not far behind the trenches and are within reach of the German guns. They don't drop many shells over. Never more than five or six a day. The further they avoid me the better. One poor beggar was killed by a shell in the town two days ago, and several injured.

Both the BEF and the German Army complained of shortages of shells and, although the Germans did have more, it perhaps explains why so few shells fell close to where Edgar Chapman was serving. Following the failure of the attack at Neuve Chapelle earlier in the year, there had been an outcry in Britain regarding the shortage of shells and, as a result, the Liberal Government had fallen in late May, and a coalition government had been formed with Asquith remaining as Prime Minister. David Lloyd George was appointed as Minister for Munitions in an attempt to solve the shell shortage problem.

Away from the Western Front, the Allies continued to press at Gallipoli. After the failure of the naval bombardment, troops had been landed at Helles and Anzac Cove in late April, but casualties were very high, even though bridgeheads were established. Then, between April and June, further landings took place at Krithia, but these were thrown back by the Turks and the British Government came under growing criticism. At the end of June, Winston Churchill, the minister who had pushed for the attack at Gallipoli, resigned and it seemed as though his political career was over. Albert Tidman was serving in the Royal Navy at Gallipoli and he had witnessed the landings in April, together with the sinking of HMS *Goliath* by a Turkish destroyer commanded by a German officer. The *Goliath* had a crew of 750, and 570 of them were drowned including her captain. Albert Tidman wrote to his mother in Eynesbury:

> We lost about eight men covering the landing of the troops, but the troops progressed all right. I shall never forget the night the Goliath went down. I had the middle watch, but it was sad to see the men struggling for their lives in the water, and all the ships showing their searchlights on the men in the water. You can't picture it at home. We did our best in trying to save a lot of them. I think we had about 100 survivors on our ship and 5 dead, the latter we buried at sea – a sailor's grave. We were not far from her. We have been in the thick of it just lately, but still the old ship is as sound as a bell. The Germans are not men, the Turk is a gentleman to the Germans. I am safe as houses. I am as brown as a berry … Don't worry about me.

Albert Tidman's scathing comment about the Germans was a direct reference to the sinking of the *Lusitania* on 7 May 1915 by a German U-boat. The liner was packed with passengers, many of whom were American, and the loss of life was huge with 1,153 passengers and crew drowning. Albert Tidman referred to the sinking of the *Lusitania* as 'foul murder', for he could not excuse the sinking of a passenger ship.

Amongst those landed at Gallipoli was the Royal Naval Division, including the Royal Marine Light Infantry. They had seen action in the opening moves of the war and had been a part of the force that had tried to defend Antwerp and stop it falling into enemy hands in 1914. At Gallipoli, Sergeant Sidney Goodman, an experienced soldier who had fifteen years' service to his credit and who had recently signed on for another six years, was one of those in action as the marines attacked at Krithia, where he was seriously injured. He did not recover from his wounds and died on 8 June. Thirty-three-year-old Sidney Goodman had only been married for a matter of months and his wife lived in barracks in Chatham, although his mother still resided in Avenue Road, St Neots. A lull in the fighting at Gallipoli followed, but in August the attack resumed with landings at Suvla Bay.

On the Western Front, the warm weather saw the trenches begin to dry out and, on 15 June, the 2nd Bedfordshires attacked near La Bassée over a period of three days, attempting to capture a farm, a crater and enemy trenches. Five officers and eighteen men were killed, whilst seven officers and seventy-two men were also wounded, including eighteen-year-old Private John Robins who was hit in the head and the spine. John Robins came from Little Staughton and had only been across the Channel for a few weeks before he went into action. His wounds proved to be serious enough for him to be transferred to a base hospital at Boulogne, where the medical staff fought for days to try to save his life. Their efforts were not enough, for he died on 23 June and a week later his parents received an official letter of sympathy from no less a figure than King George V. John Robins was the first man from Little Staughton killed in the Great War, but by the end of hostilities there were five others.

Robert Chamberlain, with the 1st Bedfords, confirmed that it was now quite warm in the trenches and he wrote in early July to express his sorrow about the deaths of Percy Watson (a fellow soldier from Eynesbury) and Martin Byatt:

> I was very sorry to hear that we had lost two of our brave heroes, who gave their lives for their King and Country. We are having some very nice weather, and it is very warm. We are in the trenches now and have been for a long time. We shall be pleased when this terrible war is over so that we can get back to our old home again, if the Lord spares us … There are a lot of Eynesbury boys out here trying to do their bit for their King and Country, but we can do with a lot more yet so as to bring this terrible war to an end. So if there are any young men in the place tell them to come and have a go instead of loafing about and talking about it.

Robert Chamberlain survived for just over a year, as he was killed on the Somme. He never did get to go back to his old home again.

Robert Chamberlain was not the only serving soldier who called upon the young men of Britain to enlist. Private John Haigh, a forty-one-year-old Yorkshireman who worked in St Neots before the war, sent the following letter from 'Somewhere in France' at the end of June:

> I thought I should be one of the oldest men, but there are men old enough to be my father, and I must say there is plenty of work left in them yet, but there is one thing that I cannot understand, that is so many married men in all the regiments we come across, then to think what a lot of young men are walking about and standing at the street corners with their hands in their pockets as much to say 'it does not matter whether England sinks or swims'. I should be ashamed to think I was not doing my duty if I were them. 'Wake up you slackers.'

The Great War was one that was dominated by artillery, and around 56 per cent of those killed at the front or behind the lines died as a result of shellfire. As such, they never saw the enemy who attacked them. Machine-gun fire and the use of the bayonet are often perceived as the embodiment of fighting between 1914 and 1918, but it was deadly artillery fire that caused casualty rates to be so high. Men were killed by red-hot pieces of metal from the exploding casement as shells blew up, by mortar bombs, by shrapnel shells or by the vaporising effect of high explosives. Staff Sergeant Whitburn Bailey of the 1st Highland Brigade, Royal Field Artillery wrote once again in early July to Mr A. Hayler, with whom he had been billeted whilst in St Neots. His letter told of the effects of shellfire and the very strange death of one soldier from an artillery shell, describing what happened after a German aircraft spotted their location:

> We hardly had time to realise our position before the shells came, four and six at a time. Everything was dust and shrapnel, and after the excitement was over we found eleven horses badly wounded – three of these it was necessary to shoot as they were past repair … four men of a neighbouring battery while sitting in their dug-out got hit, and wounded somewhat severely. We moved at night into a more safe position. You will possibly have heard that we have had one killed. Quite a young fellow … as he lay asleep in his dug-out a heavy shell pierced through, smashing his head in, and apparently killing him instantly. The most remarkable thing

was that the shell never exploded, but lay in the middle of the dug-out, and was carried out by some of the fellows, and thrown into a neighbouring ditch … It is at times difficult to realise that the enemy, ready to kill us all, is but three quarters of a mile in front.

Sergeant Bailey went on to say how different the fighting was now that the weather had changed: 'Mosquitoes, flies, and other objectionable insects are now the biggest enemy, for they torment you. The place is absolutely alive with such insects.'

At the beginning of July, Nurse Jennie Sibley was welcomed home and, when she was invited to speak at a meeting of the Sandy Sisterhood, she had the opportunity to describe her experiences in Serbia since October 1914. Jennie Sibley had been among fifty volunteer nurses who were part of Lady Paget's Unit and she was acutely aware of the dangers she would face. She recounted how Serbia was virtually surrounded by enemies, and how the only way in had been across the frontier with Greece. Upon arriving in Skopje they were given a school, which they converted into a hospital where they treated wounded soldiers. She told of the reception the unit received:

> You can well imagine the depression of the Serbians at this time, especially as they had no ammunition. Our coming seemed to herald in brighter days. Ammunition arrived. Their spirits took fresh hope and in a very short time they were in full possession of Belgrade, having taken thousands of prisoners and gained one of the biggest victories this war will ever know. Lady Paget's Unit is regarded as a mascot, having turned their dark clouds.

She went on to say how the unit worked for six months in Skopje, enduring terrible conditions for the town had no drainage or sanitation. The soldiers that they treated were in a sorry state: 'The condition was terrible – many not having been out of the trenches for four days after being wounded.' She went on to describe 'wounds ranking with pus, their bodies covered with lice, and all of them suffering frostbitten feet'. Initially there were serious communication problems as no patient spoke English, but gradually the soldiers came to trust their nurses. Conditions did not improve, though, for fevers broke out, the most serious being typhus, and it was not just the wounded that were affected. Nurses fell victim and there were fatalities, with even Lady Paget falling ill for a while. During February 1915, 2,000 Austrian prisoners died from typhus as winter hit hard with driving rain and snow. Eventually the fever abated and the unit was reinforced by others from Britain. Jennie Sibley returned from Serbia in June and the remainder of the British units were evacuated during October 1915.

Back in Eaton Socon during July were Private Edward Ashwell of the 19th Yorks and Gunner Arthur Medlow; both had seen plenty of action, Edward Ashwell at Neuve Chapelle and Festubert, and Arthur Medlow at Hill 60. Edward Ashwell was without a scratch but Arthur Medlow was less lucky, having been hit above the right eye by shrapnel at Hill 60. Eaton Socon had answered the Call to Arms well for, by July 1915, 135 men from the village were serving in the various branches of the army and navy. Of those, three had been killed and a further two were reported missing in action, while another six men from the village had been rejected as being medically unfit. One of those Eaton Socon men serving was Corporal Rodney Barringer, and he forecast an end to the war when he wrote to a friend in the village. His opinion was based upon first-hand evidence of the fighting. He said:

> I have had several letters from people who seem to think the War will be over by August, but I think 12 months next June according to what I can see of it out here. Three parts of the people I hear from in England seem to think the Germans are short of brass and copper, but they make a great mistake, the Germans keep on sending us plenty of it over, but this last two or three days they have been keeping quiet with their artillery firing.

He added that, although the weather was much better for the troops at the front, there was not much evidence of gain. What is surprising is that his last comment got by the censor, for letters were examined for remarks that might reveal plans, tactical information or opinions not felt to be conducive to the war effort.

In mid-July, the thoughts of the government turned towards the possibility of conscription when they announced plans for a National Registration of the population between the ages of fifteen and sixty-five, to take place during August. All newspapers, local and national, were asked to announce this and the *St Neots Advertiser* carried details of the scheme on 23 July. This record of names provided a database that could be used later if conscription did come in. Walter Long, the official from the Local Government Board in charge of the Register, hoped that the co-operation of local authorities would make the process much easier, and St Neots Urban District Council held a special meeting to ensure that the compilation of the Register could be effected. It was decided that the names of the unpaid enumerators would be made public, as would the districts of St Neots they would cover.

Mid-July also saw the Board of Agriculture and Fisheries advise that they had been in consultation with the Army Council regarding the shortage of men to bring in the harvest during late summer. What had been agreed was that both Regular and Territorial soldiers could be used to help where possible. Farmers were advised to contact Local Labour Exchanges for forms to apply for help from soldiers with the harvest. If any farmer wanted to obtain the services of a particular soldier, he was told to give the exact details of the regiment the soldier was serving with. Soldiers at the front knew it would soon be harvest time and they spoke fondly in their letters of the summer events they would miss. Private Walter Sherman wrote to his parents in Gransden:

> I expect that it is Gransden Feast today. I would rather be there playing cricket than here playing soldiers. I would rather be stopping the cricket ball than here dodging these shells and bullets. I don't expect you see much in the papers about Hill 60 now, we have lost that again, but not by fair means. They could not shell us off, so they done the dirty on us and gassed and we were forced to leave it.

For the soldiers in the trenches, the sight of aircraft engaged in dogfights thousands of feet above them was fascinating, and they often gazed, somewhat transfixed, as these duels reached their conclusion. Sometimes aircraft were targeted and fired upon by artillery below, as Bob Easter of Eynesbury, writing from 'somewhere in France' described:

> … one of our airmen is being shelled by the enemy. It is a grand sight to see him dodging the shrapnel as when they burst they leave a cloud of smoke. I must say they are a plucky lot of fellows; they seem to take no notice of them. One of them last Monday had no fewer than 27 shells fired at him, but I am glad to say not one of them found their mark.

Jack Allen, also from Eynesbury, wrote: 'We have aeroplanes over us continually day and night, both English and German.' The flimsy machines soaring above the trenches initially beguiled the soldiers below, especially when dogfights took place, but this changed as the role of the aeroplane altered. At first aeroplanes were used simply for observation, but by 1916 bombing and strafing were part of aeroplane tactics, as aircraft became something altogether more deadly. By 1918 they had become a very important ingredient in how both sides fought.

It was not tactical development that killed Private William Tassell on 15 July, but something altogether more sinister. An explosive bullet hit him in both legs as he was working behind the front line close to Mount Kemmel, Ypres. This was a cruel end for a man who had been so keen to fight for King and Country, and who had undergone a severe operation just to see action abroad. Bill Tassell, who was thirty-three years of age when he died, had lived for the first twenty years of his life in St Neots, had then moved to Peterborough and finally to Nottingham with his work as a gas meter tester. While in Nottingham he had joined the 1st Sherwood Foresters, a Territorial battalion, and had six years' service with them as a 'Saturday Night Soldier'. In August 1914 he was actually in camp and, when the Territorials were canvassed to see if they would serve abroad, the Sherwood Foresters responded positively. Bill Tassell was unable to go with them for he was suffering from goitre, swelling of the thyroid gland, and he was deemed unfit for service overseas. His determination to 'do his bit' can be seen in that he underwent a serious operation to try to solve the problem but, on being released from hospital, his doctor still considered him unfit for active service. Bill Tassell was very determined though, imploring the doctor to change his mind and eventually he relented, for, in January 1915, Bill joined his battalion at the front. When this happened, Florence Tassell and their two children returned to St Neots to be closer to family. Bill was welcomed by his comrades in France and during July they were in the front line, just south of Ypres. Bill found the going tough, for it seemed he had not fully recovered from his operation, and marching in full kit in the hot weather took its toll, although he hardly showed it, for when the battalion halted to rest, he spent the break helping the sick and tired. Eventually he fell ill, but medical treatment allowed him to remain at the front behind the lines, working in the rear of a wood. His comrades were entrenched in front of the wood and so he was still within range of enemy shells and bullets. Late at night on 15 July Bill Tassell's war ended, as his friend Alf told when he wrote to Florence Tassell:

> He was shot through both legs with one of those deadly explosive bullets the rotten Germans use so freely … He spoke of you and the two boys several times as he lay there lingering, and not long before he passed away he sent a message up to the trenches by a guide to me saying I wasn't to tell you. He lost a great deal of blood as the bullet pierced his main artery, and it was owing to that and the reaction, shock and worry about you that he passed away, poor fellow.

Bill Tassell's commanding officer also wrote to Florence, telling her that her husband was buried at Dickebusch and that 'He was an excellent soldier and very popular with all in his Company, and his sad end is felt by all of us'.

By the summer of 1915, wounded soldiers in their khaki uniforms were a familiar sight in St Neots and Eaton Socon. Not quite so common was the sight of soldiers in blue tunics, grey breeches and blue puttees, as happened during early August when two wounded Belgian soldiers came to Eaton Socon to visit their relations among the Belgian refugees living there. One soldier was only slightly wounded and the other had quite a sideline in making rings from pieces of German shrapnel that were soon being worn by residents of Eaton Socon and Eaton Ford. Also sporting a ring and a bracelet made from a German shell was Sapper John Bull of the Royal Engineers whilst home on leave in Eaton Socon. He had been at the front right through from Mons to Hill 60, meeting Private Leonard Bundy, and the two of them had exchanged cap badges. Leonard Bundy had gone missing in action during April and he remained so at the time of John Bull's visit home.

August saw the Gallipoli campaign renewed with vigour, and amongst those in action there were the 5th Bedfords, a Territorial battalion that contained many men from the St Neots area. The local press ran adverts for recruits for this battalion during July and August, asking for hundreds of men to come forward. The *Advertiser* added its own message on 27 August:

> As our Staff have been seriously depleted by Members of it joining the Army we shall be grateful if Correspondents and Advertisers will kindly send in their communications AS EARLY AS POSSIBLE EVERY WEEK. This will be a great help.

St Neots Red Cross Nurses, 4 June 1915.

At Gallipoli, the Allies landed at Suvla Bay which was not heavily defended, and 63,000 troops were involved. The aim was for these men to capture the area and then link up with ANZAC troops at Anzac Cove. The plan almost succeeded but a furious Turkish counter-attack recaptured Suvla Bay. The 5th Bedfords had their baptism of fire at Suvla and there were casualties, including Private William Watts of New Street, St Neots. He wrote home telling that he had been wounded as the Bedfords attacked Kidney Hill:

> We had a pretty fierce fight on Sunday, in fact I did not expect coming out alive, but I escaped it pretty well. I got a bullet through my left foot, and I left there on Monday … I do not know how many there are of us left, when I was with them they were falling like ninepins. No mistake they are some good fighting chaps, they have made their name already. We were sent out to take a hill and in less than four hours we had got it.

The attack at Kidney Hill saw the troops advance over very difficult ground, under rifle and machine-gun fire, with shells exploding among and above them. The war diary of the Bedfords describes the attack as follows:

> It was a great and glorious charge, but the position was won at terrible cost. The whole advance had been made with bayonets fixed and when the final stage was reached and the order to charge rang out the men dashed to the attack. There was no stopping these unblooded British Troops. London, Essex and Bedford Territorials charged together, but the Bedford men outstripped the Regiments on right and left and dashed into the lead, causing the line to form a crescent and sweeping everything before them. Turks went down before cold steel in hundreds, and those who were not killed turned and fled.

Also wounded at Gallipoli was Private Albert Markham of Eynesbury, whilst his brother Alfred succumbed to heat stroke and was taken to a military hospital in Cairo. The heat was fierce at Gallipoli and flies swarmed everywhere, so much so that soldiers told of their food being covered by masses of insects as they tried to eat. Not surprisingly, soldiers suffered from dysentery and diarrhoea, and they had to contend with female snipers also. Private Victor

Hill from Huntingdon Street wrote of being under shellfire, how hot it was and bemoaned the lack of tobacco. He went on to confirm that the 5th Bedfords had women firing at them, adding: 'We are in the trenches now, we were digging them yesterday, and they don't half let us have it with the shells, but only two of our boys got wounded, Sid Haynes and Bert Markham.' He finished by saying: 'It is very hot out here in the day time, but a bit cold at night. It is a very dry place, but we are close to the sea, so we all can have a good wash.' Private Fred Woodward also confirmed that Bert Markham had been wounded: 'We were digging trenches under very heavy shell and bullet fire, when one of the boys got wounded by shrapnel. It was Albert Markham.'

Further news of Sid Haynes' wounding came when his parents heard via telegram on 27 August that he had been brought back to Britain and was in hospital in Devonport. The telegram said that he was dangerously ill and his mother lost no time in catching a train to go and see him, finding him very weak and hardly able to speak. Sid Haynes had been in Gallipoli for four days when he took part in the attack at Kidney Hill, but he survived this and the hand-to-hand fighting and the bayonet charge. The very next day he was shot in the chest, the bullet going nearly through his body. He was put on board a ship to bring him and other wounded back to Britain, and it was while he was on board that the doctors managed to extract the bullet – which he kept and gave to his mother. In the very next bed to Sid Haynes was a New Zealand soldier who had also been shot – by a woman sniper lodged up a tree! Women snipers even painted themselves green to match the trees and shrubs from which they carried out their deadly work. Confirmation of the use of female snipers also came from Private Sydney Cross of the Machine Gun Section of the 5th Bedfords. His letter was received in Eaton Socon during September and told: 'It is surprising what a number of snipers there are here, women as well as men, they seem to be everywhere; they have been found with their faces and hands painted green as well as wearing green clothes.' Sid Haynes gradually recovered from his wound and survived the war.

The 5th Bedfords had a rough time at Gallipoli and readers of the *St Neots Advertiser* got a first-hand account how hard the fighting was when the paper, together with the *Biggleswade Chronicle*, published a letter from Sergeant Major Milton:

> This is not ordinary warfare. It is simply horrible. We have some chaps here who have been to France and they say that it is not a patch on this. First, there is the heat to contend with, and that nearly cooks you. Nearly everyone's face is raw already. There is no water on the place, and the dust-clouds nearly choke you. Then the high hills and boulders are larger than our houses. You have to get over them the best way you can. Another nuisance is the large number of different sorts of insects. Then there are the snipers. There are heaps of those, including women. We caught three yesterday, and one of them was a woman. They are all very good shots and they have tons of ammunition and foodstuffs, and clothes with the German Eagle on. The only thing we want out here is more men and well trained ones too … Since I started this letter I had to go out in a hurry to take part in one of the most deadly fights that has ever taken place. We lost very heavily, but we took the position, and the 5th made names for themselves. We lost more than 300 killed and wounded.

The fight that Sergeant Major Milton referred to was indeed Kidney Hill and, in late August, news filtered through that Ernest Charles Page, the son William Page of New Street, was amongst the dead. Ernest Page was in the Signalling and Wireless Section of the 5th Bedfords and his father heard of his death when a telegram arrived telling that Ernest had died of wounds on 16 August. A week later he learned more, when a letter from one of his son's comrades was delivered. It read:

Sorry to have to tell you that Ernie was wounded Sunday last in the back by shrapnel shell. Will tell you how it happened. The Signal Section, together with the Commanding Officer, were just behind the firing line, in a place surrounded by rocks, when we were suddenly shelled by shrapnel, killing one signaller, wounding four of five others, one officer, Ernie, a corporal and a scout, all injured by the same shell. How we escaped none of us can tell; it was a miracle. I expect by the time you receive this you will have read how the Beds fought, practically capturing by themselves the hill they were sent out to get, losing men and officers. Our chaps went through it fighting like demons.

The letter continued, 'I do miss poor old Ernie', and then a postscript added, 'Have since heard that Ernie is dead, but cannot believe it yet.' The letter was given to the *Advertiser* for publication, causing much sorrow, for Ernie Page had worked for the paper for a while. Twenty-year-old Ernie Page was one of William Page's three serving sons, and he was the only one to die. He has no known grave and is commemorated on the Helles Memorial at Gallipoli.

Two days later, another local man was killed at Gallipoli. Sergeant John Corbett was an experienced soldier with twelve years' service before the war. This thirty-nine-year-old re-enlisted immediately in 1914, becoming a sergeant in the Royal Field Artillery and remaining in England until July 1915 when he headed east to the Dardanelles. The Royal Field Artillery landed at Suvla Bay and went into action almost at once. On 18 August, John Corbett wrote home to his wife Nellie and their son and two daughters saying that he was well, but on the very same day he was killed, as the RFA engaged the enemy. About ten days later, Nellie Corbett received a letter from the battery captain telling that her husband had been killed at around 7 o'clock on the evening of the 18th. John Corbett was originally from Eaton Socon, where his father Jacob still resided, but he was living in St Mary's Street, Eynesbury before the outbreak of war. He was buried by his comrades and today his body rests in Lala Baba Cemetery at Suvla.

September saw no respite for the people of St Neots, as reports of more casualties at Gallipoli reached the town. Firstly, news of Private John William Mason of Eaton Socon came, revealing that he too had been wounded at Kidney Hill: 'The bullet went in the bottom of the second finger and came out of the palm. I got hit on Sunday, when a lot more of our chaps got hit. It was the first day of going into action.' Then information was received that another Eaton Socon man, Private Austin Barringer, had been hit and again the wound was to the hand. He wrote telling of his wound: 'It is only a slight one in the left hand … the bullet went through the thick part of the thumb and out the muscle so I can't move it about much.' Private Barringer was taken off the peninsula by boat and eventually made it back to Southampton in early September.

During the third week of September, news reached Eaton Ford that Rudolph Meade Smythe had been killed three weeks after arriving at Gallipoli. Rudolph Smythe was a well-known and respected figure in St Neots, having been involved in social and religious work, as well as having links to local cricket, hockey and tennis clubs. His father had been Vicar of Caxton until his death and his mother still resided in Eaton Ford. Rudolph Smythe, an officer with the 5th Bedfordshire Territorials for five years, had taken command of the Biggleswade Company when it found itself without an officer. He worked hard to make the company a most efficient one and was with

Private John Mason.

5th Bedfords Officers in 1912 – Rudolph Smythe is fourth from the right, standing.

Left: Captain Rudolph Smythe. *Above:* Plaque to Rudolph Smythe in St Neots Church.

them when they sailed for Gallipoli on 26 July. When required to spend time with his company in August, as reinforcements at Alexandria in Egypt, he was not best pleased and consequently missed the Suvla Bay landings, arriving a week later still commanding Biggleswade 'D' Company. On 13 September he was shot in the head by a Turkish sniper and, although he was rushed to a Casualty Clearing Station, he never regained consciousness and died the next day. When news of his death reached St Neots, a Memorial Service was organised for Captain Smythe and the others from the town who had fallen. Meanwhile, Rudolph Smythe's younger brother arrived in Gallipoli, having just been commissioned as an officer in the 5th Bedfords, only to learn that his brother had been killed a few days earlier. Early in 1918 Lieutenant Barlow Woollcombe Smythe would be awarded the Military Cross for bravery during the Battle for Gaza.

Confirmation of both casualties and conditions faced by the 5th Bedfords came from Corporal George Bull and Private Alan Smith. George Bull wrote:

We have lost a lot of officers and men. We keep gaining ground at night. The fighting out here is done at night. It is very hot in the day and cold at night. I often think there are some more young fellows in St Neots who could come and do their bit over here … We only get a quart of water to last us all day … We get no bread at all out here, it is all biscuits … I have not seen a house since I landed, it is all rocks and hills. I have not had a wash for nine or ten days, so you can guess how I feel … The worse thing in the daytime is the flies, you cannot rest for them … We cannot get hold of cigarettes, and the only pleasure we get is smoking.

Alan Smith wrote home to Eaton Socon from hospital in Gravesend, where he was being treated for a shrapnel wound in his right thigh: 'I am in a very nice hospital, and pleased and lucky to be alive, as the shell burst only three yards off.'

The Gallipoli campaign continued throughout October and November before ending in December, but not before another soldier from St Neots died. Thirty-two-year-old Ernest Gowler was with the 5th Bedfords and he contracted dysentery whilst fighting here. His condition was so bad that he was brought back to Britain on the same hospital boat as Private Robert Chamberlain, who had been wounded in the left leg. A letter home from him told: 'I suppose you know Ern Gowler and Charlie Knight are sick.' Ernest Gowler got back to Britain but he did not last long, dying on 17 October at Devonport Military Hospital, Plymouth. His family in Eynesbury were informed by telegram, but not before his sister, Mrs Baxter, had set off to see him in hospital. She arrived at Devonport and found herself having to attend her brother's funeral, rather than comforting him in hospital. Ernest Gowler was given a full military funeral and was buried in Plymouth.

By the start of December it was realised that the Gallipoli landings had failed and the Allies withdrew their troops from the peninsula, having suffered the huge casualties shown below:

Australia: 19,441 wounded and missing; 8,709 killed.
New Zealand: 4,852 wounded and missing; 2,721 killed.
United Kingdom: 52,230 wounded and missing; 21,255 killed.

Perhaps it should not have been such a surprise that the Turkish troops fought so fiercely to protect their homeland – after all, this was exactly what the French and Belgians were doing on the Western Front, and what the British would do if ever German Armies landed in Britain.

On the Western Front, September saw the opening moves of the Battle of Loos, a battle that the BEF did not want to fight, as the location was very unsuitable and the chances of victory were slim. The pressure for the battle came from the French, who wanted a more visible commitment from their British Allies, and the choice of Loos was pressed upon the British. Loos is a mining area that was far easier to defend than attack, with cover provided by miners' cottages and slag heaps occupied and fortified by the Germans, giving them commanding fire over the battlefield. The attack at Loos saw the BEF use gas for the first time but not too successfully, as some of the attacking troops found the gas blowing back into their faces.

Men from St Neots fought at Loos, and although some were wounded none were killed. The attack began on 25 September, following an intensive four-day artillery bombardment, and lasted until 28 September when it was called off. One of those who went into action on 25 September was Private Arthur Davies of the 1st Northants, who wrote to his brother and sister in St Neots, telling of a very lucky escape. From hospital in Aberdeen he wrote:

I have been wounded in my left hand, the bullet passing through the bottom of the thumb and coming out just below my little finger. I don't know if I shall be able to use it any more after it has healed, but it is very painful and swollen at present. I think I am very lucky being alive. I was in the big charge on Sat. Sept. 25th (in the morning), and you can bet that we gave the Germans a great surprise. We used everything we possibly could against them. As I belong to the bombing section I had to carry bombs in a Bandolier in front of me, and it is owing to this that I am alive, as a bullet struck one of the bombs and glided off. We had to do the charge, a distance of 700 yards, in short rushes. After doing about 500 yards we had just got up to make another rush when a shower of bullets came along and I received my wound.

Initially the BEF did well at Loos and captured the German front line, but reserves were too slow in being brought forward to consolidate the gains, yet the attack did show that a strongly defended trench line could be taken. One job that soldiers did not enjoy was clearing the ground over which the attack had gone in. Alf Murphy from Eynesbury was among the Bedfordshire Yeomanry who were ordered to do this work on 26 September and his account made disturbing reading for those back home. He described having to pass through the rear areas where there were dead horses killed by enemy shellfire, and then reaching the battlefield:

The worst sight of all was of course our poor dead comrades. I hope I will never see such sights again. Our work is to clear everything up. We all got in a long line and walked slowly across the ground; as we came to the dead bodies we collected all their personal belongings … when we finished work … we buried them all … Each grave is marked with a wooden cross.

Alf Murphy went on to tell of finding one soldier from Birmingham with a photograph of his sweetheart on him, together with a letter asking for her to be informed if he was killed. He contrasted the gruesome work of clearing the ground with the sight of shimmering star shells bursting above the battlefield. This work was not easy, for Alf Murphy and his comrades were shelled and shot at as they carried out their assignment.

The fighting around Loos continued into October, when Private Lionel Martin of the Grenadier Guards was wounded as the fighting abated. He was hit by shrapnel that took off a piece of the back of his skull, causing him great pain and the loss of much blood, for the introduction of steel helmets was still three months away.

While the BEF attacked at Loos, fighting carried on in other parts of the Western Front and casualties occurred on a daily basis. Attacks, shellfire and sniping continued to take their toll and two men from St Neots joined the ever-increasing total of those who fell in this way.

First of all, Private John Pearce of the 5th Battalion King's Shropshire Light Infantry was killed at Ypres on 25 September, and then Private Lewis Pope died almost a month later on 22 October, again at Ypres. John Pearce was killed as his battalion attacked German trenches close to Railway Wood. The King's Shropshires went over the top at 4.20 a.m. after a thirty-minute bombardment of enemy positions, advancing and taking the front-line German trench. The battalions that supported the 5th Shropshires did not make such good progress. A German counter-attack made it almost impossible for them to hold the captured position, and they were forced to withdraw. By 8.15 a.m. they were back in their original lines. John Pearce, a twenty-three-year-old from Weald Cottage, was killed, either during the attack or the withdrawal and his body was not recovered from the battlefield. He has no known grave and today is commemorated on the Menin Gate, Ypres.

Lewis Pope had been in the army for just over a year, having enlisted following a recruiting rally in St Neots during September 1914. After training, he had gone overseas with the 8th Bedfords, one of the battalions formed for Kitchener's New Army, and he had been at the

Private Lewis Pope, killed at Ypres, October 1915.

front about eight weeks when he was killed at Ypres on 22 October. Lewis Pope had trained as a bomber, whose job was to throw Mills bombs into German trenches as the Bedfords attacked. It was not while bombing that he was killed, though; he was seriously injured by an exploding German shell and failed to survive. His commanding officer, Lieutenant Green, wrote to Lewis Pope's father in Eynesbury, telling that Lewis 'was a man who was held in esteem by all, who was respected by his comrades and for whom I had personally a strong affection'. Lewis Pope's sister had only just received a letter from her brother when Lieutenant Green's letter was delivered telling her that Lewis was dead. The letter to his sister told how the Germans were so persistent in shelling the British trenches and recounted how he was reading the *St Neots Advertiser* his father had sent him when 'the Germans sent a shell over and smothered it with dirt, so that I had to give over. They won't let you have a minute'. Thirty-two-year-old Lewis

Pope was buried in Ypres and his body still rests there today in La Brique Military Cemetery. News of his death reached other men from Eynesbury who were serving either in France and Belgium, or Gallipoli. Private Joseph Chamberlain of the 5th Bedfords wrote home after being wounded in the ankle, telling that he had heard of the deaths of Ern Gower and Lewis Pope and how sorry he was that his friends from Eynesbury had been killed.

When troops were relieved from the trenches they spent some time in reserve behind the lines and, although this was not restful, for they were allocated labouring tasks to carry out, they did get a break from the danger of the front line. For many, football gave relaxation and relief from exploding shells and snipers' bullets. Not surprisingly there was a fair degree of wear and tear on the actual footballs, as can be seen from a letter sent from France to the *Advertiser* in November from Sergeant Davies of 'D' Squadron the Beds Yeomanry :

Dear Sir, The men of the above Squadron, who are Huntingdonshire men, wish me to ask for space in your valuable issue to beg for a couple of footballs. We have kicked to death the only two we brought to France with us.

As Christmas approached, life in the front-line trenches remained dangerous, especially for soldiers having their first experience of it. Dudley Ekins, a Private with the Canadian Mounted Rifles, wrote to his aunt in St Neots in November, telling what this introduction to trench life was like: 'The first day in the trenches a fellow sort of feels out of it, one hardly knows how to go on, but after a few hours one feels as if he has been there for weeks.' He went on to add that men quickly developed respect for German marksmanship: 'One gets to learn that Fritz as a sniper is to be watched.' Once a day, rations were dispatched to the men in the front line and usually a rations party was sent to collect the food. This was a hazardous job, for the Germans regularly shelled the communication trenches that the rations were brought up along. It was very tiring having to haul the rations up to the front through trenches that were often knee-deep in mud, as Dudley Ekins described:

We used to go out once a day for rations, in a small fatigue party, and it was a weary way from the front line to where the transports left the rations. That journey was the most dangerous of our duties as the German artillery had the range pretty accurate and shelled it periodically. Most of the casualties occurred in the communication trench. It was there that I saw the first dead man. I must have been following him up pretty closely as he was still warm, although life was extinct, the poor fellow being shot clean through the heart.

In St Neots, November saw yet another recruiting rally and again the Earl of Sandwich, Lord Lieutenant of the County, called for more men to come forward, and he even targeted numbers, asking for another 140 from St Neots and thirty-six from Eynesbury. He added that these men might not even see action, for it was possible that the war would be over before they completed their training. Little Paxton was exempt from his target for it had already sent enough men forward, whilst Eaton Socon and Eaton Ford were not mentioned as they fell under Bedfordshire local authority control at this time. As if to support the idea of more men coming forward, the first postwoman for St Neots was appointed in October 1915 when Mrs Phillips took up her new job. During the week following the recruiting rally, thirty-six men came forward and 'took the King's Shilling'. As well as recruiting rallies, the press was also used strongly in the last few weeks of 1915 to try to persuade men to enlist. On 10 December, a large advertisement for the 5th Bedfords appeared in local papers, imploring men to join up, using such emotive terms as 'Why you must join' and 'Surely there are men somewhere?' The *Advertiser* even printed a number of photographs of recruits with the 3rd Bedfords smiling and showing the thumbs-up sign. Letters from serving soldiers also increased the pressure on men to enlist and, in December, the *Advertiser* printed one from Private Francis Medlow of Wyboston. His letter seemed to intend to shame those who were hanging back, for he stressed that he was a grandfather with fifteen children, two grandchildren and he was 'doing his share' whilst others weren't. The recruiting drive did have an effect, for during the very next week another 117 men came forward.

Another grandfather was fifty-four-year-old Sapper Walter Searle of Eaton Ford, who had joined the Army Drainage Corps in October 1915. That he was accepted speaks volumes for the need for men, even if it was in a supportive role, for by using him and men of his age, the BEF could release younger men for the Western Front. In late November Walter Searle fell ill, just days after writing home to his wife Elizabeth, saying that he was 'quite well'. That changed when his wife received a telegram telling that her husband was dangerously ill in Chatham Hospital. She left Eaton Ford immediately to be with him and, although she arrived in time to see him, he died on 22 November, leaving her a widow with six children – although most were grown up. Walter Searle was buried in Fort Pitt Military Cemetery, Kent.

That these men were needed was supported by the fact that men were still being killed or wounded, even though no major offensives were now taking place, because of the onset of winter. During December the following men were either killed or wounded. On 1 December, Private Charles Bettles of the 1st Bedfords was killed when a German mine was blown. Charles Bettles was among a party that was assigned to help the Battalion Tunnelling Company as they tunnelled under German lines close to Fricourt on the Somme. The work of tunnellers was exceptionally dangerous and it was a completely different war underground – yet one that was as deadly. On 1 December the Germans blew a mine that buried Charles Bettles and Harry King, who hailed from Eltisley. Both men were killed and four others were injured, including Billy Stamford from Eynesbury, who was very upset by the death of his friend Charles Bettles. Private Herbert Mould, another St Neots man, wrote home to tell that Charles Bettles had died. Included in the letter that Herbert Mould dispatched was a photograph of the village where Charles Bettles was buried, and also a note that a wooden cross had been placed on the grave. Mr William Bettles of Eaton Socon had another son, George, serving with the Royal Irish Fusiliers, and happily he would survive the war.

Private Fred Gilbert of the Grenadier Guards was shot through the thigh but was recovering well after a tube was put in the wound, and then news arrived in St Neots that Private

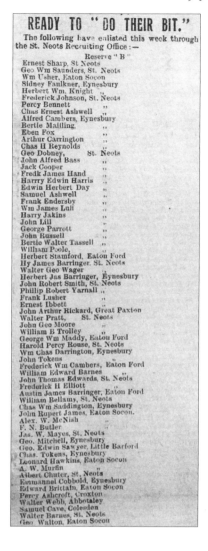

READY TO " DO THEIR BIT."

The following have enlisted this week through the St. Neots Recruiting Office :—

Reserve " B "

Ernest Sharp, St Neots
Geo Wm Saunders, St. Neots
Wm Usher, Eaton Socon
Sidney Faulkner, Eynesbury
Herbert Wm. Knight ,,
Frederick Johnson, St. Neots
Percy Bennett ,,
Chas Ernest Ashwell ,,
Alfred Cambers, Eynesbury
Bertie Mailling, ,,
Eben Fox ,,
Arthur Carrington ,,
Chas H Reynolds ,,
Geo Dobney, St. Neots
John Alfred Bass ,,
Jack Cooper ,,
Fredk James Hand ,,
Harrry Edwin Harris ,,
Edwin Herbert Day ,,
Samuel Ashwell ,,
Frank Endersby ,,
Wm James Lull ,,
Harry Jakins ,,
John Lill ,,
George Parrott ,,
John Russell ,,
Bertie Walter Tassell ,,
William Poole, ,,
Herbert Stamford, Eaton Ford
Hy James Barringer, St. Neots
Walter Geo Wager ,,
Herbert Jas Barringer, Eynesbury
John Robert Smith, St. Neots
Philip Robert Yarnall ,,
Frank Lusher ,,
Ernest Ibbett ,,
John Arthur Rickard, Great Paxton
Walter Pratt, St. Neots
John Geo Moore ,,
William B Trolley ,,
George Wm Maddy, Eaton Ford
Harold Percy Rouse, St. Neots
Wm Chas Darrington, Eynesbury
John Tokens ,,
Frederick Wm Cambers, Eaton Ford
William Edward Barnes ,,
John Thomas Edwards, St. Neots
Frederick H Elliott ,,
Austin James Barringer, Eaton Ford
William Bellamy, St. Neots
Chas Wm Saddington, Eynesbury
John Rupert James, Eaton Socon.
Alex. W. McNish ,,
F. N. Butler ,,
Jas. W. Mayes, St. Neots
Geo. Mitchell, Eynesbury
Geo. Edwin Sawyer, Little Barford
Chas. Tokens, Eynesbury
Leonard Hawkins, Eaton Socon
A. W. Murfin ,,
Albert Chuter, St. Neots
Emmanuel Cobbold, Eynesbury
Edward Brittain, Eaton Socon
Percy Ashcroft, Croxton
Walter Webb, Abbotsley
Samuel Cave, Colesden
Walter Barnes, St. Neots
Geo Walton, Eaton Socon

Left: List of those who volunteered in December 1915 printed in the local press. *Above:* Headstone of Private Charles Bettles.

George Smith had been gassed. Private Chas Norman and Corporal Chas Newton arrived home in time for Christmas, after being treated for dysentery and fever contracted in Gallipoli. Meanwhile, Private Albert Norman was celebrating being promoted to Sergeant, a deserved reward for a man who had been gassed, blown up and temporarily blinded. He arrived back home on leave at the start of December and recounted how, during the fighting at Hill 60, there was one trench that had both British and German soldiers in it and all that divided them was a steel plate.

Three days before the end of the year, the 8th Bedfords were entrenched at Ypres, close to the banks of the Yser Canal. The battalion war diary comments how the days around Christmas and New Year were fairly quiet, with very little German shelling. On 28 December the same diary records: 'Fairly quiet day Ypres and canal bank shelled – Enemy aeroplanes active.' What the diary does not tell is that Private Richard Jakins was killed by shellfire that day. Twenty-year-old Richard Jakins came from Toseland and he had enlisted at Abbotsley, although he lived with his parents, George and Camilla, in Eynesbury Hardwicke. Even though he was buried, his body became just another of those that were lost as the fighting continued, and today he is commemorated on the Menin Gate at Ypres.

Private Richard Jakins.

Jan 14 1916

Pte. Richard Jakins, 8th Beds.,
(Son of Mrs Beale, Eynesbury Hardwicke),
killed recently in France.

The year 1915 was difficult for the British Army, having to fight in offensives where success was unlikely, not being properly equipped, suffering from shortages of shells, and having to fight to show its ally, the French, that it was prepared to pull its weight. The regular army, both professional and highly skilled, was unused to fighting the kind of war that the Western Front entailed and it suffered enormous casualties, many experienced men being killed or wounded. The Territorials were raised to defend Britain from invasion, but they had volunteered to fight overseas and they too had suffered great losses. Both Regulars and Territorials had acquitted themselves well but, by the end of 1915, their numbers had been reduced dramatically. The conclusion of 1915 also saw the end of Sir John French as Commander-in-Chief of the BEF. He had come under increasing criticism following the Battle of Loos, especially with his reluctance to commit men after the initial success. He paid for this by being dismissed and was replaced by Douglas Haig.

So the second year of the war came to an end. This time there would be no Christmas Truce and fighting took place as usual. Many of Kitchener's New Armies were now nearing the end of their training and 1916 would see them called upon in considerable numbers.

THREE

⇒1916⇐
ENTER THE CITIZENS' ARMIES

I916 was perhaps the most critical and even pivotal year of the Great War. It was during this year that Kitchener's New Armies took to the battlefield in numbers for the first time, and it became the year when the BEF learned to fight the kind of war that would eventually lead to victory two years later.

As the year began, news reached St Neots that Private Rodney Barringer of the Royal Garrison Artillery had won the Distinguished Conduct Medal. At the start of January his mother received a letter in which he told how he had been put forward for the medal:

> We have had a very hot time the last few days. We have been shelled very heavily. I have never been in such heavy shell fire before. To make it worse they were nearly all gas shells. They sent us about 153 shells in 33 minutes, and after that they kept it up for several hours. One officer was killed and several wounded, and one man was killed. We had orders to leave the place, so they all went, but I hung back and stayed with one wounded man. Shells were flying all around. I was the only one anywhere near that I could see, and the poor fellow I was risking my life for trying to save, died in my arms. He had only been with us one and [a] half hours. I have been recommended for the DCM.

Later in January he got home on leave and revealed that he had been recommended for the DCM once before, when he had volunteered to stay with his battery's guns to destroy them as German troops advanced, only for British cavalry to ride to the rescue. He also said that the British lines were swarming with German spies.

In St Neots, two events took place in the first week of 1916, to support soldiers billeted in the town. A Soldiers' Dinner, comprising of beef, mutton, pork, plum pudding, mince pies and cheese, was followed by a Smoking Concert. Such concerts were very popular at the time and saw entertainment with live music, whilst the men in the audience could talk and smoke. The event was deemed a huge success by the organisers, the St Neots Recreational Committee, and it was felt that a strong bond between soldiers and the town had been forged. Most of the men stationed in St Neots were Scottish, and over the next few years they would write regularly to the families they had stayed with. Scottish soldiers found sweethearts during their stay in St Neots, and many local girls married these Territorials.

Many families were also pleased to see their loved ones return on leave from the front during these first weeks of January. One such lucky soldier was Private Lionel Martin of Russell Street, who arrived home with much to tell. He had been over in France since March 1915 with the Grenadier Guards and, although he towered over most men at 6ft 2in, he was small in comparison to others in his company, who stood up to 8in taller. For such tall men the trenches were a very dangerous place, as they had to stoop as they walked along, and one moment of lost concentration often attracted sniper fire if their heads showed above the parapet. Back home in St Neots, he told of trench raids, surviving shellfire and of his Christmas dinner of a tin of bully beef. He also spoke of how the Germans were becoming more daring in the ways that they infiltrated British trenches as spies. Whilst he and some of his chums were burying a fallen comrade, they were approached by two soldiers dressed as 'Kilties' (Scottish soldiers) who spoke with them. Later on it was confirmed that these were two German spies.

George Sawford of the Royal Army Medical Corps arrived in St Neots on 18 January, after six months at the front. He too told tales of German infiltration, with a man dressed as a major of the Middlesex Regiment being shot as a spy, and three mines exploding under the British lines and survivors seeing three men dressed in khaki escaping to the German front line just before the explosions.

Wounded soldiers were also returning from Gallipoli, reaching home after periods of treatment in base hospitals and then Britain. Private Sidney Haynes had been wounded at Suvla Bay when a shrapnel bullet hit him in the chest, penetrating one of his lungs and coming out of his back. He was nursed in a number of hospitals in Britain, but after being declared fit for duty again, the wound reopened. Home on leave, he was joined by Privates John Mason and Frank Hemmings of Eaton Socon, and Lance Corporal Arthur Hill of Huntingdon Street. Private Mason had suffered a wound to his knuckles at Gallipoli and then was hit by another bullet in the arm that left him unable even to lift a cup of tea. Private Hemmings and Lance Corporal Hill had both contracted dysentery in Gallipoli, but Private Hemmings had been very lucky not to be wounded. As a stretcher bearer during the landings, on one occasion the stretcher he was carrying was smashed by shrapnel three times in one day. He also escaped injury when a bullet went clean through his helmet, and then when he was hit by a piece of shrapnel in the neck.

Amongst the Australians who attacked at Gallipoli was Arthur Richardson, a former resident of Eynesbury, who had left eight years earlier for a new life Down Under. In January his mother received news that her son had been wounded in the hand and one of his fingers would have to be amputated. He returned to Australia as he was no longer fit for active service overseas, but he was made available for Home Defence.

Back in France and Belgium, daily shelling continued to cause casualties. In January, Privates Bertie Watts and Thomas Fletcher, both of Eaton Socon and serving with the 8th Bedfords, were wounded by shrapnel as the battalion manned front-line trenches at Poperinghe near Ypres. Then a few days later Private Fred Higgins of Eaton Ford, also with the Bedfords, was wounded and had to be admitted to hospital in Rouen.

By the start of February, the impact of the Military Service Act (conscription) was being felt, as more and more men received call-up papers. The Act saw men aged nineteen to forty-one become eligible for military service, although those under holy orders were excused. Some men, of course, did not welcome the idea of conscription and they appealed for exemption. Men could appeal on grounds of their work being vital to the national interest, of being infirm or of poor health, of hardship for their families if they were called up or if they were conscientious objectors. To deal with this situation, local tribunals were established that heard the appeals and then made a judgment. Men were either granted exemption on a temporary or permanent basis, or their appeals were turned down, making them immediately eligible for military service. Tribunals sat in St Neots and Eaton Socon and they were very busy following the introduction of conscription. Decisions could be very distressing and some men made even more terrible decisions after their appeals were rejected. One such case saw Richard Crane of Great Gransden commit suicide in March, apparently as a result of his appeal being turned down by the St Neots Rural Tribunal. His mother, Susan Crane, discovered his body hanging from a rafter in the wash-house on the morning he was due to leave to join the army.

Appeals on the ground of conscientious objection were heard in Huntingdon and those appealing were asked a number of searching questions designed to test them to the limit. The questions ran as follows:

> Supposing the Germans came to ----, and burnt your house down, what would you do?
> If you saw a German coming to kill your mother or brother, what would you do?
> Would you sit still and let them kill your mother or father?

The *Advertiser* reported in detail the hearings of conscientious objectors and, in March, printed the following letter under the heading 'A Soldier on Shirkers'. The letter was signed 'A Non Conscientious Objector – Somewhere in France'.

> Sir, I should like to draw the attention of the readers of your valuable newspaper to a recent case which came before the local tribunal. This particular applicant was granted six months exemption; what for is beyond my comprehension. In my opinion it's a shame that such cases cannot be found out. I am quite aware that all cannot come, but there are a few more in this district that might be doing a little for their King and Country. I myself should like to award such fellows with the 'Iron Cross' for their 'pluck and bravery'.

One person given little choice about joining up was Charles Ashwell of St Neots, who appeared before the town's magistrates less than a month after being ordered 'to be of good behaviour' for twelve months, when charged with being drunk and disorderly on 4 March. The magistrate advised Charles Ashwell that he was going to adjourn the case for a week and that he would sentence him then unless he had enlisted. Charles Ashwell told the magistrate that he would join up.

Perhaps there was something in the air in St Neots during early March, for Private Frank Smith also appeared before the magistrates accused of 'feloniously breaking and entering' the house of Howard Lynn in Huntingdon Street. Frank Smith had entered the house and got into bed, waking the Lynns' young son. Howard Lynn told how he rushed to the bedroom and found a 'dazed' Frank Smith. The soldier's boots, and rolled up puttees, were found on the doorstep and Howard Lynn told him to put them on and leave. Next morning they discovered that half a pork pie was missing from their larder. The magistrates heard the case but discharged the defendant, for it could not be proved he had eaten half of the pork pie!

The last week of March saw the worst blizzard known for many years, with driving snow and strong winds bringing chaos to St Neots. Traffic was disrupted by snow and fallen trees, telegraph and telephone wires were brought down and trains were delayed. The storm wreaked havoc throughout the county, but did not stop a military concert going ahead in St Neots at the Congregational Lecture Hall; many from the town braved the conditions to attend. People from all over Britain supported soldiers during March and April by contributing to the National Egg Collection for Wounded Soldiers and Sailors. The residents of St Neots District gave generously, and 6,819 eggs were donated. John Ross was one of the soldiers who gratefully received eggs, and this wounded Canadian soldier wrote to Miss Eva Cheshire of Eaton Socon thanking her:

> It was my first real good egg for a long time back … Excuse me for taking the liberty of writing to you, but I really had to tell you how I enjoyed my eggs. For believe [me], you don't see eggs around the firing line.

On the Continent, Allied commanders' thoughts were turning towards the offensives that they would undertake later in the year and, following the Chantilly Conference at the end of 1915, their focus shifted towards an area that would become indelibly etched in British military history – the Somme. In late March and early April this was still some time away, but preparations on the Somme saw raised levels of aggression in what previously had been a fairly quiet sector, before the BEF took it over from the French. The BEF had arrived on the Somme in July 1915 and soldiers arriving from Flanders were certainly pleased to be there, after the conditions they had faced at Ypres. The rolling countryside reminded many of the countryside of Britain. Private Joe Jacques of Weald Cottages, St Neots, wrote to his sister in May telling her how different it was, and yet how it still remained as dangerous as Ypres:

> The part where we are now fighting is much more hilly than the last place, all great chalk hills and we are under the ground about 20 or 30 feet in places … We get hundreds of shells every day and night, but thank God I have managed to dodge them so far. They now send us large tin canisters, which are filled up with old pieces of iron, razor blades and scizzors [sic], which do awful damage.

However, between the arrival of the BEF and the end of 1915, the hitherto peaceful nature of the area changed as trench raids, increased artillery bombardments and tunnelling made it much more violent. In the six months of 1915, over 1,600 men of the BEF were killed in action. By the end of April 1916, a further 2,034 British soldiers had died as activity in the area increased. Among the battalions who were preparing for the Somme were the 1st, 2nd, 7th and 8th Bedfords and, in just three months, they would take their part in the Big Push, as the Somme became known to both soldier and civilian back home. One soldier who had initially been with the Bedfords was (John) William Goodman, who enlisted in November 1914. Time-keeping does not appear to have been one of his strong points, as he was fined in 1915 when with the Bedfords and then reprimanded by the Border Regiment, on both occasions for arriving back late from leave. In the summer of 1915 he was gassed, and when he returned to the front he was reassigned to the 2nd Battalion, the Border Regiment. On 19 April, he was with his battalion close to Mametz on the Somme, at Mansel Copse, when a German raid took place. Twenty men of the 2nd Borderers were killed; amongst them was thirty-three-year-old William Goodman of Eaton Socon. Thirteen of the men were buried in graves that survived, but seven of the graves were lost during the continuing fighting – including William Goodman's, and today he is commemorated on the Thiepval Memorial to the Missing. William's father, George, found out that his son had been killed at the beginning of May, when he received the dreaded brown envelope from the War Office.

Other soldiers wounded during March and April included Privates Walter Stamford and Lionel Martin. Walter Stamford had a very close call, being hit by a bullet that went through his throat and came out of the back of his neck. He wrote to his wife in Cambridge Street telling her that he had been wounded by a German sniper as he guided men out of the firing line and back to billets. Grenadier Guardsman Lionel Martin was wounded at Ypres when a German shell exploded directly into the dugout he was occupying with nineteen other soldiers. Eight of these died, including one of Lionel Martin's close friends. Writing home, he told that he had a slight wound to the head and that: 'One of my pals had a leg off, and both feet, and was hit in the head. He had some rum and smoked a cigarette and chatted to me as he lay on a stretcher. He died in hospital.' He also told that two of those who died were brothers who joined up together and died together.

Better news of local serving soldiers came in the *Daily Mirror* of 18 April 1916, with news of the award of the Distinguished Conduct Medal to nineteen-year-old Private J.B. Hawkins of Eaton Socon, together with his photograph. The glad news regarding Private Hawkins was tempered by the sad tidings concerning Private Charles Evans with the 4th Battalion, the Royal Norfolks in Egypt, serving with the Mediterranean Expeditionary Force. He had contracted dysentery, dying on 26 April, and his mother and father, Ann and Charles, heard this in early May when a letter arrived at their home in Russell Street. The letter was from twenty-seven-year-old Charles Evans' commanding officer, telling that he had been buried with full military honours in the desert, close to the Suez Canal. Captain Steel consoled Ann Evans, saying: 'Although your son had been with us but two or three months we had realised that he was of the stamp that gives a good account of itself in battle.'

At around the same time, information reached St Neots concerning other soldiers on the Western Front and further afield. First it was learned that two brothers, Thomas and George Freshwater, had been wounded; Thomas with a gunshot wound to the buttock in France and George wounded whilst with the Persian Gulf Expedition. Then news arrived that Seaman John Joyce had survived the sinking of HMS *Russell* in the Mediterranean, and that nineteen-year-old Private John Chandler and twenty-nine-year-old Samuel Hedge of Toseland were missing, believed killed on 19 April. Both soldiers were serving with the 8th Bedfords, and on the 19th, as they raided enemy lines, they came under German shellfire near the Yser Canal, Ypres. Thirty-two Bedfords were killed, ninety-seven were missing believed killed, and sixty-five were wounded. The information about both men changed in early May; Samuel Hedge's death was confirmed, but the news of John Chandler came as a relief to his parents, for he was a POW in Germany. As his parents were mourning, a letter arrived in their son's familiar handwriting, saying: 'You may be thankful that I am alive … there are 35 of us Bedfords here – all that was left of a company, the others killed, wounded or buried. How I got through that bombardment I don't know.'

On 21 May, daylight saving was introduced in Britain for the very first time, giving an extra hour of daylight to help with the war effort. It was estimated that the measure would allow a saving of around £2.5 million. The measure would last until 1 October and, although the dates have changed, daylight saving remains with us today as a reminder of the Great War. The extra hour, as well as cutting back on gas lighting, meant that there would be another hour's daylight in which to bring in the harvest. At a meeting of the Hunts War Agriculture Committee in early May, the idea of using German POWs as workers was discussed. With true 'British fair play' it was agreed that if this happened then the POWs would be licensed, fed and paid.

In France, the build up to the Somme continued and mining became a very significant feature of this escalation of fighting. Mines were a very effective way of destroying enemy trenches, sapping morale and gaining a considerable advantage if the crater could be occupied, for the lip gave an elevated position that overlooked the enemy. Private Len Shaw, the son of the postmaster of St Neots, told of seeing mines being detonated:

We are anticipating a very lively time as this front is very, very, very hot just now … It is a sight to see a mine sprung from anywhere close by. The column of fire … shoots up into the air over 70 feet, and the earth literally belches forth huge stones, earth, parts of the trench, revetting, etc. The rival bombers then scrap of course for possession.

In May, Len Shaw escaped injury when a grenade burst near, but just days later he was not so lucky when, in a bayonet charge against the Prussian Guards, he was hit in the chest; paper and a book in his pocket deflected the bullet. Then he was hit by shrapnel and he had to spend three days in a shell hole without food and only half a bottle of water. Eventually he crawled back to his own lines and was taken to hospital for treatment. He explained:

The piece of shell had gone through my side pocket, and taken part of a corkscrew and a box of matches through my leg, entering at the thigh and coming out near the groin. I have two rubber tubes through my leg now.

Len Shaw's wound was so bad that his doctors thought he would not pull through and his family were contacted. His father travelled over to France to see him and, although his son had a wound the size of a tennis ball in his groin, he did recover. Indeed, how much better he was can be seen as, when his father left for home, Len Shaw said to him: 'Don't forget to send the *Advertiser*.'

The newspaper in early June continued to give much space to the war and war-related stories, ranging from details of local conscientious objector cases at the tribunals to the shocking news that the Secretary of State for War had died. On 5 June, Lord Kitchener was on board HMS *Hampshire*, which was taking him to meet the Russian leaders. Just off the Orkneys, and in a force 9 gale, the *Hampshire* struck a German mine and sank, with the loss of Kitchener and 643 of the crew. Only twelve survived the cold, rough seas and Kitchener's body was never recovered. Tributes flooded in from King and Country, but perhaps it was the men of the New Armies who felt the loss most, just as they were about to be blooded on the Somme. Throughout Britain, Kitchener was mourned and the King described him as 'a great soldier' who had given forty-five years of service to the state. The chances to drink to the memory of this great man were reduced, though, for many pubs were running short of beer, forcing them to close for two days a week. Clearly the large number of men who were with the army was having an effect upon both farming and production, and on 8 June a meeting was held in the Magistrates' Room in St Neots to discuss the use of women for farm work.

In France, preparations for the Somme continued and casualties increased. Sapper Kenneth Knights was wounded badly when a shell exploded close to him. He wrote to his brother, Revd Knights: 'On June 2nd, a high explosive shell sneaked up behind me and bit me in the leg; the wound is not serious but it is rather painful.' He was brought to Chatham Military Hospital and the wound proved to be far more serious, for three weeks later news reached St Neots that the leg had been amputated. Other soldiers told of the increase in the number of high explosive shells being used by the Germans. Private Sidney Medlock told that 'Fritz' has 'a new sort of trench bomb, somewhat bigger than before, three feet long, one foot across and weighing 210lbs' and that it exploded 'shaking the ground like an earthquake'. Gas shells also rained down on the men in the front line, as Private Joseph Baker of Eynesbury told: 'Those gas shells are cruel, your eyes are as bad as if someone had thrown lime in them.' Private Baker was well informed about other soldiers from St Neots for he received the *Advertiser* each week and was clearly upset at Len Shaw's wounding. He also told how the drowning of Kitchener had distressed the men in the trenches. The *Advertiser* continued to print details of the tribunals that considered men's requests to be exempted from conscription. The men at the front were not impressed by some of the reasons given to avoid conscription, or of the tribunals that met specially to deal with conscientious objectors. Private Sidney Medlock spoke of wanting to see 'conchies' deal with shellfire, whilst Private Alex Proudlock told: 'We don't know whether to be amused or disgusted at some of the so-called reasons of the "hope to be exempted" who appear before the Tribunals. They must be apologies for Britishers.'

The men in the trenches were also aware that a great sea battle had taken place early in June at Jutland, and they and the citizens of St Neots read about it first-hand when a letter from Frank Rowlett, a former resident of the town, was included in the *Advertiser* of 28 June. Frank Rowlett was aboard a destroyer and wrote:

> The first thing we knew was that the big warships were firing as hard as they could. We could not see the German ships at first as we were so low down in the water and it was rather misty. Shots were splashing all around and we saw two of our large vessels go down, but we did not know which they were. One of them sank in flames.

He went on to tell how his ship had fought with a German cruiser and that it was very fortuitous that they had escaped:

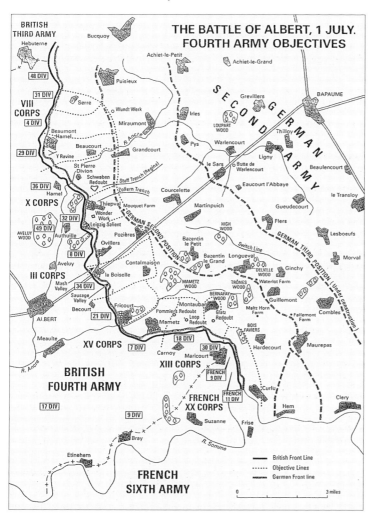

Map of the Battle
of the Somme,
July-November 1916.

One shell caught our bridge, killed two signallers and telegraphmen, wounded the coxswain, and knocked the captain right off the bridge. Part of our bridge was carried away, and the foremost funnel and mast. A second shot went through the second funnel, and missed the boiler by a couple of inches.

That his ship survived was, in his view, down to his skipper, Captain Trelawney.

On 26 June, Edward George Henry Montagu, 8th Earl of Sandwich, died, aged seventy-six, in the Cottage – a small villa in the grounds of Hinchingbrooke House where he had lived for much of his life. Throughout 1914, 1915 and 1916 he had campaigned vigorously for men from Huntingdonshire to enlist, and had spoken with gusto at many recruiting rallies throughout the county. His death saw the area lose one of its most colourful characters and good friend of the late King Edward VII.

On the Somme, the scene was now set for what many see as the most infamous battle of the Great War. The original plan was for German trenches to be bombarded for five days, thus destroying any effective resistance. Heavy rain extended that to a seven-day bombardment, and by Saturday 1 July all was ready for 100,000 British troops to make their mark by advancing through and beyond the German lines. What is sometimes overlooked is that these men were all volunteers, whether original BEF, Territorial or Kitchener's New Army. By the end of that day, 57,470 of them had become casualties, with 19,420 dead. It was, and remains, the worst day ever experienced by the British Army in terms of those killed, wounded and missing. The battle continued for another 148 days, by which time the advance would be roughly 6 miles, but Bapaume, the first day objective, had still not been taken. Men from St Neots fought on the Somme and were amongst the casualties that by November had risen to over 400,000 with around 125,000 dead.

As the troops prepared to go over the top on that bright and sunny Saturday morning, the level of bombardment increased for three hours after sunrise, and men who survived told of their ears bleeding as the sound of explosions reached a crescendo. Heavy artillery, mortars and shrapnel shells rained down on the German lines and some men even admitted feeling sorry for the Germans on the receiving end of it. What was unknown was that the Germans, in the two years they had been on the Somme, had built dugouts, sometimes 30ft below ground, which were impervious to anything other than a direct hit by high explosive shells. Consequently, most German soldiers were safe and ready to face the British advance. When the barrage stopped the British had to get across No Man's Land before the Germans emerged from their deep dugouts to set up their machine-guns. Although the men were told that there was no need to run, as the Germans would have been obliterated by the seven-day barrage, many battalion commanders did tell their men to cross as quickly as they could and these battalions enjoyed most success on 1 July.

Amongst the battalions that went forward in the southern part of the battlefield were the 7th Bedfords, and the 2nd, who were in support, both containing men from St Neots and the surrounding villages. Nineteen-year-old Albert Childerley from Eaton Ford had been in France for around ten months, and this former butler was the first local man killed in the Battle of the Somme. In the days leading up to 1 July, both sides shelled the other's trenches heavily and on 30 June Albert Childerley was badly wounded. Indeed, in those days before Zero Hour, as the advance was referred to, almost as many men with the 2nd Bedfords were killed as when the attack went in. Albert Childerley did not recover from his wounds and was buried at the casualty clearing station at Gailly. Then, as the Bedfords were about to advance on 1 July, a German shell fell in a front-line trench where Private Richard Ball of Eaton Ford was about to go over the top. His friends, Corporals Bason and Hickson, and Private Warboys wrote to Richard Ball's mother: 'It was during the attack, and the Germans were shelling, and one shell came in the trench. Dick got hit and was taken to hospital where he passed away.' Dick Ball had been determined to serve his country and had enlisted as soon as war was declared. He was discharged in November 1914 because of defective eyesight but after treatment he re-enlisted, being accepted into the 3rd Bedfords, a battalion that was used to train men for overseas service. In late September 1915 he was sent to France and Flanders to the 2nd Bedfords and, in the nine months until his death, saw plenty of action, being buried alive for two hours after a shell exploded close by and then having his greatcoat blown off him on another occasion. His luck ran out on that first day of the Somme when he died of wounds. He is buried at Peronne Road Cemetery, Maricourt.

Slightly further north on the battlefield, the 15th Battalion of the Durham Light Infantry attacked towards Shelter Wood, supporting the Kings Own Yorkshire Light Infantry. As the DLI went forward, they came under heavy enemy fire and Second Lieutenant Clifford Skemp Haynes of Croxton led his men onwards after every other officer had fallen. Officers on 1 July wore a different uniform from ordinary infantrymen and they presented inviting targets for German marksmen. Clifford Haynes fell as he led his men, charging the enemy. His parents, Revd and Mrs Haynes, received the sad news about eight days later and, perhaps more tragically, so did his wife of just three months. Lieutenant Haynes' body was lost as the battle continued and today his name joins 72,000 others on the Thiepval Memorial.

At Ovillers, about a mile north of Shelter Wood, just across the Albert/Bapaume road, the 8th Battalion Yorks and Lancs Regiment went over the top at 7.30 a.m., initially making some progress. Many of these men were ex-miners from Rotherham but in their ranks was Lance Corporal Charles Roland Cropley of Avenue Road, St Neots, a twenty-two-year-old who was training to be a train driver before he enlisted. As the battalion advanced it suffered heavy losses, as the week-long barrage had failed to destroy the German positions there. The advancing troops fell in large numbers. Initially Roland Cropley, as his family called him, was posted as missing – but that changed. His company commander wrote to Roland Cropley's mother:

> A very heavy machine gun fire was opened on us; and I'm afraid your son was amongst one of the brave lads who laid down his life for his country. Only 30 men returned out of the whole company, so you may imagine what a hard time we had. There is the faintest hope that he may have been made a prisoner of war, but I'm afraid it is very improbable.

Captain Runbold's words proved to be true and Roland Cropley's body was never located. Today he is commemorated on the Thiepval Memorial.

Shortly after Roland Cropley's Company attacked, the 2nd Battalion, West Yorks Regiment also went over the top at Ovillers. Even before they were out of their front-line trenches they had lost 250 men to German artillery and then, as they tried to cross No Man's Land, a further 180 fell. Among those killed in action was twenty-seven-year-old Sergeant Sidney Hoitt, a regular soldier married to Rose Mardlin of Eaton Socon. He had been in Malta at the outbreak of the war and reached the Western Front in October 1914. On 1 July he had shown great bravery in the failed attack and was awarded the Military Medal posthumously. Once again, his body could not be recovered from No Man's Land and he too is remembered on the Thiepval Memorial. Both the 8th Yorks and Lancs and the 2nd West Yorks were part of the 8th Division that attacked on the first day of the Somme; altogether their total casualties for 1 July were 5,121 officers and men.

So five men, either from or associated with the St Neots area, died in the first twenty-four hours of the Battle of the Somme. Others were perhaps more fortunate, surviving and being able to tell their tale. Private Walter Gale of St Neots was wounded on 1 July as his battalion, the 2nd Royal Berkshires, also went over the top at Ovillers. He wrote home giving a remarkable account of the attack:

> It was a terrible time we had the day I was wounded; a week last Saturday, and the first day of the attack. My Battalion was the first over the top in the attack, and they didn't half give us something, they were waiting for us. I did not reach the Germans' first line before I was hit and went down. I crept into a shell hole, along with one of our sergeants who was wounded. This was 7.30, and we expected we should have to lie there until dark, as they were shelling so hard, but by about 11.00 the sun was burning my wound so that it was nearly driving me mad, so I could stick it no more, and started to crawl back to our trenches, which was a long job.

A few days later his father received another letter at his Victoria Terrace home giving more information:

> I received my wound, which is shrapnel in my right buttock … Our guns had been fairly quiet all night, but at 6.30 they started for an hour's bombardment before we went over, and it was as if all hell had been let loose. The Germans did not take it lying down though, and gave us plenty of iron rations to be going on with, which killed and buried a terrible lot of our lads. I was just caught by the legs once while the two men next to me were completely buried, and had to be dug out. Just before 7.30 we got over the top and laid down in front of our

wire, where we had to wait for 'A' Company to come up on our right. They had a distance of 200 yards to come to get up to us, so we had some few minutes to wait, which seemed like hours, as they were shelling us all this time and had their machine guns on us too. The lads were wanting to be getting on the move, and as soon as we got the signal from our officer we were up and away for the German lines. I don't know what the other lads' feelings were like while we were lying there, but I know I was a bit shaky and excited. But as soon as we got on the move I had quite forgotten that, and my only thought was to get to the German trench as quickly as possible. But luck was against me, and when I was hit I was within 50 yards of their wire … and crawled into a shell hole that was nearest to me – there were plenty of them – and started to scratch it deeper with my hands.

Many others were wounded as the attack went in and continued in those first few days of July 1916. Privates Walter Adams and Albert Jakes from Eaton Ford were both wounded and brought home. They were joined by Privates Archy Manning and Ernest Cook, who told:

A big piece of shrapnel entered the back of my left hand, went right through in a slanting direction, came out at the bottom of my little finger, and has broken that to pieces. A shell burst at the back of me. It is really wonderful that I am alive. We had just passed the second line of German trenches.

Private Cook of the 6th Queens Battalion was wounded close to where Sidney Hoitt and Roland Cropley had been killed at Ovillers; the Queens made more progress as they attacked before dawn, yet still achieved no breakthrough.

Private Henry John Potter from Eaton Socon, serving with the Sherwood Foresters as they took part in the 'Big Push', also told of his experience:

Well I suppose you have read of the great advance which commenced last Saturday, and it was a day I shall never forget. We gave old Fritz a good push that day, although we found him very strong on our front where we were, having to fight against some of Germany's best troops, and we lost many brave officers and men. It was a sad sight to see so many comrades, dead and wounded, lying on the field. It is wonderful how I got through it all without a scratch. Fritz kept up a perfect hail of rifle and machine gun fire, besides the artillery. The position we had to take was very strong. I tore my trousers and puttees all to rags on the German barbed wire. I was glad to be able to take part in the first phase of the great advance.

By the end of July, the BEF had pushed the Germans back around two miles and were fighting a bloody battle trying to take High Wood, Trones Wood, Bernafay Wood and Delville Wood. The 1st Bedfords were one of the battalions ordered to attack High Wood and amongst their number were Privates Robert and Jim Chamberlain of Eynesbury, and Herbert Mould of St Neots. The fighting here was truly awful and Professor Richard Holmes in his book, *The Western Front*, describes it as being 'ghastly by day, ghostly by night, the rottenest place on the Somme'. The 1st Bedfords had a hard time of it here and in three days lost sixty-four NCOs and men, killed between 26 and 29 July. One of those killed was Private Robert Chamberlain, and his brother Jim, who was also in the 1st Bedfords, wrote home:

My Dear Mother, I am very sorry to have to tell you that Bob is dead, he got killed in the afternoon on 27 July. He was hit in the neck with a piece of shell, but, dear mother, he was buried as nice as you can expect, and Herbert Mould buried him just behind the firing line; but I do hope, mother, you will not worry yourself too much, as it nearly breaks my heart to have to tell you such sad news … Poor old boy, but I hope he has gone to a better place.

Thirty-one-year-old Robert Chamberlain had been on reserve in 1914 and was called up immediately, going to his regiment on 6 August 1914. He was wounded at Mons and Hill 60, and had even been recommended for a Military Medal for Gallantry. Although Herbert Mould buried him, the grave was lost as the battle raged and today his name is found on the Thiepval Memorial.

Brothers James and Thomas Currington of Yelling had three sons each, all of whom were serving with the Bedfords on 27 July, and five of the six were either killed or wounded. Thomas Currington's son Albert died and both William and Ernest were wounded, whilst James Currington's son William was killed and Walter was wounded. The only one of the six cousins not killed or wounded that day was Joe. Ernest survived for another ten months before he was killed at Arras in 1917. None of the three who died has a known grave; Albert and William are remembered at Thiepval and Ernest at Arras.

Also in action with the 1st Bedfords in late July was Private Theodore Rowlett, and he was wounded once again. In 1915 he had been hit in the chest and right shoulder at Hill 60, and then wounded in the hand and head, and he had also been buried twice when shells exploded close by. Now he was again a casualty close to Trones Wood, being wounded in the left leg, with his kneecap shot off. Three weeks later his war ended when the leg was amputated.

At the end of July a tragic event took place closer to home, when Martin Riseley, a Lance Corporal with the 95th Canadian Infantry, was killed. Martin Riseley had lived in Duloe before moving to Canada, but returned to fight for the mother country. He arrived in England after training and had been back for just seven weeks when he died. After visiting his parents in Eltisley he caught a train heading south. At Hatfield he got off to go to the toilet and as he tried to get back on the train it started to move away. He fell under its wheels and was shockingly injured. He was taken to St Albans Hospital where one of his legs was amputated but he died on Monday 31 July.

On 4 August, the second anniversary of the outbreak of the war, the people of St Neots showed their support and solidarity when a public meeting was held in the Market Square. Those who turned out were addressed by speakers from St Neots Urban Council: one of them, Mr Samuel Hinsby, whose son was being treated for a shrapnel wound, told them:

> On this, the second anniversary of the declaration of a righteous war, this meeting of the Citizens of St Neots records its inflexible determination to continue to a victorious end the struggle in maintenance of those ideals of liberty and justice which are the common and sacred cause of the Allies.

After the singing of 'God Save the King', those attending made their way to St Mary's Parish Church for a service where Archdeacon Hodgson stressed that St Neots was 'united in our love for our country, our King, our sailor lads and our soldier boys'.

On 15 August, two more local men were added to the growing list of the dead when they went into action with the 1st Battalion, Ox and Bucks Light Infantry close to Mouquet Farm and Pozieres, which had become the targets for the Allies after the capture of Ovillers on 17 July. Skyline trench was the objective and the battle was fierce, with the ground becoming smashed by artillery bombardment; where friend or foe trench line ran was almost impossible to ascertain. Late on the 15th, Sidney Warner and Frank White went into action and both were killed outright by shellfire. Sidney Warner had enlisted in September 1915, joining the Hunts Cyclist Battalion, but he transferred to the Ox and Bucks Light Infantry in 1916. On 15 August, he was in a group of men carrying Mills bombs up to the jump-off trench when they came under heavy German artillery fire and he was killed. Sidney Warner's body was never recovered and he left a widow of just two months behind in St Neots. His brother Bert was also wounded but he recovered. Frank Marchant White, who went by the nickname 'Flitter', had an eventful time during the summer of 1916. He married Jane Violet Berry of Eaton Socon on 15 July and then went back over to France. He had enlisted in 1915, also joining the Hunts Cyclists, but again he opted to be transferred to a battalion that could serve overseas, as the Hunts Cyclists were stationed in Britain for the entire war. He too found himself in the Ox and Bucks Light Infantry, in the same battalion as Sidney Warner. One month after his wedding he was killed on the Somme; his wife heard of this when she received a letter from Second Lieutenant T.H. Rover that read:

> I am very grieved at having to inform you of the loss of your husband, Pte F White 1484. He was killed on 15th August, when we were in action, by shell fire … I am very sorry indeed that this should have happened, especially as he had not been long with the Buckingham Battalion and I should like to give you my own personal sympathy.

Both Sidney Warner and Frank White are commemorated on the Thiepval Memorial.

Two days later and much farther away, Private Corbett Jesse Barringer died of malaria contracted whilst serving in Salonica with the Royal Army Medical Corps at the 40th Casualty Clearing Station. Twenty-year-old Corbett was the son of James and Kate Barringer of Eaton Socon and he was buried in Mikra British Cemetery in Thessaloniki. Another son, Frederick, had joined the army and was undergoing training with the Essex Regiment. He was sent over to France and Flanders in 1917 and went into action at Cambrai in late November.

Back on the Western Front another tragedy took place on 18 August, again close to Skyline Trench where Sidney Warner and Frank 'Flitter' White had died three days earlier. The 5th Warwicks, a Territorial battalion, attacked at 5 p.m. and, despite fierce German resistance, they successfully advanced with the help of a smoke screen and a machine-gun barrage, taking both the enemy position and 425 prisoners. Within the ranks of the 5th Warwicks was nineteen-year-old Private Harold Carrington, the son of George and Grace Carrington of Brook Street, St Neots. Harold Carrington had initially joined the Hunts Cyclists in October 1914 but had transferred to the Warwicks. As the Warwicks attacked, this popular young man died. His mother received the following missive from Lieutenant Colonel Mann of the Warwicks:

> Dear Mrs Carrington, I regret to have to inform you that your son, No. 377, Pte H G Carrington was killed in action on 18 August, during an attack on the enemy's trenches. Your son's conduct was most gallant during the attack, and it only remains for me to assure you of the deepest sympathy of myself, the officers and men with your great loss.

Harold Carrington's death was witnessed by Arthur Irons of Eynesbury who was also with the Warwicks. Writing to his father, John, he told: 'We took 800 prisoners. Young Carrington went under, and several Hunts got wounded, but I am all right. Both Frank Neal and I have been made Sergeants.' The loss of Harold Carrington was deeply felt in St Neots by the many people who knew and liked him. He does have a known grave and is buried in Ovillers Military Cemetery.

Others wounded in these dark days of mid-August were Private Fred Pearson of Eynesbury, Sergeant George Corbett, and Private Walter Eversden who was hit when a shell exploded, injuring him and others from the 1st Bedfords. Walter Eversden had originally been one of the Hunts Cyclists but had transferred to the Bedfords, and was in a fatigue party when the German shell fell. He was struck in the face, causing a slight wound to the mouth, and he walked for a couple of miles to get treatment in the company of another slightly injured St Neotian, Private George Day. Less fortunate was thirty-two-year-old Corporal William Bembridge Bennett, who was killed in action on Saturday 26 August with the 7th Northamptonshire Battalion. William Bennett was a Lincolnshire man who had moved to St Neots, working in Barritt's jewellers before he enlisted. He was buried in Allonville Communal Cemetery on the Somme.

Private Harold Carrington.

On the very next day, 27 August, the 8th Battalion Royal Warwicks attacked close to Pole Trench near Mouquet Farm, called either 'Mucky Farm' or 'Moo Cow Farm' by the Tommies or Aussies who fought to capture it. The 8th Royal Warwicks attacked in the evening but ran into their own artillery barrage, causing them to veer to the south, and in doing so they were counter-attacked by German infantry. Amongst the 8th Royal Warwicks were two men from Eynesbury, again initially with the Hunts Cyclists but now with the Warwicks. As the Germans counter-attacked, Private Frank Jakes and Sergeant Frank Neal were among the Warwicks who fiercely fought back until their numbers were so small they had to withdraw. In the confusion that followed, both men were posted as wounded and missing in action. Later this changed to 'killed in action' and their bodies were never recovered, both joining the 72,000 names of the missing on the Thiepval Memorial. News of twenty-one-year-old Frank Neal reached St Ives, where his parents lived, and at first it was reported that he was wounded and in hospital but that proved to be incorrect, much to the regret of James and Alice Neal. Elizabeth, the mother of twenty-three-year-old Frank Jakes, was equally distressed to receive news of her son's death.

Perhaps news of all of the casualties on the Somme was causing some men to have serious doubts about a life in the army and some quite literally disappeared during the summer months of 1916, failing to respond to their call-up papers under the Military Service Act. Recruiting officers took the unheard of step of printing the names of men who had not responded and, on 1 September, the *Advertiser* printed a front page notice asking for information about local men who had not received or had ignored their call-up papers.

The new month saw no let up in the number of casualties and on Saturday, 2 September, men from the 1st Bedfords were working to repair front-line trenches and prepare assembly trenches for the attack the next day. Saturday was fine and sunny, if a little windy and unusually quiet for the Somme. As the Bedfords worked into the early evening, the Germans dropped occasional shells on their lines. One of these hit the parapet where 'B' Company were working and exploded. The Bedfords' war diary describes the shell as 'peculiar', saying it burst 'in reddish light, and formed no crater'. It did wound nine men though, one of them badly. He was twenty-two-year-old Private George Day, the son of William and Emma Day of Cambridge Street, and he had been in the army since September 1914, when he joined the

'Have you seen these men' notice from August 1916.

MILITARY SERVICE ACTS, 1916.

THE RECRUITING OFFICER, HUNTINGDON,

asks for information regarding the following Men, as to whether they...............

(a)   Have joined the Army;
(b)   Are exempted from the Provisions of the Military Service Acts, 1916 ;
(c)   Are in possession of a definite Certificate or Badge exempting them from liability for Military Service ;
(d)   Are in a Reserved Occupation ;
(e)   Have removed to another District Etc., etc.

THE ABOVE INFORMATION is required to complete Records in Recruiting Offices, and any communication will be treated in strict confidence.

LIST.

Name.	Age on Registration	Last known Address.
WATTS, ARTHUR JOHN	25	Ramsey St. Mary's, Hunts.
NEWMAN, WILLIAM	34	17, Russell Street, St. Neots.
CORNISH, DAVID WILLIAM	19	Straw Press, Ramsey, Hunts.
SAMWAYS, AR. HENRY	21	Paxton Hill, St. Neots.
MOULDER, STEPHEN HENRY	22	43, Ermine Street, Huntingdon.
MANNING, WILLIAM	31	The Bell, St. Ives, Hunts.
BIRCHAM, GEO. FREDK.	37	South Lodge, Great Paxton, St. Neots, Hunts.
BURTON, HARRY	23	147, Palmerston Road, Woodston, near Peterborough.
WOOTON, DAVID	26	Green's Row, Middleton Street, Yaxley, Hunts.
BASS, JOHN THOMAS	22	c/o Mrs. Parish, Holme, Hunts.
TOWERS, JOSEPH WILLIAM	31	Little Whyte, Ramsey, Hunts.
MAYES, WILLIAM IRONS	27	Brook End, Keyston, Hunts
GRAY, ARTHUR EDWARD	54	Taylor's Farm, Somersham Fen, Hunts.
DICKINSON, ALFRED	35	28, Coneygree Road, Stanground, near Peterborough.
GOWLER, GEORGE	40	Ridley Fen, Hunts.

Recruiting Headquarters,
5, Ermine Street, HUNTINGDON.

August 30th, 1916.

Hunts Cyclists. By 1916 he was with the Bedfords and had fought through the early stages of the Somme. Now, on this quieter than usual day, he was so badly injured that he died of his wounds. He was buried in Bronfay Farm Military Cemetery.

On 3 September, the Allies resumed their attack and for three days the battle for Guillemont raged. Guillemont was south of the Albert/Bapaume road and about a mile from Trones Wood where the Bedfords had fought so hard in July. Amongst the battalions that went into action on 3 September were the 14th Royal Warwicks and within their ranks was Private Frank Whittet, the son of baker Alfred Whittet of St Neots. At noon, the 14th Warwicks attacked slightly to the south of Guillemont and managed to secure a section of the German trenches at Wedge Wood. Later in the day the wood was taken by the 1st Bedfords, but in this initial assault Frank Whittet lost his life. His father was told at first that he was wounded and missing in action, and the last that was seen of him was when he stopped to help a wounded comrade. Later he was confirmed as being killed, but once more the outcome was no known grave. Frank Whittet's route to commemoration on the Thiepval Memorial was a familiar one for he had also transferred from the Hunts Cyclists to a battalion serving overseas. William Storey, who was also serving with the 14th Warwicks, again after transferring from the Hunts Cyclists, was another wounded on 3 September. He had been with a patrol checking an enemy dugout when the occupants threw out a grenade which exploded behind him. After treatment, he returned to St Neots on leave and told: 'All the things in my trouser pockets were blown out, with the seat of my trousers and pants, and the tail of my shirt.' William Storey recovered from the wounds to his back, but this son of Inspector Walter Storey of St Neots would not see the end of the war.

On the very next day, three men from St Neots were killed as the 1st Bedfords continued the assault at Guillemont and were charged with capturing Leuze Wood just beyond Wedge Wood where Frank Whittet had died. The Bedfords advanced late on 3 September, entering Wedge Wood, where they found thirty of the Warwicks still alive and whom they promptly relieved. The next day did not start well for the Bedfords, being shelled by their own artillery and forced to withdraw from two captured front-line trenches. A fierce bombing struggle followed as the Germans tried to retain their positions; the Bedfords eventually won this clash, yet at a cost. The casualties were recorded when the fighting ended on 6 September and showed the Bedfords had gone into action with twenty officers and 610 men, and had come out with three officers and 321 men. Privates Cyril Barrett, Herbert Mould and Harry Searle were among those who went forward on 3 September but were not alive when the Bedfords took their roll call on 6 September. All three died on Monday 4 September and all three have no known grave. Cyril Barrett died instantly when he was struck by a German bullet as he went to help a wounded friend, and the two were buried side by side. Herbert Mould and Harry Searle were killed in the brutal fighting in Leuze Wood. The ages of these three men spans three decades, for Cyril was twenty-three, Herbert was thirty-two and Harry was forty-two.

Private William James Chamberlain was hit in the right hip at Leuze Wood and he wrote home to Eynesbury telling of this, and of seeing Herbert Mould die instantly when he was shot in the head. Then further information reached St Neots from Private Robert Lambert who had worked at the *Advertiser* before the war. He had joined up with Cyril Barrett and had formed a strong friendship with Cyril and three others from London, Barnsley and Kettering. He wrote home, telling:

Three of them were together at the time, and from what I can gather, Cyril was the first to get hit. One of the other two went to pull him under cover and he got hit, and the remaining one, in endeavouring to get them both in, received a bullet also. I believe death was instantaneous – machine gun bullets. Herbert Mould too has gone. Only the week previous he was relating some of his experiences to me, and saying he had been out since from the commencement and hoped now he would manage to get through.

After the capture of Guillemont, the BEF shifted its attention to Ginchy, about half a mile further on, and Private Lionel Martin of the Grenadier Guards was wounded once again. Fighting at close quarters and with bayonets, he was bitten on his cheek by a young German and then he was hit by a machine-gun bullet. Writing home, he told:

> The wound was made by a machine gun bullet going through my left leg between the knee and the ankle, just catching the bone. I got it whilst in action … We took about 100 prisoners that night. I did not know for some time after I was hit that I had been wounded. I thought I was only bruised and felt nothing for eight hours. When I took my puttees off I found my leg bleeding.

Private Harry Sharman from Eynesbury, also with the Grenadier Guards, was wounded on 15 September close to Ginchy. His letter home told:

> I am pleased to get away from the trenches for a time. I got hit in the right shoulder. My word it was a great sight to see the boys going over the top, but don't know how many of them pulled through, I was not there long enough to know, as I was wounded just as the attack started.

The attack on 15 September was the start of another major offensive on the Somme that saw the BEF use its secret weapon, the tank. There was much debate regarding the most opportune time to introduce the tank, some being of the opinion that its impact would be lost if used in a dribble rather than en masse, as the Germans might be able to devise defences against the tank if just a few were initially used, and then there would be no breakthrough that could lead to victory. By September 1916, Haig could not afford to wait, and thirty-two of the monsters moved forward on that Friday morning, but nine of them broke down before reaching the jump-off point, and only fifteen reached enemy lines. Those that did go forward had mixed results, generally enjoying more success in the middle of the area attacked than at the flanks, and the village of Flers was captured. The British press later reported in glowing terms: 'A tank is walking up the high street of Flers with the British Army cheering behind.'

The impact of the tank was considerable, for although the vast majority broke down on that first day of use, they did have a severe psychological effect upon the Germans, who were shocked at the appearance of these metal monsters. For over two years the British had explored ways in which the impregnable barrier of the enemy's trenches, with their swathes of barbed wire, could be breached. Vehicles with huge caterpillar tracks, armoured roving vehicles and gun-mounted trains all came under consideration before the 'landship' was decided upon. Their development and production was a closely-guarded secret, and the name 'tank' derived from the attempt to disguise them, as they were shipped to the front as water tanks. Two types of tanks were used on the Somme, the male and the female. The male tank was bigger and armed with a 6-pounder gun, whilst the female's main armament was a heavy machine-gun. The conditions inside the machines were terrible, not only being cramped with a crew of up to eleven, but also exceedingly hot. These early machines had a top speed of 4mph, and were steered by the slowing or stopping of one of the tracks, whilst the other one continued to move. The noise inside was dreadful and crew communication was only possible by shouting, written notes, or signs. The petrol engine's heat and fumes made life within the tank uncomfortable, to say the least, for ventilation was minimal. There was no suspension and the ride for the crew over uneven ground jarred their bones; the 6-pounder gun had to be moved manually to be aimed and fired. However, the tank did bring something extraordinary to the battlefield, and it was able to traverse the extended coils of German barbed wire, thus offering a fascinating glimpse of possible victory.

In the build-up to the mid-September attack, the 8th Bedfords raided the German trenches just beyond Leuze Wood in an area dominated by the Quadrilateral Redoubt. On 14 September, the Bedfords bombed their way along 100 yards of enemy trenches at 6 a.m. but could not hold on to them. Twelve hours later they attacked again but failed to take the Quadrilateral, sustaining more casualties, even though the Germans were driven from their advanced posts. One of the casualties was twenty-one-year-old Private Jack Howe of Eynesbury who had joined up in November 1915 and, after training, had gone overseas six months later. Now he was wounded, and although he was taken to No. 21 Casualty Clearing Station at La Neuville, near Corbie, he could not be saved, succumbing to the gunshot and dying on 14 September. He was buried at La Neuville, next to the Casualty Clearing Station. The chaplain with Jack Howe at the end was J.M.S. Walker and he wrote to the family: 'He was brought into this Hospital on September 14th, suffering from a wound in the back, but he did not live long, he passed away the same day at 5.10pm. I do not think he suffered.' Chaplain Walker also told the family that he had some wild flowers from near Jack Howe's grave if they wanted them. Jack's brother Fred was serving in the BEF and his younger brother George enlisted in time to fight during 1918, surviving until five days before the war ended.

The BEF's attack on 15 September is known as the Battle of Flers-Courcelette and was a major Allied push that lasted until the 22nd. This offensive was the first large-scale one since 1 July and involved British, Canadian and New Zealand troops who were charged with breaking the German line. By the end of the Flers offensive the BEF had suffered around 30,000 casualties, and one of those killed was Raymond Asquith, the son of the Prime Minister. For St Neots there were considerable casualties, with many wounded and five men killed during the offensive. On the 15th, three men were killed as the 8th Bedfords attacked the Quadrilateral Redoubt at 6.20 a.m. However, the artillery bombardment preceding the attack failed to neutralise the German positions and then the three tanks that were supposed to support the attack did not turn up. The attacking Bedfords ran into cruel machine-gun fire as they approached the Quadrilateral and amongst those killed were Privates Walter Newton, Albert Page and Charles Pindred, all of St Neots. News reached the town in late September. Initially twenty-one-year-old Walter Newton was reported as missing in action, believed killed, but later the true circumstances of his death were told by a comrade, Private Marnes. He described Walter Newton's incredible bravery, as soon after the advance began he was shot in both legs and his comrades told him to stop, but he refused and kept up with the attack. He had not got much further when he was shot again, but still insisted on moving forward and reached the German trenches. There, as he was placing his rifle on the parados of that trench to resist any German counter-attack, he was shot in the head and died. The parents of Albert Page did not hear of his death until early October,

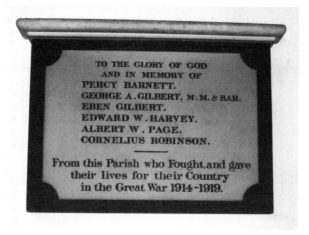

when they received a letter from his company commander, telling: 'He was a brave lad, well liked by all who knew him, and a great loss to his company.' Thirty-two-year-old Charles Pindred, the son of Edward and Charlotte Pindred of Cambridge Road, was also first reported missing. All three men have no known grave and are remembered on the Thiepval Memorial. A fourth man to die on

Memorial from Hail Weston Church.

15 September was Private John Chapman, the son of Jesse Chapman of Luke Street, Eynesbury. He was in Canada in 1912, but had returned to fight for his country of birth. On 15 September, he was killed when the 8th Middlesex went into action at 1.40 p.m., attacking from Leuze Wood to support the 7th Middlesex, who were trying to capture Bouleaux Wood. The 8th Middlesex were forced back to their jump-off positions in Leuze Wood in the face of strong German resistance. John Chapman was one of five brothers serving, but he was the only one to die and today his name can also be found on the Thiepval Memorial.

Although only four men from St Neots died on 15 September, many others were wounded then and in the days that followed. They included Private Teddy Harvey of Eynesbury; Privates Tom Fletcher and Herbert Hawkins of Eaton Socon; Private Joseph Waldock of St Neots, who had both legs shattered and his back injured by shrapnel; Private Chas Jones of Eynesbury, who was wounded for a third time; and Private Ted Medlock of the 1st Bedfords, who was hit in the right foot. When Ted wrote home from hospital in Cardiff, he told of the struggles near Leuze Wood: 'Then we took the ridge close by Leuze Wood, it is all right taking the ground, but it is the worst holding it after they have got the range on you with their 5.9's.' George Sawford, a Private with the Royal Army Medical Corps, was in hospital at Le Havre suffering from shellshock, whilst Private Albert Franklin from Eynesbury had a close call when shrapnel struck his steel helmet and ricocheted, wounding his hand. The man standing next to him was killed. Another Eynesbury man, Arthur Irons, had recently been promoted to Sergeant but his time in exercising his new duties did not last long for he was captured during the fighting at Flers, spending the rest of the war as a POW. Sergeant Richard Jakins of Great Gransden fought at Flers with the Royal Field Artillery and spoke of seeing many local men. He saw first-hand the tanks and even went inside one, as he told in a letter of 24 September:

> The tanks are here and have been in action. I have seen four of them, and been inside one.
> They are queer things to look at and go over anything. You should have seen them after the
> action, hundreds of bullet marks all over, but the bullets did not penetrate them, just scratched
> them, that was all.

At Flers, the offensive ground to a halt after a week, but not before another man from St Neots died. Thirty-one-year-old Ernest Fisher had joined the 2nd Battalion, the Royal Fusiliers, after returning from Canada and he was killed in action on 22 September.

Three days later the 1st Bedfords attacked at Morval and, as they advanced to capture a sunken road, thirty-two-year-old Arthur Tokens was mortally wounded, dying the following day. Arthur Tokens had volunteered in September 1914 after a recruiting rally in St Neots and he was posted overseas in early 1915. He had then fought at Ypres, Festubert and Loos before being wounded on the first day of the Somme. After recovery, he returned to his battalion just before the attack at Morval where he was fatally wounded in the head, the arms and the side. In the attack at Morval an extraordinary event occurred which led to Private Thomas 'Todger' Jones winning the Victoria Cross. Todger Jones was so incensed when one of his pals in the 1st Cheshires was shot dead by a German sniper that he went out to get revenge. He killed the sniper and two Germans who were shooting at him, even though they had a white flag. He then attacked a German dugout where he shot two officers and captured 102 Germans. Remarkably, Todger Jones came through all of this unscathed apart from bullet holes in his tunic and helmet. He survived the war and lived until 1956.

Casualties were certainly very high for the first three months of the Somme. In Mid-September some of those wounded soldiers who were being treated in St Neots gave a concert at the Pavilion. The soldiers performed piano solos, sang songs, recited stories and acted out sketches. The concert, organised by Sergeant Pendry, was a great success with every seat sold and people even turned away. At the same time, the 'War Gifts' fund was set up to provide gifts

Jump-off trench, Thiepval Wood. Archaeologists have recently excavated the area from where the 7th Bedfords attacked in September 1916.

Schwaben Redoubt photographed in 2008. The tree line is where the redoubt was situated; the BEF had to attack uphill to capture it. Tom Adlam won his VC here.

for all St Neots and Eynesbury soldiers and sailors. It was suggested that collections could be made in St Neots and that further entertainment could take place at the Pavilion to raise funds. While attention was being focused on helping those serving their country, a letter arrived on 11 September addressed to the people of St Neots, advising them to concentrate upon the skies. The letter from Alan Chichester, the chief constable, read:

> I think the inhabitants should know the importance of strictly conforming with the Lighting Regulations, annoying as they must be to us all. During a recent raid in an adjoining county a Zeppelin, on noticing a single lamp in a field, was distinctly seen to alter its course, wheel round, and drop four bombs within about a hundred yards of the light. Further comment is needless.

Over the next few months, local policemen would act quickly upon the chief constable's advice and a number of citizens were brought before magistrates for negligence regarding lights.

On 26 September, the BEF switched its focus of attention to Thiepval Ridge and the Schwaben Redoubt, which dominated the northern area of the Somme battlefield. The Schwaben Redoubt was a complex of trenches, deep bomb-proof dugouts, and command posts. On 1 July the Schwaben Redoubt had been captured by the 36th Ulster Division, but their courage and bravery had not been enough for them to hold on to it. They were the only division north of the Albert/Bapaume road to take all of their objectives on that first day but their success was their undoing, for supporting divisions were unable to make the same headway, and the Ulsters found themselves isolated and under attack from three sides. They had to retreat, leaving the Schwaben Redoubt back in German hands. Now at the end of September, the BEF would try to capture it again and also take Thiepval, where the 32nd Division had been so badly cut down on 1 July.

Attacking on 26 September, the 12th Middlesex came under savage fire from defending Germans as they assaulted Thiepval, and for a while they were held up – until a tank arrived that literally crushed the enemy's resistance. In the hard fighting at Thiepval, two men from the 12th Middlesex won the Victoria Cross. Private Fred Edwards, an Irishman, showed great bravery when he bombed a German machine-gun position as the Middlesex fought their way along an enemy trench, and Private Robert Ryder used a Lewis Gun to clear an enemy trench, advancing through a hail of bullets. Both men survived the war and became the best of friends. In the fighting at Thiepval, Private Charles Medlow – aged nineteen, and only at the front for a month – was killed. Charles Medlow was from Wyboston but lived in Eaton Socon; his father and two brothers were also serving in France. He is buried in Heath Cemetery on the Somme.

The Schwaben Redoubt presented a formidable challenge for the BEF to capture and the task was given to the 18th Division, which included the 7th Bedfords: the 'Shiny Seventh'. During the fighting, Second Lieutenant Thomas Adlam won the Victoria Cross when he stormed a German machine-gun emplacement even though he had been wounded in the leg. Tom Adlam came from Salisbury but, after the war, he settled in Sandy, Bedfordshire for some time, becoming the chairman of the British Legion there between 1922 and 1926. The 'Shiny Seventh' advanced on the 28th without artillery support, hoping that this would surprise the Germans, and 'A' and 'B' Companies were to use the bayonet and the Mills bomb to penetrate and capture the north-west section of the heavily-fortified redoubt. When they came under murderous German machine-gun fire, and were pinned down, Tom Adlam reacted and won his VC. Two local men in the 7th Bedfords fell during the taking of the Schwaben Redoubt.

George Cooper was a Private in 'D' Company, whose job was to clear out German trenches after they had been passed by the advancing 'A' and 'B' Companies. Sometimes enemy troops would hide or play dead and then shoot the Tommies as they continued to advance. 'D' Company was given this task and they methodically worked their way along captured trenches and dugouts, clearing them as they went. This was dangerous work, especially as the men ran out of Mills bombs to throw down into the dugouts, and during this operation eighteen-year-old George Cooper was killed. By rights he should not have been serving overseas, for soldiers were supposed to be at least nineteen to do so. George Eversden was with 'A' Company, who had the unenviable task of attacking without artillery support and he was lost as the men went in. Both were declared missing, believed killed in action, but it was not until 1917 that their families received official confirmation. George Cooper was from Eaton Socon and he has a marked grave at Mill Road Cemetery that sits on the site of the Schwaben Redoubt, but George Eversden from St Neots does not and is listed at the Thiepval Memorial.

On 29 September, the 18th Division's assault on the Schwaben Redoubt continued and another local man, Private Frank Pepper of 'B' Company, 7th Bedfords was killed. Frank Pepper was initially listed as missing but the battalion war diary later recorded him as being killed, although no grave was ever identified. He is listed on the Thiepval Memorial. For one of Kitchener's Battalions, the 'Shiny Seventh' had acquitted itself very well at Thiepval and the Schwaben Redoubt, taking positions that the Germans believed were impregnable. For the remainder of 1916 they were not in front-line action but remained as support.

The capture of the Thiepval Ridge was a significant event, but the fighting on the Somme did not stop and raged for two more months. Soldiers from St Neots featured again and many were wounded as the Allies gnawed away at the Germans' positions across the Albert/Bapaume road. Seventeen-year-old Harry Byatt, another under age soldier who should not have been serving overseas and whose brother Martin had died just a year earlier, was wounded in these days on the Somme. He had joined the Hunts Cyclists in 1915, before transferring to the 1st Bedfords.

Privates Bert Page and Alfred Ashford were others wounded during October. Arthur Ashford's steel helmet saved him from serious injury when German bullets struck it, resulting in only a slight wound to the right ear. From Great Paxton came news that Private James Bryan was wounded, when his father received a card from their twenty-three-year-old son, serving with the 10th Queens, in which he also expressed his sadness regarding the death of another local soldier: 'Sorry to hear [of] young Searle's death – another sorrowful home.' James Bryan was referring to Harry Searle, who had been killed at the beginning of September. The Bryan family had certainly had their share of bad news, for Jack Bryan, the twenty-year-old brother of James, had died near Arras in May 1916. Within days of the receipt of the card from their elder son, James and Kate Bryan heard that he too had died of wounds and had been buried with full military honours. Early in the New Year, Mr and Mrs Bryan received a photograph of their son's grave from the War Office, and today his body rests in Étaples Military Cemetery.

These men from the town were not the only ones who came under enemy fire during October. Nurse Jennie Sibley had returned to the front and was now in Salonica, treating wounded men of the Allied Salonica Force. Writing home, she told: 'We were under fire seven times during our 1st, 2nd, and 3rd week here by hostile aircraft guns.'

In Britain, food prices were rising as a result of the German U-boat campaign and Asquith's government responded by giving an increase in Old Age Pensions, so that couples now received 19s 6d, while single pensioners now got 12s 6d per week. Shortages would get even worse when the German High Command decided that unrestricted submarine warfare would resume on 17 January 1917, following the Somme. The battle had become one of terrible attrition and this convinced the Germans that they could not win the war on the Western Front. Unrestricted submarine warfare seemed to be the only solution that would bring Britain to its knees.

As the fighting continued on the Western Front, tragedy struck closer to home when, on 21 October, thirty-nine-year-old Private George Angell died at Huntingdon County Hospital. He was serving with the Royal Ordnance Corps, Clothing Depot who were stationed in the town, shifting large bales of clothes, when the chain holding one of them broke, causing the bale to fall on him. His leg was broken, gangrene set in and on the 25th this man from the Isle of Wight died. He was buried in Huntingdon Cemetery.

The number of wounded soldiers back in the county of Huntingdonshire also brought the following request from Howard Coote of the Lord Lieutenant's Office in Huntingdon: 'An appeal has been received for rough, strong Walking sticks for Wounded and partially Disabled Soldiers; these sticks are wanted in very large numbers [in fact thousands] in various Military Hospitals.' Added to that number of wounded soldiers was Private Archie Gilbert of Eaton Ford, who was hit by shrapnel in the jaw and neck on 22 October. At first it was reported that he had been killed but his wife, who worked at Cooper's Nursery at Brampton, quickly informed the local press that this was incorrect. Apparently he was unable to speak to confirm his identity following the shrapnel shell burst and it was only whilst in hospital that this Private with the Royal Warwicks was able to tell those treating him who he was.

Also wounded was Lance Corporal Albert Caress from Eynesbury, who had been in action throughout September and October and had witnessed the tanks in action at Flers. In late October he had been wounded, three days after a bullet that struck the telephone he was carrying also ripped through his tunic without injuring him. Lance Corporal Caress was in the 1st Bedfords, as was Herbert Mould, who had been killed on 15 September, and his letter home, telling of his own wound, also told of his sadness of the death of his friend:

> I knew Pte. Mould in civilian life. I also served 14 months with him out here, and a more joyful fellow I have never met, he was the life of the Regiment and was liked by both officers and men alike. He would also set a good example under shell fire, as cool as a cucumber and feared nothing. I saw him in an engagement we took part in, in July, 1916, sit on the parapet with shells and bullets flying all around him, and he didn't move a muscle, but was singing nearly all the time. He helped bury Pte. R Chamberlain, of Eynesbury, the same day.

In early November, the local press reported an altogether stranger incident that had taken place at Ravensden, near Bedford when Colonel James Sunderland, the JP for the area, was fined £5 for shooting a mascot of the 3rd Bedfords in Howbury Park. On 11 October the Bedfords were carrying out manoeuvres on land owned by Colonel Sunderland, who arrived at the Bedfords' field kitchen demanding that the battalion's mascot, a terrier, be given to him, for he said the dog had chased rabbits on his land. Private Arthur Horne, who was working at the field kitchen, refused to hand over the dog but Colonel Sunderland, who was armed with a shotgun, fired the gun, killing the terrier. Private Horne told how Colonel Sunderland was very agitated, with white froth on his whiskers as he shot the mascot, and that the colonel had stamped on it. Colonel Sunderland was also fined £2 for assaulting Private Horne as he tried to protect the terrier.

On the Somme, autumn changed to winter as the weather deteriorated and rain fell throughout the first week of November, making the trenches very muddy and restricting any Allied advance. The last actions of the Battle of the Somme started on 13 November as the weather worsened, with snow falling as the troops attacked across half-frozen mud. The chosen location for this last action was north of the river Ancre, an area that had been fairly quiet since 1 July when the BEF failed to take Serre or Beaumont Hamel, suffering terrible casualties in the attempt.

Among the battalions that attacked on 13 November were the 1st Cambridge and the 4th Bedfords, and within their ranks were men from St Neots who would not see the conclusion of the assault, referred to as the Battle of the Ancre. The 1st Cambridge did well and reached their objectives without much difficulty. Casualties were light, for they suffered only sixty-three men wounded or killed, and they dug in to consolidate. However, amongst the casualties was Lance Corporal Edwin Day, a thirty-four-year-old postman from St Neots, who lived at

Pear Tree Cottage, Huntingdon Street with his wife, Eliza. Edwin Day had served as a regular soldier in India before the war and was 'on reserve' until early 1916, when he returned to the Colours. On 13 November he was killed, as Lance Corporal Sidney Rose of Eltisley told:

> We were in the big advance last week. In the mist I got lost, but I got where I had orders to go. We advanced nearly a mile deep, and took a lot of prisoners. I got several myself, and it was grand sport poking them out of dug-outs with our bayonets. Lance-corpl. Day, who was in the St Neots Post Office, was killed in the attack by a sniper who happened to get left behind in the mist. Tell his people he won't snipe again, a pal of mine blew half his head off the first shot. Day was shot through the heart, and suffered no pain.

The 4th Bedfords attacked at 6.45 a.m. and came under heavy German fire, suffering many casualties and having difficulty advancing. It was a dangerous job trying to clear the German front line close to the river, as both friendly and enemy shells rained down, but the Bedfords bombed their way along. Private Arthur Sears was amongst those who were killed during this fighting. He is buried in Serre Road No. 1 Cemetery, but Edwin Day has no known grave and is commemorated on the Thiepval Memorial.

The fighting at the Ancre lasted until 18 November, by which time the BEF had taken Beaumont Hamel where the Newfoundlanders had been mown down on 1 July, but the Germans still held Serre at the northern end of the battlefield. Any visitor to this section of the Somme battlefield today cannot fail to be moved by Serre Road No. 3 Cemetery, where eighty men are buried. The graves are either inscribed 1 July or 13 November, for every man buried here fell in these two failed attacks at Serre.

The Battle of the Somme has to be seen as tragic in terms of the number of British and Empire troops that were killed, for around 125,000 died, but the British Army that emerged from the battle knew how to fight, having learned painful yet significant lessons that were put to very good use in the remaining years of the war. The British Army that went into the Somme was, to the main, an amateur one. The army that emerged from this difficult and harrowing experience was a professional one that would go on to win the war. Both infantry and artillery tactics developed hugely as a result of the Somme, changing the way in which the BEF fought, especially during the final 100 Days of the war. What consolation this was to the bereaved families whose fathers, husbands and sons had died on the Somme is another matter.

Many miles to the north of the Somme, the war continued on a lesser but equally dangerous scale and, on 25 November, twenty-eight-year-old Ted Flint, a Corporal with the 10th Battalion, the Lincolnshire Regiment, died of wounds near Armentières. Ted Flint had been born in Eynesbury where his parents still lived, but after he married Eva Darrington of Wyboston they moved to live in Coventry in 1913. He joined up at the same time as his brother George and went over to France in 1916 where he had quickly shown bravery, being promoted after his work in No Man's Land whilst out with a wiring party. Then, in late November, he was killed by shellfire as his platoon sergeant's letter told Eva Flint:

> He was hit from a bursting shell. I was with him when he died. The Battalion doctor was with him when he died. He was unconscious until he died and had no pain whatever. He was loved by every man in our platoon, and our officer thought a lot of him.

During November, the British public saw soldiers at war for themselves when the film, *The Battle of the Somme*, was shown throughout the country. This was the first time ever that real images of war were seen by the public and many must have recognised the faces of their loved ones, sometimes in captured moments before they went over the top, perhaps to die. Some of the film was staged but much footage was real, including an actual attack on 1 July close to

Hawthorn Ridge. The film featured soldiers from the Bedfordshire Regiment in which men from the St Neots area served. This film had a profound effect throughout the country, showing men before, during and after battle. At one screening, the words 'My God they're dead' were heard. The film was shown at the St Neots Pavilion in March 1917.

At the start of December, twenty-one-year-old Fred Woodward, who had been with the 5th Bedfords, lost his fight against the dysentery he had contracted at Gallipoli. He had arrived back in Britain in late 1915 and had been treated at Ipswich in a convalescence home for some time. After returning home he continued to suffer the painful effects of the disease and eventually passed away peacefully on 4 December. The following day he was buried in Eynesbury Old Cemetery and the service was conducted by Pastor Hazelton, who had led the Sunday school that Fred Woodward had attended as a child. His former comrades in the 5th Bedfords, when they heard of his death, held a collection and Private Joe Chamberlain wrote to Fred Woodward's parents, sending a postal order to ask if they could purchase a wreath on behalf of his comrades.

At the start of December, Herbert Asquith resigned as Prime Minister and was replaced by David Lloyd George, who at once took a much more 'hands on' control of the war than his predecessor. A War Cabinet was set up consisting of Lloyd George, Lord Curzon, Anthony Bonar Law, Lord Milner and Arthur Henderson and it met daily, with the aim of co-ordinating the political, diplomatic, economic and military components required for success. Conscription and rationing were both the work of this cabinet, but over the next two years there would be issues between its leader, Lloyd George and the Commander-in-Chief of the BEF, Douglas Haig.

In December 1916, Haig published his report of the Somme and in it he stressed that the three main aims had been achieved, notably:

> To relieve the pressure on Verdun.
> To assist our Allies in the other theatres of war by stopping any further transfer of German troops from the Western Front.
> To wear down the strength of the forces opposed to us.

Historians still argue today about the Somme and whether it was a turning point in the war or a charnel house that did little apart from kill so many of those who heeded Kitchener's call in 1914. Whatever view one takes, what is true is that a considerably weakened German Army emerged and, during late 1916, it started to make plans to withdraw to the east to a more easily defended position.

As for the BEF, it was also weakened, for the loss of a quarter of a million men on the Somme was a serious blow and their replacements in 1917 would be conscripted men and those who had responded to the Derby Scheme. What is also true is that at the close of 1916, the end of the war seemed no closer than it had done at the end of 1914 or 1915.

FOUR

~1917~
SOLDIERING ON

I916 was a cruel year for the people of St Neots and the surrounding villages, with thirty-five men killed or dying of wounds. This pattern continued throughout 1917 and the number of those killed doubled before the end of the year, bringing more sorrow to an already grieving local population.

The year began badly at the St Neots Paper Mills on 1 January when Reginald Basson fell into machinery that he was cleaning. The machinery continued to turn and both of Reginald Basson's legs were mangled; they were amputated below the knee at Huntingdon Hospital. Sadly, within a week he passed away, leaving a young wife and four children. Within the town, the National Egg Collection for Soldiers continued but there were grumblings when the price of beer increased at the start of the month. In Eaton Ford, the Cousins family, who had lost one of their five serving sons, Frank, in 1915, had better news of his brother Ernest, who was reported missing in action during December. In early January they heard that he was a POW in Germany.

Less welcome news reached Eaton Ford in the second week of January, when Mr Leader Murfin heard that his youngest son had died on Boxing Day 1916. William Murfin was a Private in the 9th Battalion, East Surreys, but was attached to the 72nd Trench Mortar Battery when he was killed in action. Trench mortars delivered a deadly load and they usually attracted an equally deadly response from the enemy's own version, the Minenwerfer. Both sides' mortars fired large canisters containing enough explosive to destroy many metres of a trench. British Tommies feared the destructive power of 'Minnies', as they called the German trench mortars, and they also did not relish their own trench mortars firing, for they drew an unwelcome enemy reaction. William Murfin became one such casualty on 26 December close to Loos, for there was no Christmas Truce in 1916.

Over in France and Flanders, the men in the trenches were suffering from one of the worst winters in living memory and soldiers struggled to keep warm. Private William Cole wrote to the *Advertiser* telling how wintry it was: 'It has been bitterly cold out here, some of our chaps have had their clothes frozen on them.' The paper was also full of thank you letters from soldiers at the front who had received parcels from the citizens of St Neots and the villages over the Christmas and New Year period. The letters came from everywhere that British soldiers were fighting, not just the Western Front. One came from Salonica, from Private Arthur Bellamy, telling how he had fought in Serbia and was now getting acclimatised to Salonica. Apart from saying how grateful he was for his parcel, he also told how George Bettles, a fellow St Neotian, was with him in the Balkans but was in hospital suffering from dysentery. Certainly local people were very generous, and the Eaton Socon War Funds Auction in January raised almost £94, which was £18 above the previous year's total, at a time when prices were rising.

Mercifully, there were no local men killed during January but that changed during the first week of February when two, Leonard Haynes and Arthur Moran, died. Leonard Haynes, a Wyboston man serving with the 8th Battalion, the Buffs, was killed in action on 6 February close to Mazingarbe. News of his death was received in mid-February and then a letter arrived from one of his comrades, Arthur Webb, telling Leonard Haynes' wife:

> I write to tell you that your husband, Pte. L. Haynes was killed in action early yesterday morning, shot through the head by a machine gun bullet. Although he had been with us only for a short time, and although I have not known him for very long, yet that time was sufficient for us to realise and appreciate his worth as a soldier and his qualities as a man.

Leonard Haynes died close to Loos and today he rests in Philosophe British Cemetery. Twenty-nine-year-old Arthur Moran from Eynesbury had been awarded the Military Medal for gallantry earlier in the war and had originally been with the Bedfords, but had transferred to 34th Trench Mortar Battery, Royal Garrison Artillery. Close to Armentières, on 6 February, he too was hit by enemy fire and died of his wounds. His wife, Amelia, received news of his death in mid-February at their London home, as did his parents, William and Hannah, in Luke Street, Eynesbury. In just over six months they would hear that their other son, Able Seaman William Moran, had been killed in an air raid over Chatham in Kent.

Just over a week later, twenty-six-year-old Private Sidney Faulkner was among the 6th Battalion Northants Regiment who attacked at Boom Ravine, near Miraumont. The 6th Northants and the 11th Royal Fusiliers were the assaulting battalions and they went into action at 5.45 a.m. in conditions that were far from ideal, for an improvement in the weather had seen the snow thaw and the ground become very muddy. Indeed, some of the Northants soldiers' rifles and Lewis guns clogged up as the men lay for hours in mud before the attack. Although Boom Ravine was taken, the attack was not a success and casualties were high, with virtually all of the Northants officers being killed or wounded; then German troops counter-attacked strongly, using specially trained marksmen. The Northants and Fusiliers casualties were 129 killed, 448 wounded and 163 missing. Later, a captured German officer told that a deserter had betrayed the attack, so a court of enquiry was held. The result of the enquiry was indecisive, but what was certain was that Sidney Faulkner had been killed as the Northants attacked. Confirmation of his death did not reach his parents' home in Montagu Street, Eynesbury until April. Sidney Faulkner's body was never recovered and today he is commemorated on the Thiepval Memorial.

The fighting continued close to Boom Ravine and twenty-one-year-old Private Albert Darrington from Wyboston, who had volunteered in 1915, went forward with the 4th Bedfords as they went forward in support near Miraumont. They came under enemy fire as they tried to get across barbed wire and Albert Darrington was amongst the 113 Bedfords who received fatal wounds, although for him it would be days later that he succumbed to them in a military hospital at Étaples.

On 26 February, another local man serving with the 4th Bedfords died three weeks after being wounded. Thirty-four-year-old Lance Corporal Frank Huckle was hit by shrapnel in both legs on 7 February near Miraumont. After being wounded, he lay out in No Man's Land and the wound in his left leg deteriorated as he suffered from exposure when the temperature fell. He remained in the open for some time before stretcher bearers could bring him in and, when they did, he was taken to No. 1 Canadian Hospital – but it was a week before he was strong enough for the surgeons to operate and remove the four pieces of shrapnel. At first it seemed that he was doing well and the operation had succeeded, but his left leg became septic and it was necessary to amputate the whole leg. The Sister in charge of his ward asked him if he wanted his parents, wife and children to be informed how serious things were, but he said, 'No, I do not want to frighten them in any way.' The operation took forty-five minutes; when he was taken back to the ward he developed purulent bronchitis because of the septic condition of his leg. Three hours after the operation he died and he was later buried at Étaples Military Cemetery. Frank Huckle was a well-known and well-liked man throughout the St Neots area, and an accomplished sportsman, playing in goal for both St Neots and Huntingdon football teams. He had worked for the Post Office since 1898 and today his name and that of his fellow worker, Edwin Day, appear on the plaque in the St Neots sorting office. Frank Huckle had joined up on 15 June 1915, but before then he had belonged to the St Neots Volunteers where he instructed other men in basic military skills. His grief-stricken wife had only received a letter from him on the day before he died, in which he played down the seriousness of his condition. The next letter she received was from Sister Stacey telling that he had died.

Towards the end of February, the Germans withdrew from the Somme to take up a stronger position on the newly-constructed Hindenburg Line. As they retreated, the BEF advanced tentatively, coming across some malicious and deadly surprises left behind. Dugouts were booby trapped, animals were slaughtered and water supplies were poisoned. The Germans were determined not to leave anything behind that the Allies could use and this scorched earth policy shocked the advancing troops. The booby traps they left were ingenious and claimed many lives. One British Tommy saw a piano in a dugout and, when he started to play, it exploded, killing him. Tempting wine bottles were attached to explosives by wire, while stoves had gun cotton hidden inside them. The results caused Allied soldiers to be very cautious as they moved forward and occupied enemy trenches and dugouts.

Far away from the bitter cold of the Western Front, some men from St Neots were serving in East Africa and for them heat was the problem. They were grateful for parcels from home although these took quite some time to arrive. Norman Seward received one such parcel from his father four months after it was sent. These men were part of the East African Expeditionary Force and they were engaged in the very difficult task of defeating the German commander Paul von Lettow-Vorbeck, who was a most resourceful master of guerrilla warfare, resisting the Allies and fighting on until two weeks after the war in Europe ended in 1918.

In St Neots, snow fell regularly throughout March, and on the Western Front winter continued to hold its grip, but the Allied commanders' thoughts were turning towards a Spring Offensive. The bad weather continued into April when the Allies made their next attack, this time at Arras. The battle was forced upon the British commander, Douglas Haig, in support of the offensive of Robert Nivelle, the debonair new French Commander-in-Chief. Nivelle had become a national hero at Verdun when his troops had recaptured Fort Douaumont from the Germans. He was quickly perceived by the French as a man who could win the war and he had now persuaded the French and the new British Prime Minister, David Lloyd George, that he could do this on the Western Front. Nivelle's mother was British and he had a very persuasive tongue, convincing David Lloyd George of his plan. Field Marshall Douglas Haig was ordered to place the British Army under French control for this campaign, much to his displeasure. The plan for a massive French attack on the Aisne required a British supporting/ diversionary attack at Arras, but it was virtually doomed from the start when a French officer, who was captured prior to the attack, had on his person details of the offensive, and therefore the Germans were ready and waiting. Haig did not favour Nivelle's plan but was overruled by David Lloyd George, and the BEF had to carry out the attack at Arras.

The British attacked on Easter Monday, with the Canadian Corps securing a memorable victory at Vimy Ridge. This was the first time that the Canadians had fought together as an army and their planning and execution were outstanding. Attacking in driving snow, they took the whole of the German front line that overlooked the Douai Plain and, under their excellent commander General Arthur Currie, they forged a formidable reputation for themselves with this success; by the end of the war the Germans were very wary when the Canadians were opposite them. Today, those who criticise the BEF are keen to point out that the most effective troops within the BEF were either Australian or Canadian, often discounting British troops. However, those critics fail to recognise that a huge percentage of the men of those two Imperial and Dominion forces were actually born in UK and had emigrated before the war. At the outbreak of hostilities, they had quickly volunteered to come to the aid of the mother country, as is evident from the number of ex-St Neots residents from both Canada and Australia who fought during the war.

As the Allies prepared for the offensive, troops continued to move into and out of front-line positions and were subject to the daily 'hate' artillery bombardments. Two weeks before Arras, Privates Sidney Hart and Alfred Ashford were killed during such actions. Twenty-two-year-old Sidney Hart was one of those soldiers who had answered the call for men from afar. In 1915 he had left for Canada but had enlisted in the 46th Canadian Infantry, the Saskatchewans, who were nicknamed the 'Suicide Battalion'. On 22 March he died a couple of hours after being wounded. His family, who lived in Duloe, received the sad news that their son had been killed and buried shortly afterwards, and today he rests in Villers Station Cemetery, close to Vimy Ridge where, two weeks after his death, the Canadians would forge such a reputation for themselves. His father received a letter in early April from Chaplain Cummings of the Canadians telling that Sidney Hart 'died of wounds one and a half hours after he was hit, but never regained consciousness. He suffered little or no pain, and passed away peacefully at 4 o'clock on March 22nd.' Alfred Ashford was three years younger than Sidney Hart and had joined the Hunts Cyclists in late 1915, before being transferred to the 14th Warwicks. On the day after Sidney Hart's death, he too was killed. Alfred Ashford had gone overseas in 1916 and was wounded in the head on the Somme, being hit in the right ear as the Warwicks defended a trench they had just taken. After recovering he returned to the front, but was severely wounded by shellfire on 23 March and was taken back through the lines where surgeons amputated his right leg; unfortunately the wounds and the shock were too great and he died. A week later, his father George, who lived in Huntingdon Street, heard his son was dead.

April 1917 was a difficult month for the families of local men serving at the front, for by the end of the month twelve more men were dead. The first was Private George Mailing of the 11th Suffolks who died of wounds on 7 April, two days before the battalion attacked at Arras. Twenty-four-year-old George Mailing had enlisted in St Neots in 1916 and his parents, Charlotte and Alfred, heard of his death in the middle of April when the dreaded brown envelope was delivered to their Cambridge Street home. In May two more letters arrived, giving more information about his death. The first was from a Sister at the casualty clearing station where he had been taken; it said:

> Your boy was admitted on 7th April, 1917, in the morning, and died the same evening at 10.15 pm. He was very badly wounded in both legs, nothing could be done in the way of operation and all other remedies were in vain. He left no message, as he was too ill.

The second letter came from one of his comrades, H. White, and read:

> It came as a great shock to us all, as we thought he wasn't wounded so badly … It was on Easter Sunday, and George was walking down the road, when a big shell landed a few yards away. He was wounded in both legs and was picked up at once by some RGA men. He was very plucky and explained to them how to bandage him up. He was away from the Dressing Station in less than half an hour, so no time was lost, and everything possible was done for him.

On the following day, 8 April, and much farther afield in Palestine, Captain Ernest Paine, the grandson of two local businessmen, William Medland and Jabez Paine, was with the 17th Battalion, Machine Gun Corps Motors that used armoured cars. This thirty-eight-year-old was killed in a tragic accident.

In France, the Battle of Arras officially began on 9 April and initially proved successful for the British, but by the middle of May it came to a halt. For the French the offensive was hardly successful at all, as by the end of the campaign their armies were close to mutiny and their commander-in-chief, Robert Nivelle, had been sacked. However, Arras was not without gain, for the BEF was able to employ tactics that had been developed on the Somme to good effect. Men from the St Neots area fought here and died. William Dean was a policeman in Biggleswade until December 1915 when he joined the army and was assigned to the 2nd Bedfords, where he reached the rank of Corporal. On 9 April, the 2nd Bedfords went into action in driving snow and William Dean was hit in the abdomen, receiving severe gunshot wounds. For some days doctors tried to save his life, but he passed away on 14 April, and was buried in Warlincourt Halte Cemetery. His wife of just ten months, Nellie, heard from one of the Sisters treating him that he had died, hardly being able to speak during the time he was with them. William Dean was twenty-four when he died and both his grieving wife, who lived in East Street, and his father from Ackerman Street, Eaton Socon, mourned.

On the same day, Easter Monday, the Royal West Kent Regiment, the Queens, were also in action at Arras and Private Herbert Reed of Eynesbury was luckier than William Dean, for although he was wounded by shrapnel in the nose, wrist, forehead and right leg, he survived.

Not so fortunate was Eaton Ford man Jack Searle, who had joined up eighteen months earlier and was with the 8th Bedfords, just to the north of Arras at Loos. On 18 April, the Bedfords were three days into the assault to capture Hill 70 and when they went forward were met with heavy machine-gun fire from concrete pillboxes, followed by a fierce artillery bombardment. Nine men were killed and thirty-three others

Wooden cross marking the grave of Corporal William Dean. Wooden crosses initially marked graves before the white headstones of the War Graves Commission were introduced.

were wounded. Among the dead was twenty-one-year-old Private Jack Searle who had been overseas for about a year and had fought on the Somme. In May, his mother received a letter from his company's quartermaster sergeant that read: 'We cannot do much to ease your sorrow, but maybe it will comfort you to know how much we miss Pte Searle. Fearless and courageous, he was always a hard worker.'

Five days later, Corporal Frederick Hazelton was killed when a German shell exploded as the 1st Bedfords attacked at La Coulotte, close to Vimy. The German position was especially well defended and the Bedfords faced accurate and withering machine-gun and trench mortar fire. Frederick Hazelton fell as the Bedfords advanced and, as the battle raged, his body was lost. He had joined the Hunts Cyclists in June 1916 and from there had been transferred to the 1st Bedfords. His father was Pastor John Hazelton of the New Baptist Church, St Neots and he had every reason to be proud of his son, the first boy from the town to win a free scholarship to Huntingdon Grammar School. Although he had worked as a clerk in the offices of Paine & Co., Frederick had kept his connections with his church, where he was a Sunday school teacher and librarian. He was just twenty-three when he was killed on that Monday near Vimy and today he is commemorated close by on the Arras Memorial. A month later, his father received a letter from C.H. D'Arigdon, the commanding officer of 'A' Company that Frederick Hazelton was with. It told John Hazelton that his son 'was killed during an advance on the enemy trenches. A big shell fell almost at his feet and killed him instantly'.

Corporal Herbert Balls of Eaton Ford was also in action with the 1st Bedfords at La Coulotte and, at the end of the day, he was listed as missing. At first it was believed that he had been captured by the Germans and was a POW, but later that was changed to 'killed in action'. A letter from Lieutenant Hanssen of the Bedfords was received by his mother Caroline, telling more about what may have happened to him. It included the following:

> With the utmost gallantry, a portion of the battalion penetrated far into the German lines. Unfortunately another portion of the attack was held up, and many of the splendid fellows (among whom your son has always been prominent) were surrounded and compelled to surrender.

His body was never recovered and twenty-two-year-old Herbert became the first son of James and Caroline Balls of Rose Cottage to die, for his brother William was killed ten days later. When the roll call was made for the Bedfords at the end of 24 April, Private Frederick Adams was amongst those classified as missing. It would not be established until the start of 1918 that he had been captured by the Germans and had died on 27 April. Frederick Adams was one of five Eaton Ford brothers serving and he was not the only one to die during the war.

As the fighting continued at Arras, Private Wilfred George Reynolds from Eaton Ford became another casualty on Saturday 28 April. When local papers reported his death, it was first recorded that he had gone missing and his

Lance Corporal Wilfred Reynolds.

Private Thomas Durham
and his wife, Emily.

demise was not confirmed until October 1918. However, in 2009, fresh evidence surrounding the nature of his death came to light when the Eatons Community Association asked local people for any information about the men on the Eaton Socon War Memorial for a booklet they were producing. William Reynolds, it transpired, had been sniping at the Germans from a church, and when the enemy returned fire they could not dislodge him so they called up artillery support that blew the church up, killing this Lance Corporal with the 4th Middlesex in the process. William Reynolds had enlisted in April 1915 and had been overseas for a year and a half, so by 1917 he was quite a veteran. His body was never recovered and today he is remembered on the Arras Memorial. Also wounded and missing on the 28th was Sergeant George White of the 10th Lincolns, just over eight months after his brother had died on the Somme. In March 1918, confirmation was received that this former postman was also dead and, like his brother, has no known grave.

On 29 April, the BEF attacked again at Oppy and the 4th Bedfords were ordered to assault and capture enemy trenches there. They succeeded but were furiously counter-attacked and lost the trench, only to attack again and take it once more. They then sought to consolidate their position and came under constant shellfire for the rest of the day, suffering more casualties. Private Thomas Durham of 'C' Company was one of those killed that Sunday, but it was not until October that his wife, Emily, and his five children had confirmation that he was dead. Thomas Durham was a 'yellabelly', as folk from Lincolnshire are known, for he had been born in Spalding in 1880 where his parents, who came from Eaton Socon, were employed as farm workers. When they returned to St Neots, Thomas worked on the land and then at Paine's Brewery. He had joined up in 1916 and a year later he was dead, but again no body was recovered and his name can now be found on the Arras Memorial. Killed in the same action was Private Corbett Smith, who had been brought up in Eaton Socon but lived in Northampton at the outbreak of the war. He had enlisted at Bedford in February 1916 and was then sent overseas in June. His stay at the front was short for he came back to Britain suffering from trench foot, but recovered to return to France in August. He fought during the later stages of the Somme, was wounded close to Thiepval and was then hospitalised in England before heading back for Arras.

On the same day, Private Herbert Gregory of the 13th Royal Fusiliers was killed in action less than a month after arriving in France. He was a Norfolk man who had married a local girl, and his wife learned that her husband was missing in particularly sad circumstances. Jane Gregory knew that her husband carried a photograph of the two of them together, and in May she received this photograph through the post from a soldier who had picked it up on the battlefield at Arras. She then heard officially that he had been killed, but that changed to missing in action. Then in late May another official letter arrived at their home in New Street, telling that he was indeed dead. Both Herbert and Jane Gregory were thirty years old and they had two young children. Herbert Gregory's body was recovered and he rests today in Chili Trench Cemetery near Arras.

The twenty-ninth of April 1917 was the worst day of the war so far for the people of St Neots, for two more men were killed, one at Arras and one at Gaza in Palestine. Lance Corporal Wilfred Carlton with the 1st Battalion Royal Berkshires was initially posted as missing, but that was later changed to 'killed in action'. Wilfred Carlton was another who took the route to the front via the Hunts Cyclists, joining at the start of October 1914. He has no known grave and his name sits with so many others on the Arras Memorial. Sergeant Frederick Humphries was an Eaton Socon man with the Egyptian Expeditionary Force that was trying to drive the Turks from Palestine and so capture Jerusalem. The key to this was the capture of Gaza, a fortress that dominated Southern Palestine and, without its fall, there could be no progress for the Allies. The initial battle in March had been without success and Gaza was not taken. At the very point that the Turks had abandoned their defence, the attack was called off. The attacking troops of the EEF (Egyptian Expeditionary Force) could not understand why they were being pulled back and it would take two further assaults in April and October for Gaza to be captured. In April, the second attempt to take the stronghold failed even though tanks and gas shells were used to support the attack. Gas proved to be unsuccessful, as the heat caused it to disperse without effect, whilst the soft sand clogged up tanks' engines. Fred Humphries had initially been with the 5th Bedfords but, by April 1917, was with the newly-formed 162nd Machine Gun Corps as the EEF pushed forward at Gaza. This oft overlooked theatre of fighting was quite remarkable, for the majority of the British troops here were Territorials or mounted yeomanry and the conditions they had to fight in were very different from the Western Front, with searing heat, swarms of flies, and lack of water. The enemy they faced was equally as dangerous as the Germans. 'Johnny Turk', as the Tommies labelled their adversary, had proved to be a formidable foe in Gallipoli and the same was true in Palestine, especially the Anatolian Turks, as Fred Humphries discovered. He was killed by a high explosive shell, when pieces of metal from the casing flew through the air and caught him in the neck. His mother received a letter from Company Commander Cedric Relley, telling:

> Your son was killed at about 10 minutes past 12 yesterday afternoon by a piece of H.E. shell, which struck him at the base of the neck, his death was practically instantaneous. The doctor tells me that he cannot have suffered in any way.

He was buried with a comrade killed by the same shell explosion and rests today in Gaza War Cemetery.

Back at Arras, the 18th Division prepared to attack in what was known as the Third Battle of the Scarpe; amongst their number were the 7th Bedfords, the 'Shiny Seventh', who had been out of the front line for about a month. Now they were about to go over the top again at dawn on 3 May and Privates Charles Saddington and Charles Tokens, both Eynesbury men, were among those who advanced. From the beginning the attack did not go well, with problems with the artillery bombardment and supporting tanks, and the advancing troops then came under heavy enemy machine-gun and artillery fire before the attack halted in front of the German barbed wire. The Bedfords had to fall back to their own trenches, but Charles Saddington and Charles Tokens were not with them. Both men had been killed in action during the advance and their bodies were not recovered from No Man's Land. Charles Saddington was thirty-two and a well-known figure in the town, having been Scoutmaster in St Neots for almost nine years. His widow, Millicent, presented a portrait of her husband to the Scouts as a memorial to him six months later and this was hung in the headquarters of the Scouts. Charles Saddington had joined up in July 1916 and had been posted overseas six months later, writing home regularly, always in a positive way. The last letter that his wife received told how he was looking forward to coming home on leave, but then the next letter informed her that her husband was dead. It came from Second Lieutenant Driver and read:

> I regret to inform you that No. 30818 Pte. Saddington, C. W., your husband was killed in the Battle of Arras on the 3rd May. He suffered no pain, being killed instantaneously, and at the time was doing his duty like a true British soldier.

Three brothers from the Tokens family of Eynesbury had been serving in the BEF in 1916 and now, a year later, only one of them, John, was alive. Arthur had died on the Somme and now Charles was declared missing at Arras, but that changed later to 'killed in action'. John Tokens survived the war.

On the same day, Privates John Crowe and Percy Watts went forward at Arras with the 1st Battalion, the Royal Berkshires, a regiment they had joined from the Hunts Cyclists in 1915, and both were killed in action. John, the twenty-two-year-old son of John and Harriet Crowe of Cambridge Street, was not officially declared dead until the start of the next year and his body was never recovered. Percy's final resting place was also lost, so the Arras Memorial is the only place in France where they are commemorated. Also on 3 May, William Balls, a Private with the Royal Fusiliers, who had been wounded in the thigh in 1916, went missing in action and it was not until July that his death was confirmed. So within less than two weeks, two of the four Balls brothers had died.

On 8 May, two more local men fell at Arras – Sergeant Walter Edwards and Private William Storey. Walter Edwards had been born in Eynesbury in 1886 but had left for Canada in 1911, settling in Ontario. Five years later he was back in Britain after joining the 19th Battalion, Canadian Infantry and thence overseas to France. In January 1917 he was wounded, but then in the latter stages of Arras he was killed in action. By that time he had been promoted to Sergeant and was with the 19th Machine Gun Section, specialising in the Lewis Gun. He fought at Vimy on Easter Monday, coming out without a scratch and, in April, he wrote to his mother in Eynesbury telling of his promotion and that all that was wrong with him was a slight cold. Eight days into May that changed when he was killed at Arras. William Storey was one of two sons of Inspector Walter Storey, the other being Harry. Both had

Private William Balls.

been wounded in 1916 and now William was dead, as two letters from the 14th Warwicks that were delivered at the Storey home in New Street told. The first came from Lieutenant Wood, the second from Private Mashford, and both explained that shellfire had killed William Storey. Lieutenant Wood's letter told:

> During our spell in the front line trenches we experienced considerable shelling from the enemy artillery, but it may be of some consolation to you to know that your son maintained a cheerful endurance until the end throughout that trying period, and met his death fearlessly, that he preserved a soldierly determination to the last is evident from the fact that he was cleaning his rifle in view of a probable crisis, when a shell landed in the trench causing the instantaneous death of your son and his friend Ernest Cope. We buried them both in soldiers' graves behind our trenches.

The second letter from Private Mashford read:

> Being your son's companion, and the promise we made, I felt it my duty to write. He was killed by a shell, instantly, so he did not have any pain. I think I saw him take his last breath, as I was beside him. It was a shock to me and I miss him very much, as he was my best pal I had out here, we always shared in everything. I do not know how I escaped, as there were four all together.

Although both William Storey and Ernest Cope were buried, their graves soon became lost and today these friends' names sit close to one another on the Arras Memorial.

May continued to exact a deadly toll for the St Neots area, for on the 9th, twenty-two-year-old Private John Gilbert from Roxton, serving with the 1st East Surreys, died as they attacked near Oppy Wood. The East Surreys had gone forward at 7 p.m. on the 8th, had attacked at 2.30 a.m. on the 9th with the aid of a creeping barrage, and then fought through the rest of the night. Sadly John Gilbert was killed during the attack. Then, on 17 May, a tragic event took place when twenty-one-year-old Able Seaman William Higgins was drowned while rowing out to HMS trawler, *Killdeer*. He had volunteered at the start of the war, serving as a member of the Royal Naval Reserve and carrying out patrol and

Eaton Socon Roll of Honour War Shrine.

escort duties in the North Sea and to Russia. His body was recovered and buried in Bedford Cemetery, and today he is commemorated on the Eaton Socon War Memorial as he had lived in the village with his Aunt, Mrs Lovitt, for two years before his tragic accident.

In Eaton Socon, a war shrine was unveiled during the second week of May, just outside the west entrance gates of the churchyard. The shrine took the form of a polished oak tablet, with a pointed canopy and the letters RIP inscribed on a cross. It was headed: 'Roll of Honour, 1914-1917' and listed the twenty-four men from the area who had died so far; it read as follows:

Capt. R. M. Smythe, Beds. Regt.
Pte. J. Anderson, Berks. Regt.
Pte. C. Bettles, Beds. Regt.
Pte. A. Childerley, Beds. Regt.
Pte. W.G. Cooper, Beds. Regt.
Pte. A.D. Townsend, Beds. Regt.
Pte. C. Barringer, R.A.M.C.
Pte. W. Murfin, E. Surreys.
Pte. C. Payne, Beds. Regt.
Sergt. J. Corbett, R.F.A.
Pte. W. Green, Beds. Regt.
Pte. A. Darrington, Beds. Regt.
Sergt. S. Hoitt, W.Yorks.
Corpl. L. Bundy, Canadian In.
Lce.-Corp. F. Cousins, Beds. Regt.
Pte. W. Goodman, Beds. Regt.
Pte. C.W. Medlow, Middlesex.
Pte. R. Ball, Beds. Regt.
Pte. H. Usher, Northants Regt.
Pte. W. Searle, R.E.
Pte. H. Carrington, Hunts. Cyclists
Pte. F. White, Hunts. Cyclists
Pte. L. Haynes, E. Kent.
Corpl. W. Dean, Beds. Regt.

Sadly, by the end of the war another forty-eight men from the village had their names added to the Roll and all would later be inscribed on the Eaton Socon War Memorial.

Back in France, the fighting at Arras continued. Twenty-three-year-old Trooper Edward Bardell, brother of Mrs Wildman of the Two Brewers, Eaton Socon, who was serving with the Household Battalion and was wounded in April during the assault of the Roeux Chemical Works, died of his wounds on 24 May. In 1921 his was one of the names etched on the Eaton Socon War Memorial.

Five days later, another Eaton Socon man, twenty-three-year-old Private Jesse Cooper of the 1st Berkshires, died of wounds. His wife Gladys heard this when she received a letter from the Berkshire's padre, telling:

We have been in the line and under pretty severe shell fire for some days, and on 28th May, when a party was going out late in the evening, a shell dropped among them, wounding a good many. Your husband was hit in the side and thigh. We got him down at once to the doctor's aid post, where his wounds were dressed, and he was carried back to the field ambulance, but soon after his arrival there he died.

Most of the work to repair and strengthen trenches was carried out at night, with the equipment used for this being carried to the front line, and then working parties went out when darkness fell. Such work was especially dangerous, for the Germans shelled communications trenches as they knew men would be working their way along them in preparation for the night's work. Jesse Cooper was in such a party when he and fourteen others were wounded by enemy artillery. Jesse had originally joined the Hunts Cyclists but had transferred to the Berkshires. He had survived the accidental exploding of a grenade in England and had been wounded during his first stint in France. When he came out of hospital he married Gladys Irons, four months before he died. Now she was widowed.

Those who worked for the *Advertiser* were saddened in May when they found out that one of their former co-workers had been killed at Arras. Arthur Hogg had worked as a compositor in the *Advertiser*'s office in St Neots, although he and his wife lived in Peterborough. On 13 May he was killed in action with the 2nd Suffolks, but news of his death did not reach his former colleagues until late May. Arthur Hogg had been married just fifteen months and, on the very day that he died, his wife gave birth to a son whom she named Arthur Henry.

Somewhat better news reached St Neots at around the same time, concerning Corporal Sidney Fisher who had gone missing in April whilst fighting in Palestine. Towards the end of May, his mother heard from him via a card from Jerusalem saying he had been captured by the Turks and was being treated well. He had been wounded by shrapnel on 27 March and, together with fifty other wounded men, had been captured by the enemy when the British had withdrawn. He was very pleased to have been taken by the Turks, for he had been stripped of everything by Bedouins before the Turks found him. Three pieces of shrapnel had gone right through his left leg but had missed bone and, although he could not yet walk, he was recovering well.

April and May were months that were particularly hard on the folk of St Neots, but June was kinder as just two soldiers died. Such a figure is surprising, since the BEF launched a major offensive on 7 June at Messines Ridge, Ypres where, for the first time in the war, casualties of the attackers were fewer than those of the defenders. The attack began when nineteen mines exploded under the German front line and General Herbert Plumer, who commanded the British 2nd Army here, reportedly remarked to his officers on the eve of the battle: 'Gentlemen, we may not make history tomorrow, but we shall certainly change the geography.' Plumer was very popular with the soldiers of the BEF, for his planning was meticulous and he was no 'donkey' as some of the BEF's generals were labelled. He did not risk the lives of his men in futile attacks. Plumer's 2nd Army advanced at 3.10 a.m., supported by tanks, gas shells and a creeping barrage that gave excellent protection. What they found surprised them, for around 10,000 German soldiers had been killed as a result of the mine explosions and the advancing British troops faced very little opposition. When the artillery barrage ceased, the Germans quickly manned forward trench lines and set up their machine-guns. Therefore, when the mines exploded many were exposed and hundreds were atomised where they stood, whilst others were found by the advancing BEF without a mark. The shock of the explosion had killed them and it seemed as if they were sleeping when the BEF entered enemy trench lines. Within three hours, all of the initial objectives were taken in this resounding success for the BEF. The noise of the exploding mines was heard in Southern England, and the story has been told that the Prime Minister, David Lloyd George, heard the rumble as he was working in his study in 10 Downing Street.

Private Sidney King from Eynesbury wrote home telling his wife about Messines, describing the battle:

> I have been in a great attack on the Germans, and they have had [to] go back a long way.
> I have had many a look over the trench this last nine months at No Man's Land, but at last we
> went over the top … and then up went the mines, and then off went the Artillery, which said

we were to advance. I shall never forget it, the earth was like a volcano, and the flames leapt hundreds of feet into the air, but on we went for the position set out for us. Many were the great deeds done that morning, and many a Tommy found his last resting place, but the Good Lord spared me to get through, and the Huns were hurled back from the trenches they had held for two and a half years … I have been told over 7,000 prisoners were taken.

Other men from St Neots fought at Messines, but the first casualty in June came much closer to home when Frank Whiddett died of consumption in Eaton Ford. Frank Whiddett had been a regular soldier who had fought with the 1st Bedfords right from August 1914, seeing action at Mons and all of the early major battles. At one stage he had been buried alive after a shell explosion but was dug out, and later he had been gassed. He had then developed consumption and was treated in a sanatorium for a year and a half. In the autumn of 1916 he moved to the Barley Mow public house, Eaton Ford, with his wife Kate and their three children, in the hope that life there with country air would help his condition. Sadly this was not the case and this former sergeant of the Bedfords died on 8 June. He was buried with full military honours in Eaton Socon churchyard, as two buglers from his regiment played the 'Last Post'.

Sergeant Frank Whiddett.

As the month progressed, storms hit the Huntingdonshire area badly and then news of heavy casualties reached St Neots – but this time within Britain, when London was attacked on 13 June by German Gotha bombers, killing 162 and injuring over 500. Among the dead were eighteen children from Upper North Street School on the East India Dock Road. The bombing of London continued throughout the autumn of 1917 and into 1918, for the German High Command felt that this, together with the U-boat campaign, would bring Britain to her knees before millions of American troops could have an effect on the Western Front after the USA had declared war on Germany in April.

In France, towards the end of June, Private Herbert 'Jimmy' Lovitt was killed in an attack on enemy trenches close to Oppy Wood. The 1st Bedfords captured the German trenches but Jimmy Lovitt died during the attack and was buried just behind the front line. Jimmy was nineteen and had volunteered in 1916 when under age, joining two older serving brothers. He had immediately shown a real flair for soldiering as a first-class bomber, and while carrying out this dangerous job he was killed. His father, Frank, heard of his son's death in early July and that he had been buried at the front by a fellow St Neotian, Corporal George Bellamy. Other soldiers were perhaps more fortunate during June, as Percy Reynolds of Eaton Ford, who was reported missing in action, was confirmed as being a POW, whilst George Bettles and Arthur Dobney were both back home in St Neots. George Bettles was on leave, following an attack of malaria contracted whilst in Salonica, and Arthur Dobney was invalided out of the army. At the same time, news also arrived that Fred Sharman of Russell Street had been promoted from Sergeant to Second Lieutenant in the Grenadier Guards.

At the end of July, the BEF resumed the offensive at Ypres and this continued right through until November, by which time this Third Battle of Ypres had become known by the name of the small village that sits on a ridge overlooking Ypres – Passchendaele. However, before the offensive began, men from St Neots died in Mesopotamia and in Flanders. Twenty-four-year-old Private George Colbert was serving with the Army Service Corps when he succumbed to heat stroke and died on 16 July. George Colbert had been born in Wellingborough but lived in St Neots, as did his wife Ida and his parents George and Elizabeth. News of his death reached them in late July, telling that he had been buried in Baghdad. Five days later more local parents received similar distressing news, when Bombardier Claude Cheshire of the Royal Field Artillery became a casualty of an artillery duel close to Ypres. Claude Cheshire had joined up in the summer of 1915 but had fallen ill whilst overseas and had spent time recovering, before returning to active service during February 1916. Now he was killed in action and the sadness that his parents, Frederick and Jane, felt was compounded in less than a month when their elder son, Frederick, also serving with the artillery, died of wounds at Ypres. The two brothers had even managed to meet up at Messines just after the attack in June but now, within the space of thirty-five days, both were dead and Mr and Mrs Cheshire had lost their only two sons: Claude, aged twenty-one, was killed in action on 12 July and Frederick, aged twenty-four, died of wounds on 16 August. Frederick Cheshire was a married man and this talented sportsman's death was particularly hard for his wife and two young children. Frederick Cheshire Snr had worked as the police sergeant at Eaton Socon for some years, but in 1917 he and his wife were living in Shefford, a few miles away. The grief and sadness they all must have experienced in the summer of 1917 is hard to imagine.

Shells, trench mortars and rifle grenades remained a constant menace and source of death or wounding along the Western Front, accounting for the majority of casualties suffered by both sides. Private Eben Norman was one such casualty when a rifle grenade exploded, wounding him in the left foot and the right shin; the injury was bad enough for him to be brought back home to Bradford Hospital. The outcome was that he lost one of his toes but strangely, in the idiom of the day, the local press reported that 'he was going on nicely'. Better news in mid-July concerned Company Sergeant Major Alfred Smith of the Royal Fusiliers, recommended for and awarded the Distinguished Conduct Medal for bravery. At around the same time, news reached St Neots that another local man, Sergeant Fred Davies of the Royal Berkshires, had been awarded the Military Medal for 'coolness and organising an advanced post' during fighting in April. Sergeant Davies was another who had started out with the Hunts Cyclists but had been transferred to the Berkshires during the Battle of the Somme in 1916.

Less welcome news was that Private George Smith of Montagu Street, Eynesbury had been killed with the 8th Bedfords close to Lens on 22 July. George Smith had the job of carrying water to the trenches and then dispensing it along the front line, often coming under enemy shellfire. His wife received a letter from Corporal Joe Mardlin telling how her husband had died:

> I am sorry to say [he] was killed today by a shell bursting quite near to him. He was just outside the aid post in the trenches and talking to a machine gunner, who I am also sorry to say was killed by his side. I myself was just inside the aid post … I hope it will be a comfort for you to know he suffered no pain, as he was killed instantly … His body at present is quite close to me as I am writing these few lines to you.

George Smith was buried and rests today in Philosophe British Cemetery.

Just a week after the death of George Smith, Private Frank Hemmings of the 2nd Bedfords died of wounds at Ypres. Reports had been received that the Germans had withdrawn from their front-line trenches to the north of Ypres and two patrols were sent out on the night of 28 July to establish if this was true. When they returned they had suffered eight men killed, seventeen wounded and four missing. Frank Hemmings was among the wounded, succumbing to his injuries and dying on what was his twenty-second birthday. Frank Hemmings was from Eaton Socon and had seen a fair amount of action before his fatal wounding at Ypres for, after volunteering in 1914, he had fought at Gallipoli before transferring to the 2nd Bedfords. He was buried by his comrades and today his body rests in Dickebusch New Military Cemetery.

Two days later, the next stage of the Third Battle of Ypres began in earnest. The British troops that attacked on 31 July, the 5th Army, were under the command of Hubert Gough, the youngest General in the BEF, and he was now given the task of driving the Germans from Passchendaele Ridge. Gough had a reputation as a 'thruster', which meant that he was not afraid to push his men forward, even if resulting casualties were high. The British Army that attacked on 31 July had certainly evolved since the Somme and its composition had changed also, now being a mixture of volunteers and conscripts. For some men, Passchendaele would be their first taste of battle, whilst for others it would mean drawing upon the experiences gained on the Somme and at Arras.

When Gough's 5th Army attacked it was buoyed by the success of Messines but, as with every attack, the soldiers were both fearful and nervous. A ten-day bombardment preceded the attack before the troops attacked at 3.50 a.m., following a creeping barrage, one of the developments from the Somme which gave advancing soldiers much greater protection as they crossed No Man's Land. A wall of shells exploding around 50 yards in front of them meant that the enemy had to keep under cover, and that the advancing troops could get amongst the Germans without coming under the kind of machine-gun fire they had faced on the Somme. The infantry had also become far more efficient since the catastrophe of 1 July 1916, and now fought in specialised platoons, using fire and movement tactics. It certainly worked on Tuesday 31 July, for the British advanced over a mile. However, if the British had learned from the Somme, so had the Germans and they employed the tactics they had tried to use on the first day of Arras in April, notably defence in depth and counter-attack. As the Germans counter-attacked the weather turned, with heavy rain falling, and for the next ten days little fighting was possible. Indeed it was so bad that even supplying the troops occupying the positions captured on 31 July was a mammoth task. The mud that will always be associated with Passchendaele worsened as the rain continued to fall, and attacks became more difficult. On 10 August, and then again on the 16th, the BEF attacked, this time at Langemarck but without any real success. Plumer's 2nd Army now replaced Gough's 5th Army as the instrument of the British advance, and Plumer immediately reverted to the tried and tested tactics of Messines, meticulously planning the next stage of the attack.

One of the battalions attacking on 31 July was the 2nd Bedfords and within their ranks was thirty-year-old Private Fred Higgins, who was a veteran in comparison to many who went into action that day. After volunteering in 1915, he had fought at Festubert and Loos, and was wounded early in 1916 close to Lens. After treatment, he returned to France for the later stages of the Somme, before going on to fight at Arras and Messines. Now, as the Bedfords fought their way towards Pilkem, he was killed on 2 August by a German shell; although his comrades buried him in a grave marked with a wooden cross, it was lost as the fighting continued and today his name can be found on the Menin Gate. His aunt, Emma, heard of his death when the chaplain of the battalion wrote to her in early August. Fred Higgins had lost his wife in 1912 and had moved back to Eaton Ford from Bedford in 1912. His children – Elizabeth, aged ten, and Albert, aged eight – were now orphans.

A week later, twenty-one-year-old Leading Signalman William Gill of Eaton Ford was part of the crew of the destroyer, HMS *Recruit*, as she patrolled in the North Sea. The *Recruit* was a new ship and had only been launched in late 1916 but, on 9 August, she struck a mine and sank with the loss of fifty-four lives, including William and Rose Gill's son. He had joined the navy in 1911, had served with the Mediterranean Gibraltar Patrol, had fought at Jutland in June 1916 and now was drowned when the *Recruit* sank. His body was never recovered and William Gill is remembered on the Royal Navy Memorial at Plymouth and, closer to home, at Eaton Socon.

Back at Ypres, the fighting continued and casualties mounted. On 14 August, Lance Corporal Jack Cooper was added to the list of those killed in action, following that of his brother Jesse who had died of wounds just three months earlier. Jack Cooper had enlisted in the summer of 1916 and had joined the prestigious Public Schools' Battalion, the 16th Middlesex. At the start of the war, this battalion had been formed as an elite group with men going through an application procedure but, by 1916, they had lost so many men that recruitment was no longer selective, and Jack Cooper was among their ranks as they attacked at Ypres. The Middlesex had advanced two days earlier to establish positions on the banks of the Steenbeek, a small stream that was now the size of a small river following all of the rain. This stream had to be crossed if the BEF was to take its objective, the village of Langemarck.

Lance Corporal Jack and Private Jesse Cooper. Jack is seated.

Two days later, Jack Cooper suffered a fatal wound as the Middlesex consolidated the position, as his wife Sarah heard when she received a letter at their home in Cambridge Street, St Neots. Chaplain G.M. Wheeler wrote: 'He was brought in here quite unconscious with a shell wound in the head and he never regained consciousness. He laid down his life as a brave soldier, and I am glad to say suffered no pain.' Chaplain Wheeler went on to say that all of Jack Cooper's effects would be sent on and that Sarah Cooper would be able to obtain a photograph of his grave if she contacted the War Office. Thirty-two-year-old Jack Cooper had only just returned to the front after being wounded in February. Now he had not been so fortunate, and he was buried in Mendinghem Military Cemetery at Poperinghe, close to Ypres. There were other local soldiers wounded on 16 August, including Private Fred Pearson from Eynesbury, who was hit by a bullet in his right arm; Private Ernest Coleman of Eaton Ford, who had received a serious gunshot wound to the back; and Private Thomas Norman of St Neots. Although all would bear the scars of their wounds for the rest of their lives, they survived.

As the fighting raged at Ypres, news of more casualties reached St Neots. Tom Sharman, a gunner with the RFA, was wounded in the face when a German shell struck his gun, splitting it in two. Writing home to Eynesbury, he told that he was lucky that the shrapnel piece did not strike higher as it would have hit him in the eye. Private Jesse Bundy of Eaton Socon was another wounded and his wife heard how 'his injuries are luckily fairly slight, the bullet passing through his right arm, grazing his chest and neck'. Sergeant George Corbett, with the Bedfords at Ypres, had certainly had an eventful time so far during the war. In 1916 he had been wounded and had also suffered from trench fever, frozen feet and a dose of gas. Now in 1917 he was wounded again in the left hand and thigh, with bone being hit, and he needed quite some time to heal – yet recover he did, surviving the war, unlike his brother John who died at Gallipoli.

Another survivor was Gunner George Hemmings of the Royal Garrison Artillery, unlike his brother Frank who was killed at Ypres just days earlier at the end of July. George Hemmings wrote home towards the end of August, telling:

I am still alive and well … I was in the battle of Messines. What a sight when the mines went up. I was also in the battle of Ypres … We are all hoping the war will end this year, as we have all had enough of this life.

At the same time that Gunner Hemmings' letter reached Eaton Socon, news arrived in St Neots that Corporal William Ayres of the Royal Engineers had won the Military Medal at Messines. In late August he was presented with it by his commanding officer.

If the information about Corporal Ayres was welcome when it was received at his East Street home, then the same could not be said at the home of John Bartlett in Huntingdon Street, for his wife, Alice, heard in early September that her husband had been killed by shellfire on 24 August. Three letters arrived within a short space of time: from his platoon officer, from the chaplain of the Bedfords and from Albert Norman who was close to him when he was killed. Albert Norman's letter told how John Bartlett had 'died an instantaneous and painless death, being killed by a shell'. Second Lieutenant Haynes confirmed this and told that three men had been killed when the German shell fell into the trench occupied by the Bedfords, adding: 'He has been taken from the line and will be properly buried in a cemetery behind.' Chaplain Provis told Alice Bartlett that her husband's platoon had been heavily shelled throughout the afternoon of 24 August but John had stayed at his post and had behaved very well under such a bombardment. The war diary of the 1st Bedfords confirmed all of this, telling: 'In trenches Front line was heavily shelled with 5.9s & 8 inch on 24 inst casualties 3 O.R. Killed 4 O.R. wounded.'

John Bartlett was thirty-five and, after joining the Beds Yeomanry, had transferred to the 1st Bedfords on Christmas Day, 1916. Now, eight months later, he was killed close to Arras in one of the daily artillery duels many miles south of the main area of fighting at Ypres. He was buried and rests today in Roclincourt Cemetery. His brother, William, also served and was badly affected by trench fever, but he survived.

At Ypres, the rain that had relented since 16 August now started to fall heavily and the battlefield once again became a quagmire across which the 8th Royal Warwicks attacked on the 27th. Amongst their number was twenty-one-year-old Lance Sergeant Harry Oldham, the son of John and Martha Oldham of Church Street. In August 1914 he had joined the Hunts Cyclists, but had transferred to the Warwicks with whom he had seen front-line action at Arras and now Ypres. On the 27th, the 8th Royal Warwicks were charged with taking Schuler Farm but they failed to take their objective. Harry Oldham was initially reported as 'missing in action' but this changed in November when he was officially declared killed. Unsurprisingly, his body was never recovered from the mud that was 3rd Ypres; today his name is among the 35,000 men with no known grave who are commemorated on the back wall of Tyn Cot Cemetery. Harry Oldham had two serving brothers, Jack and Frederick, and both survived the war.

The family of Harry Oldham was devastated by news of his death, but two St Neots wives were relieved to hear, at the start of September, that their husbands were alive but were POWs, after going missing on 31 July. Frederick Hand and Thomas Norman were both wounded and captured on the first day of 3rd Ypres, and had found themselves in a German hospital in Ghent in adjacent beds. Fred Hand wrote to his wife at their home in Windmill Terrace on 5 August, but she only received his postcard on 7 September:

Just a few lines, as I expect you have been worrying and wondering where I am. Well, I got wounded in the bottom of my back and taken prisoner on July 31st, but don't worry, I am treated well. Norman, the milkman, is with me.

Thomas Norman wrote to his wife at their home in Albert Terrace on 11 August, but again it took over three weeks for his letter to arrive: 'I got shot through the hand, it is going on all right. It is eleven days since I was captured.' William Markham, a Private with the London Regiment, was also wounded and captured at Passchendaele, and again it was not until September that his mother in Eynesbury heard of this. Another in hospital, but this time in France, was Private Percy Stamford of Eynesbury. His parents, from Huntingdon Street, heard in late September that he had received a wound to the right thigh but was recovering well.

September saw the impact of Germany's unrestricted submarine warfare bring about a shortage of sugar, and St Neots Urban District Council put in place a scheme for its distribution that required the local population to apply to buy it. Back in Flanders, the struggle to take Passchendaele Ridge continued, and on Friday 14th the 1st Battalion of the London Regiment, the Royal Fusiliers, attacked at 3 a.m. to the north-east of Ypres, close to St Julien where the Germans had first used gas in 1915. In their ranks was twenty-eight-year-old William Herbert Barker of Cambridge Street. He had joined up in October 1914, originally with the Hunts Cyclists and then the 8th Bedfords, before being assigned to the 1st London. Their objective on 14 September was a German trench the Allies called Winnipeg. Four and a half hours after the Londons' attack, the Germans counter-attacked and among the casualties was William Barker. His wife Hilda heard of his death in late September and today he rests in Tyn Cot Cemetery, the largest Commonwealth War Graves Cemetery in the world, that sits across Passchendaele Ridge.

For the next seven days hardly any rain fell at Ypres, so the ground began to dry out once again, and on 20 September Plumer's troops attacked but, true to his doctrine, his men only advanced as far as was safe, and then waited for the inevitable German counter-attack that was destroyed by his artillery. The attack, known as the Battle for the Menin Road Ridge, went in just before 6 a.m. and local men were involved. Private Will Stapleford was one who was wounded, as he told his mother in a letter received in early October:

> Just a few lines to let you know I have been wounded in the right foot. I got hit on 20th Sept … I was in the big push when I got hit. Three of us got put down by the same shell; my mate, I and my platoon officer.

In the ranks of the 10th Queens was Private Ernest Murfin from Eynesbury, a nineteen-year-old who had joined up under the Derby Scheme and had been on the Western Front for just a year. The Queens went over the top at 5.40 a.m. and immediately came under enemy machine-gun fire. The war diary tells how the Queens 'advanced about 50 yards when they were met with heavy fire from two machine-guns which did great havoc'. However, they were able to work around these killing machines and succeeded in silencing them and taking their objective. When the roll call was taken later in the day, Ernest Murfin did not answer and for some time his fate was unknown. In October, his mother and father wrote asking for information and received a reply from Major Reginald Bonson of the Queens, but he was unable to give any real news of their son: 'Unfortunately, the officer commanding the Company was wounded, and I have made enquiries, but nobody knows or saw your son after a certain hour on Sept 20th.' A few days later, John and Mary Murfin heard from the War Office that their son was indeed dead. His body was recovered later and today rests in Hooge Crater Cemetery, Ypres.

Many miles to the south of Ypres, daily shelling continued to take its toll. On 23 September such a German bombardment accounted for thirty-five-year-old John Bunnage, a Private with the 8th Battalion, the Royal Fusiliers. On that day, a company of the Fusiliers was entrenched at Monchy, close to Arras, and although the Battle of Arras had ended some months earlier, this daily barrage was a deadly reminder that no front-line position was safe. John Bunnage was killed on the night of 23 September; his father heard of this when he received a letter from Corporal J. Munro, telling: 'No doubt it will relieve you a lot to know he suffered no pain. I myself was next to him when he was killed by a large portion of shell.' Corporal Munro went on to say that John Bunnage had been buried behind the lines and his grave remained secure. Today he rests in Monchy British Cemetery.

Three days later the BEF attacked at Polygon Wood at Ypres and George and Alice Ashford of Huntingdon Street lost their second son, Fred, just six months after the death of their first born, Alfred, at Arras. Nineteen-year-old Fred was a Private with the 7th Sherwood Foresters, whose objective was to capture a number of German blockhouses – which they did, but the Germans then counter-attacked and Fred Ashford was killed. His body was never found and today his name can be found on the back wall of Tyn Cot Cemetery. On the same day, the 9th London Battalion attacked at 5.50 a.m., advancing in a thick mist which caused them to lose direction. They came under heavy fire, especially from a German pillbox, but they persevered until they were counter-attacked. Private Arthur Cousins of Eaton Socon was one of the Londons who died that day and, like his brother Frank, who had died at Ypres over two years earlier, he has no known grave; Frank's name is on the Menin Gate and Arthur's at Tyn Cot.

October began with a number of soldiers returning to St Neots, some wounded and others invalided out of the army. Fred Brace from Eynesbury and Eben Norman of St Neots saw their war come to an end because of injury, and Stanley Smith from Eaton Socon, a Private with the Worcesters, had his put on hold after being wounded in the back and hospitalised back in Blighty. Over in Flanders, the battlefield at Ypres had dried out considerably during September, but ominously the rain returned on 2 October and fell steadily for the next eleven days, just as the BEF began the final push to take Passchendaele Ridge. The ground quickly became a quagmire and progress was slow and laborious. Trench lines became almost indistinguishable and soldiers moved from shell crater to shell crater as they advanced through the glutinous mud. In terms of soldiers killed, the first few weeks of October were kind to the people of St Neots and the surrounding villages, for there were no fatalities. Indeed there was even cause to celebrate in Eaton Ford when news arrived that Private Frank Cook of the Warwickshires had been awarded the Military Medal and been promoted to Lance Corporal.

On 12 October, the battle for Passchendaele began in earnest; among those attacking was the New Zealand division, within whose ranks was thirty-nine-year-old George Dean, a man who had been born thousands of miles away in Eaton Socon. George Dean, the youngest son of John Dean, was living and working in New Zealand in 1914 but, together with thousands of others, answered the call for help from the mother country. In the summer of 1916 he was with the 1st Battalion, the Otago Regiment, that landed in Britain and then went over to the Western Front. On 12 October 1917, the New Zealanders formed the left flank of the attack, and, going in at 5.25 a.m., they met with very fierce German resistance, including uncut barbed wire, machine-guns and pillboxes. As they advanced, it was noticed that there was a small gap in the German wire which they made for, but here they faced murderous machine-gun fire. Three waves of the New Zealanders tried to break through, but could not do so and had to dig in where they were. Among the many casualties was thirty-nine-year-old George Dean, whose body was not recovered; today he is remembered at Tyn Cot Cemetery. So, barely six months after his nephew William had died, George Dean joined the ranks of the fallen.

For the next nine days it was fairly quiet at Passchendaele before the attack resumed in earnest on 22 October. However, the rain continued to fall and men who fell off duckboards were in serious danger of drowning in the mud. Water was not the only thing falling from the skies though, and both sides shelled each other with dedication and intensity. On 19 October, the 7th Bedfords moved forward as relief for the Royal Fusiliers, and what they found was not a front-line trench but rather a series of water-filled shell holes. There were few duckboards and the men had to stand deep in mud, whilst enduring severe enemy shelling, until they were relieved on the evening of the 20th. On the morning of that day, a German shell had killed five of the Bedfords and seriously wounded two others, including Lance Corporal Charles William Ward, on this, the day before his thirty-eighth birthday. 'Flash' Ward, as he was known to his comrades, was taken back for treatment but he died two days later. In early November, a letter from Captain Phillips reached his wife at their Brook Street home telling of her husband's death:

We were holding the front line on the Flanders battle front and just before dawn on that day the enemy put down his usual artillery barrage. One shell fell into the small piece of trench dug and occupied by the section which your husband commanded, killing five and wounding two, of which your husband was one. His platoon immediately sent for the stretcher bearers, who came up, dressed him and carried him away in spite of the heavy artillery fire. He reached the dressing station, where his wounds were dressed and [he] was sent to the Casualty Clearing Station. It was with great sorrow that the Company and myself heard two or three days later that he had succumbed to his injuries, for there was no more popular man in the company than 'Flash'.

His death left his wife to raise their six children on her own. 'Flash' Ward rests today in Mendinghem Military Cemetery, close to the Casualty Clearing Station where he died.

Also in action in these first few days of the renewed attack were the 15th Sherwood Foresters, including Bernard Hugh Penfold who had risen from the ranks by 1917 to become an officer. Initially he had fought as a Private but had quickly shown leadership qualities and had been given the chance for officer training, which, when completed, saw him commissioned as a Second Lieutenant in the Sherwood Foresters. On 22 October they attacked at Houthulst Forest, a couple of miles to the north of Passchendaele Ridge, and their war diary records that they lost one officer and fifteen other ranks killed, together with 180 men missing. Bernard Penfold was that officer. His body was never recovered from the mud of the battlefield and he is commemorated at Tyn Cot. Before the war he had worked for Barclays Bank at both Huntingdon and then St Neots. He left a wife and three young children.

On the same day that Bernard Penfold died, thirty-two-year-old Private Samuel Smith of the 8th Norfolks went over the top with his battalion at 5.35 a.m., as rain fell steadily. The 8th Norfolks were in lead position as the attack went in at Poelcapelle with the objective of taking Noble Farm and the Brewery. In order to help the advancing troops, a 'Chinese attack' was employed which was designed to fool the Germans as to the exact location the assault was coming from. Wooden figures that could be raised and lowered added to the confusion and German troops rushed to man their front line in expectation of an attack that was not forthcoming. Instead, British artillery that had ceased just before the feigned attack now bombarded the German front line, catching many more enemy troops unprotected. The ruse worked, for the Norfolks captured the Brewery, with a second wave of the 10th Essex moving through and beyond the Norfolks to Noble Farm. Initially, Samuel Smith was posted as wounded and missing, and for almost a year there was uncertainty about his fate, but in September 1918 he was officially declared dead. Samuel Smith had been born in Eaton Socon but was living in St Neots in 1914 at 68 Russell Street with his wife, Adelaide, and, when conscripted in the summer of 1916, he was the proud father of a son, Sidney. Samuel Smith's body was never found and today he is commemorated at Tyn Cot.

Sapper George Gaunt.

On the very next day, another local man was added to the growing casualty list when Sapper George Gaunt, the son of William and Caroline Gaunt of River Terrace, Eynesbury and the husband of Lucy Gaunt, was killed. He had left Eynesbury to work in Surrey at the Epsom Asylum, and it was there that he had enlisted. The work of sappers was as dangerous as that of any soldier, as they worked at a variety of tasks, including trench work, mining and construction, in or close to the front line. Therefore their casualty figures were high, as artillery barrages, sniper's bullets and mortars took their toll.

Lucy Gaunt and her son Maurice visiting George Gaunt's grave in Ypres.

On 23 October, George Gaunt joined the list of those sappers killed, together with eleven others from the 11th Leicesters, Midland Pioneers. They were killed whilst digging under German trenches in the attempt to set a mine and blow up part of the German front line. George had only been overseas for six weeks when he died. He is buried in Ypres Reservoir Cemetery and his grave has the word *mizpah* inscribed at the bottom. *Mizpah* is a Jewish word meaning emotional bond between people who are separated, and it seems likely that his widow asked for it to be inscribed there.

Other local men were more fortunate in these first days of the battle for Passchendaele Ridge and survived their wounds. Sergeant Chas Sharman was hit in the thigh by shrapnel, and Privates Lionel Martin and Stanley Smith were both brought back to Britain for treatment in hospital. At Ypres, the fighting lulled for three days until the BEF attacked again on 26 October – but in those quieter days, Private Cyril Kisby of the 14th Warwicks was killed. Cyril Kisby came from Lincolnshire but had worked in St Neots in Armstrong's Drapers and had lodged in Bedford Street.

When the fighting resumed on the 26th, four more local men died, two from Eaton Socon, one from St Neots and one from Eynesbury. Lance Corporal Robert Drake was in the same battalion as Cyril Kisby and he was sniped as he went over the top on that Friday morning with the 14th Warwicks. In the confusion following the attack, his grave was lost. Jack Drake, as he was known, was another whose military career had begun with the Hunts Cyclists in 1915, but a year later he transferred to the Warwicks and found himself on the Somme. Now he was killed as the Warwicks attacked north of Gheluvelt towards Passchendaele Ridge at 5.40 a.m. Twenty-four-year-old Jack had been in Canada in 1914 but had returned home to Eaton Socon where his parents ran the post office on the Green.

The second Eaton Socon soldier killed on the 26th was thirty-two-year-old Private Fred Thornton of the 2nd Battalion, the Queens, who also attacked close to

George Gaunt's headstone.

Gheluvelt. As the Queens advanced, they were met by heavy enemy machine-gun fire and shelling, and were driven back to their starting position. Fred's wife Alice heard of his death when she received a letter from Captain W.G. Gibson of the Queens, telling that he 'was hit by a piece of shell during the recent advance, death being instantaneous' and that he 'did not suffer in any way'. Although he had volunteered in June 1915 when the Bedfords Recruiting March had come through Eaton Socon, he had not been sent overseas until just a month before he was killed. Once again there was no identified grave, even though Captain Gibson told how Fred Thornton had been buried with others killed from his company.

The third local man to die on 26 October was Private William Ashwell of St Neots, who was with Cyril Kisby and Jack Drake in the 14ᵗʰ Warwicks, following transfer from the Hunts Cyclists. William Ashwell had enlisted at Huntingdon towards the end of December 1915. Six months later he married Margaret Davis, who was widowed when her husband was hit by a German bullet as he advanced that Friday morning. He too has no known grave.

Private George Childs of Eynesbury had been wounded three times before he went over the top on 26 October, and bore scars on his right shoulder, his face and his left thigh. He was one of the few regular soldiers surviving, having been in action since Mons, initially with the 1ˢᵗ Bedfords but by 1917 with the 2ⁿᵈ Border Regiment. As with many soldiers returning from wounding, he was allocated to a regiment that needed 'topping up' and so found himself with the 2ⁿᵈ Border Regiment as they attacked south of the Menin Road at Gheluvelt on Friday, 26 October. The troops had a difficult task, having to advance over a marsh, cross the Krommebeck stream waist-deep in water and mud, and then face enemy pillboxes that bristled with machine-guns. The Borderers enjoyed some success, but were eventually driven back almost to their jump-off position by a German counter-attack. George Childs was killed just ten days after his twenty-sixth birthday, but this was not confirmed until early 1918 when his mother heard from the Red Cross. Private J. Mitchell gave the Red Cross a report which said:

> We went over at 6.00am and took our first objective, and then had to fall back to near our front line, which we held. On the way over I was alongside of Childs. I saw him hit about the groin. He crawled into a big crater where a lot of other wounded were … Some Germans were in a pill box near the crater, and they were sending rifle grenades towards the crater.

Another report told of George Childs being hit in the thigh and his wound being dressed by stretcher bearers, but he did not make it back to the dressing station. He too has no known grave.

Twenty-four hours later, Private William Chapman of the 1ˢᵗ Bedfords died as a result of his fourth wounding of the war. William Chapman had survived over three years at the front before he was fatally wounded, in late October, when hit in the neck by a German bullet. He had enlisted back in September 1914 and had served as a stretcher bearer since then. The three wound stripes that he wore on the sleeve of his tunic spoke volumes about the dangerous work carried out by stretcher bearers as they tried to help the wounded in No Man's Land and front-line trenches. Now, after getting through both the Somme and Arras, it was his turn for stretcher bearers to be called when he was shot near Zillebeke, Ypres. He was taken back through the lines and treated at a Canadian Casualty Clearing Station, but his life could not be saved and he was buried at Lijssenthoek Military Cemetery. Thirty-seven-year-old William Chapman had been born in Eltisley but was living with his wife in St Neots in 1914. News of his death reached St Neots on 4 November when his father, Samuel, received a letter at his Huntingdon Street home.

On 28 October, nineteen-year-old Bertie Waldock, a Private in the 9ᵗʰ Leicesters, was killed by enemy shellfire. Bertie had joined the army in February 1917 and had gone overseas later that year. He had initially been with the Army Service Corps but had then been drafted into the Leicesters where he served in the transport section, bringing food and ammunition to the front lines. Bertie's mother, Ada, heard of his death when she received a letter from Captain

Pascoe of the Leicesters, telling: 'He was killed suddenly by a piece of shell passing through his heart, and so his death was painless. He had only joined our battalion about three days before, and so it seems harder that he was taken.' Captain Pascoe went on to say that Bertie had been buried and that his diary was being forwarded, but the grave was subsequently lost.

Much better news arriving in St Neots in late October concerned brothers Arthur and Alfred Smith, who were both awarded medals for gallantry. Arthur, a stretcher bearer with the Royal Warwicks, won the Military Medal, whilst his brother Alfred, a company sergeant major with the Royal Fusiliers, had won the Distinguished Conduct Medal at Arras in June, but this was only now confirmed. In 1918 Arthur won a Bar to his MM when capturing a German machine-gun nest. Then it was learned that Private Sidney King from Eynesbury had also been awarded the Military Medal for Gallantry as a stretcher bearer. Private King had carried out his duties without regard for his own life over a period of four days, bandaging the wounded and carting the injured from the battlefield as enemy artillery fire rained down. Another stretcher bearer, Private John (Jack) Haynes of Wyboston of the Warwicks, also won the Military Medal. Sadly, in six months' time Jack Haynes was killed close to Ypres. Finally, the Military Cross was won by Chaplain James Tunstall, who was the Wesleyan minister in St Neots before the war. For sixty hours he had attended the wounded between 4 and 7 October at Broodseinde under heavy enemy shellfire, and he managed to bring many of those injured to dressing stations. He stayed at his post until all of the wounded had been brought in and treated.

Private William Cooper of Eaton Socon was with the Royal Fusiliers during the fighting for Passchendaele Ridge; he had a remarkable escape when he survived a piece of shrapnel hitting him in the back and coming out under his right arm. He wrote home to tell his wife of this and said that he was in hospital in France. John Chamberlain of Eynesbury, a Private with the Bedfords, was also wounded badly in late October and lay out on the battlefield for twenty-four hours in the pouring rain before he was brought in. For some time the wound in his left thigh gave his doctors serious concern but he pulled through. More fortunate was Gunner Joseph Baker, also from Eynesbury, who wrote home, telling: 'I have had several of my pals killed at my side, but I never received a scratch.' He also described how the rain made progress difficult, causing 'plenty of mud, knee deep' and saying how saddened he was to receive the *St Neots Advertiser* and read of so many local men being killed or wounded.

As the BEF slogged towards Passchendaele Ridge, the 4th Bedfords went forward on 30 October as the fight to take the ridge continued. Within their ranks were Privates Oscar Boon and Fred Foster and, by the time the battalion came out of the line on 1 November, both were dead. Oscar Boon was the younger brother of Edgar Boon, killed at the start of 1915 at Ypres; Oscar was initially reported as wounded but sadly that changed and he died almost three years later in the very same place. The 4th Bedfords attacked at 5.50 a.m. but as they struggled forward through the cloying mud they were hit by a savage German artillery barrage and suffered many casualties, only managing to advance between 150 and 200 yards, in which time they suffered casualties of fifty-two dead, 180 wounded and twenty-three missing. Twenty-year-old Oscar Boon had survived the Somme and Messines but now he fell at Ypres and, unlike his brother Edgar, he has no known grave. Fred Foster of Eynesbury was twice Oscar Boon's age, being forty years old when he was killed. He had survived the attack of the previous day but was fatally wounded by a stray bullet on the 31st. His sister heard from one of his comrades that he 'had just come through a great battle when a stray shot killed him instantly'. He was buried at La Brique Cemetery at Ypres.

October had been truly awful for the people of St Neots and the surrounding villages for this month had seen the highest number of casualties so far during the war, and although November was kinder in terms of those killed, it did not start on a good note. On the second day of the month, and thousands of miles away from the Western Front, twenty-two-year-old John Darrington of Wyboston was killed in action during the Third Battle of Gaza in Palestine.

The 5th Bedfords, nicknamed the 'Yellow Devils', were trying to capture the fortress of Gaza, the key to a successful advance northwards to Jerusalem, and were fighting the Turks, an enemy as deadly as the Germans. During the fighting, John Darrington's rifle jammed and, as he looked up, he was shot in the head by a Turkish sniper. The fighting at Gaza was brutal, with the Turks raising a white flag at one stage and then proceeding to open fire with a machine-gun as a platoon of the Bedfords advanced, killing most of them. Other 'Yellow Devils' were killed by their own artillery as they advanced too quickly. Gaza fell to the British on 7 November and John Darrington was one of those buried in Gaza War Cemetery.

In Flanders, the final push to take Passchendaele Ridge began on 6 November and, true to form, after dull but dry weather for just under a week, it started to rain as the troops attacked. Many soldiers even began to think that heavy artillery fire caused the rain to fall, as it continued until the fighting ceased on 10 November, when the Ridge was in British hands. Estimated casualties for the BEF over the 100 days of the campaign vary, but it is generally accepted that around 250,000 men were killed or wounded in the fighting that brought an advance of 5 miles. On the day the offensive was called off, twenty-seven-year-old Albert George, a Lance Corporal with the 2nd Battalion, Lancashire Fusiliers, was killed, just over two years after enlisting. Initially he was with the Army Service Corps but, as the front-line battalions began to suffer more and more casualties, he was transferred to the Lancashires. Albert George was born at Goodwick, close to Eaton Socon, but when war broke out he was a baker in Kettering with a wife, Nellie, and a young son, Cyril. Albert George was one of nine men with the Lancashires killed in these last days of the fighting for Passchendaele Ridge, and sadly his last resting place was lost, so today he is commemorated at Tyn Cot. Shortly after Albert George's death, his brother Harry arrived home on leave in Eaton Socon from the Middlesex Regiment to complete his recuperation from wounding.

A PRESENT FROM PALESTINE

'TO THE ALLIES WITH GENERAL ALLENBY'S COMPLIMENTS'

THE TURKEY:- "I wonder what Wilhelm said when he heard of this!"

Cartoon showing Turkey's loss of Gaza, 1917.

Some three weeks after the end of 3rd Ypres, nineteen-year-old Sidney Luff, the only son of Stephen and Eliza Luff of Eynesbury, was killed in one of those daily barrages that so epitomised the Western Front. He had been with the Hunts Cyclists before transferring to the 2nd Royal Berkshires, with whom he was wounded by shrapnel in the left leg in November 1916; this had necessitated hospital treatment for seven months. He returned to duty, fighting at Passchendaele, and was killed three weeks after the battle ended on 2 December. His name can be found at Tyn Cot on the back wall.

By the middle of November, with winter fast approaching, it was usual for the level of fighting to abate – as was the case at Ypres in 1914, and the Somme in 1916. However, Douglas Haig was not yet done with 1917 and, on 20 November at Cambrai, tanks en masse were used for the first time with stunning initial effect. Over 300 tanks went forward at 6.20 a.m., after a surprise hurricane bombardment from around 1,000

Lance Corporal Albert George.

guns, and achieved a breakthrough, with a 5 mile advance. Lessons had been learned from 3rd Ypres, with aircraft being a key feature of the assault, and they targeted, bombed and strafed German artillery and troops. The artillery on 20 November employed a technique known as 'predicted firing', which was certainly a great step forward from the Somme, for the gunners made use of aerial observation, increased understanding of trajectories, gunnery training and improved shells.

Linked to calculating the positions of German guns via flash spotting and sound ranging, the surprise bombardment on the morning of the attack was especially effective. The change from destructive to neutralising bombardment was a significant development, and would play a crucial role in 1918. If the effects of this artillery bombardment shocked the Germans, then the impact of an attack of over 300 tanks staggered them. The Germans were suspicious that an attack might be in the offing, but the BEF cleverly disguised the movement of tanks to forward positions by drowning out the noise of tank engines with aeroplanes flying over the front lines as the tanks advanced. Planning for the attack incorporated improved co-ordination of infantry, tanks, artillery and aircraft, which saw the BEF break the Hindenburg Line at Cambrai. When news of this reached Britain three days later, church bells were rung for the first time in many a year, and it was felt that victory was close. However, the higher ground that was Bourlon Wood was not taken and this had serious repercussions.

These tactical developments today would be described as 'all arms fighting' and they prompted a savage counter-attack from the German 2nd Army on 30 November. Here the Germans showed that they had developed their own tactics, and the use of 'storm troopers' featured prominently. This tactic had been two years in the developing and had been honed in fighting on the Eastern Front and saw crack troops advance quickly, skirting any serious resistance which was to be mopped up by other German troops assigned to follow the storm troopers. It was used with devastating effect just four months later when the Germans launched their Spring Offensive, the Kaiser's Battle. By the end of the first week of December 1917, the German 2nd Army had recovered the vast majority of the territory lost on 20 November. Cambrai saw casualty figures of around 40,000 for both the British and their German foes, but had also given both sides a tantalising glimpse of how the war might be won.

News of Cambrai casualties reached Britain in early December but, for St Neots, the first recorded death on 27 November came as a result of a wounding seven days before the actual battle began. Twenty-three-year-old Private Walter Cook was serving with the 12th Kings Liverpool Battalion when he was badly wounded on 13 November as enemy trench mortars rained down near Gonnelieu. The battalion retaliated and the German mortars fell silent,

DOING SOMETHING FOR HIM

THE KAISER:- "You must do something for me"
THE DENTIST:- "Certainly, Your Majesty" *(Aside).* "There are a few Million Americans who mean to do something for you soon, and when They've done it you'll have something worse than a toothache."

Cartoon published to show the impact of America's declaration of war on Germany in 1917.

Above: Lance Corporal Arthur Dobney. *Left:* Lance Corporal Arthur Dobney after being declared unfit for duty overseas. Here he is pictured as a military policeman in the UK.

but too late for Walter Cook who ended up in hospital at Rouen. His injuries were so extensive that he could not be saved, as the matron of the Red Cross Hospital told Walter's wife Flora: 'He had been unconscious all the day before, and died very peacefully. We were in such hopes that he would pull through, but his wounds were so many and the bleeding left him very weak.' Matron Riddell sent his pocket book, watch and cigarette case to his wife and let her know that he had been buried in Rouen, where he rests today.

Another Eaton Socon man died just before Cambrai. He was thirty-year-old Arthur Dobney, who had served for some time with the Bedfords before the war. He had re-enlisted in September 1915 but was not classified as A1 and so was deemed not fit for service overseas, being therefore assigned to the 3rd Bedfords, a 'reserve' battalion that spent the war on home defence and as a training battalion for men who were fit to go to the front. In early 1917 he became seriously ill and pleurisy saw him hospitalised for many weeks, leading to his discharge from the army. He returned to Eaton Socon, dying there two days before Cambrai, and was buried in St Mary's churchyard.

When the Germans counter-attacked at Cambrai, nineteen-year-old Geoffrey Addington was in the firing line as the 2nd Battalion, Durham Light Infantry were attacked close to Gouzecourt. As shells rained down, Second Lieutenant Addington was killed by an explosion while carrying a wounded man to safety at Cantaing. The Durhams' war diary for 30 November recorded: 'Enemy heavily shelled our line causing a number of casualties. 2nd Lt. Addington killed.' A week after Geoffrey Addington died, his parents, John and Ada, received an official telegram at their Eaton Ford home telling of their son's death just four weeks after his arrival in France. He had been commissioned in July 1917, after passing out of Sandhurst where he had become very adept in using Mills bombs, and he did in fact turn down the opportunity of becoming a Special Bombing instructor there in favour of going out to the Western Front. Geoffrey Addington was buried in Ribecourt British Cemetery, 6 miles south-west of Cambrai, and back in Eaton Socon a brass plaque in loving memory of him still adorns the south wall of St Mary's Church, although this is a replacement, as the original was destroyed when the church was severely damaged by fire in 1930.

Also facing the full fury of the German counter-attack was nineteen-year-old Frederick Barringer, entrenched with the 235th Company, Machine Gun Corps at Villers Guislain to the south of Cambrai. The German attack took the BEF by surprise, and storm trooper tactics drove the British back. Frederick Barringer was wounded in his left side, and was among around fifty men captured by the Germans. No news was received about him for four months, until his father James heard that his younger son had died on 30 December, a month after his capture. The letter from the War Office that reached their Eaton Socon home gave shellshock and his wound as the causes of death. James and Kate Barringer had now lost both their sons within the space of fifteen months. When the War Graves Commission began their work in the 1920s, Frederick Barringer's body was brought to Le Cateau Military Cemetery, where it rests today.

Other Eaton Socon soldiers serving abroad were fortunate in late November and early December, for they were in receipt of special parcels sent from the parish, containing soap, a pair of socks, a khaki handkerchief, a chocolate cake, cubes of Oxo, spearmint chewing gum, cigarettes and a tin of cocoa. As Christmas approached, these gifts were very welcome. Within a week, the Urban Council for St Neots and Eynesbury met to discuss sending similar parcels to soldiers from the town. Throughout Britain, the U-boat campaign was now having an impact and there were shortages in many areas, not least in the import of tea, and the International Stores prompted the people of St Neots to change their breakfast habits by drinking coffee instead. In the town, wounded soldiers from the Voluntary Aid Detachment Hospital gave a concert for their nurses and families on 19 December. Four days later, a memorial service was held at Eaton Socon Church for the forty-three men from the parish who had fallen in battle.

As 1917 closed, the war showed no sign of ending and the optimism of some serving at the front had waned, for Passchendaele changed the mood of many soldiers. Quite what 1918 would bring was anyone's guess, for although American troops were arriving in Europe in their thousands, they were not battle-hardened, and Russia's exit from the war meant that hundreds of thousands of German veterans were now released from the Eastern Front. In Russia, Petty Officer Ernest Ireland of St Neots was with an Armoured Car Squadron that had been supporting the Russians. Now that Russia had left the conflict, these men had to get back to Britain, and it was not until 1918 that they managed this, having to negotiate their exit with the newly-ruling Bolsheviks and then crossing the North Sea in a patrol boat. Ernest Ireland arrived home around 15 February 1918, after two years away, and was a most welcome sight for his family.

Meanwhile, Douglas Haig came under increasing pressure from David Lloyd George after Passchendaele and Cambrai, and the Prime Minister would have replaced him if a suitable candidate could have been found. The BEF itself was changing, as more and more conscripts filled its ranks. Many were just nineteen, and 1918 would exact a heavy toll of these young men.

Private Fred Barringer.

FIVE

⁓1918⁓
FROM DEFEAT TO VICTORY

At the start of 1918, the toll of the Great War for Huntingdonshire was made public, with the release of figures showing that up to the end of 1917, 646 men had been killed in action, whilst another 106 had died of wounds. These figures did not include Eaton Socon, for at this time the parish was part of Bedfordshire. Sadly, by the end of the conflict these numbers increased significantly. On the first Sunday of January, 'The Day of National Prayer' saw a large congregation gather in the parish church in St Neots to pray for men at the front, and perhaps those prayers were heard, for in early January news filtered through that many soldiers missing during the fighting at Cambrai were alive. Postcards from Privates Frank Harvey and John Barringer confirmed their capture by the Germans and they were now POWs, much to the relief of their families in Eynesbury and Eaton Ford respectively.

More good news followed when it was learned that local men had been awarded medals for bravery. Private Harold Markham of the Essex Regiment won the Military Medal at Cambrai even though he was gassed and shellshocked, but by Christmas he was back at the front. Then two officers of the Royal Field Artillery were awarded the Military Cross. St Neotian Lieutenant Douglas Vernon Tomson won his medal when the group of signallers he commanded came under heavy machine-gun and artillery fire. Around half of his men were wounded but he continually encouraged them to keep repairing the signal wire as shells broke it, and then he captured twenty enemy troops, using only his revolver. Just three months later, Lieutenant Tomson was wounded in the neck during the German onslaught that so nearly won them the war, and again his bravery was recognised for he was awarded a Bar to his MC. Lieutenant Victor Desborough was the brother of Mrs F. Butler, Eaton Socon, and he won his Military Cross when enemy shelling destroyed an ammunition dump close to his battery, injuring both the gunners and horses. As shells continued to fall, he organised the recovery of both men and horses.

January brought flooding to the St Neots area and there were concerns over the safety of drinking water so residents were advised to boil it before use. At Gamlingay, an inquest into a fatal air crash confirmed just how dangerous aircraft were in these formative years of the Royal Flying Corps. The pilot, Second Lieutenant Henry Hall from Northamptonshire, was killed in the crash as he lost control in fog. Aircraft were a familiar sight in the skies around St Neots, with planes regularly landing and being guarded by the St Neots contingent of the Hunts Volunteers. Percy Smith, a printer, was one such volunteer and on 1 January this Eaton Ford resident was asked to help start a grounded plane by turning the propeller. As he did so he slipped and two fingers of his right hand were struck off as the propeller engaged.

In France and Flanders no new major attacks took place, but the daily routine of shelling and trench raids continued and, of course, there were casualties. During the first week of January, news reached St Neots that Able Seaman Sam Smith was wounded by shrapnel in the right shoulder and leg, and Able Seaman George Basson had gunshot wounds to his left shoulder and head. It may seem odd that a sailor was serving at the front, but the Naval Division served as soldiers on the Western Front from May 1916 until the end of the war. Then, on 5 January, as the 2nd Bedfords were in the front line at Polderhoek, Ypres, Lance Corporal Charles Day of Eaton Socon was killed by shellfire, just as he was about to exit the trenches to go home on leave, even having his leave pass on his person. Charles Day was one of five men with the 2nd Bedfords killed that day, just over three years after he had volunteered. His grave was lost during the continued fighting and today he is commemorated at Tyn Cot.

Corporal Jack Cheeseman of Maltman's Villa, Eaton Socon was seriously wounded in January as part of one of his feet was blown off by an exploding shell. He was brought back to Blighty to hospital in Salisbury where his wife was able to visit him. This was the third time he had been wounded, and he had also been gassed on another occasion. News of other injured local soldiers came in mid-January and Privates Leslie Stocker, Herbert Breed and Ralph Abbott were wounded in the back, hand and thigh respectively.

On 18 January, nineteen-year-old Private Frank Oakley was also injured when the 9th Suffolks came under fire at Fremicourt, close to Cambrai. Frank Oakley was one of those who had responded when the Bedfords Recruiting March passed through Eaton Socon in the summer of 1915; initially he was with the 3rd Bedfords in Britain, until he was sent overseas to the 9th Suffolks. A week after he was wounded, his mother Alice received a letter from Captain England of the Suffolks, telling her that her son had been killed in action: 'Death was instantaneous, so he suffered no pain.' Only two men were wounded during the three days the Suffolks were in the front line and only Frank Oakley did not survive. He was buried at Beaumetz Cross Roads Cemetery, close to Cambrai.

News of other men was perhaps better. The parents of Private William Sharp of St Neots heard that their son was a POW in Germany, after receiving a letter telling of his wounding

Huntingdonshire's Fighters.

The "St. Neots Advertiser" publishes the following: The 5326 Huntingdonshire residents in the Army and Navy are contributed by the following parishes. (Of the total number 4 are women):—

Parish	No.	Parish	No.
Alconbury	56	Keyston	14
Alconbury Weston	32	Kimbolton	96
Abbotsley	19	King's Ripton	22
Abbots Ripton	22	Leighton	30
Alwalton	14	Molesworth	7
Brampton	106	Midloe	1
Buckworth	12	Morborne	8
Brington	2	Old Weston	7
Bythorn	13	Oldhurst	14
Barham	7	Orton Longneville	20
Buckden	104	Orton Waterville	15
Broughton	27	Offord Cluny	25
Bury	37	Offord Darcy	42
Bluntisham	36	Paxton, Little	12
Coppingford	3	Paxton, Great	23
Catworth	34	Pidley	24
Covington	4	Raveley, Little	6
Caldecote	1	Raveley, Great	11
Chesterton	15	Ramsey	494
Colne	23	Stukeley, Great	36
Connington	29	Stukeley, Little	35
Diddington	18	Staughton, Great	86
Denton	6	Spaldwick	22
Easton	6	Stow	11
Ellington	17	Southoe	17
Eynesbury	135	St. Neots	282
Eynesbury Hardwick	8	,, Rural	2
Elton	68	St. Ives	329
Earith	159	Somersham	121
Fenstanton	84	Sawtry	107
Fenton	3	Stilton	45
Folksworth	6	Sibson-cum-	
Fletton Rural	198	Stibbington	14
Farcet	102	Stanground	144
Gidding, Great	26	Toseland	11
,, Little	4	Tilbrook	29
,, Steeple	5	Tetworth	1
Great Gransden	37	Upton	11
Grafham	15	Upwood	26
Godmanchester	272	Woolley	6
Glatton	8	Waresley	19
Huntingdon	442	Woodhurst	18
Hartford	50	Wyton	12
Hamerton	12	Wistow	42
Hail Weston	25	Warboys	174
Holywell-cum-		Woodwalton	20
Needingworth	32	Woodston Rural	140
Houghton	32	Water Newton	11
Hilton	34	Winwick	10
Hemingford Abbots	30	Yelling	25
,, Grey	75	Yaxley	170
Holme	35		

The population of the county in 1911 was 55,577.

Numbers of those from Huntingdonshire serving in 1918. Eaton Socon is not included as it was in Bedfordshire then.

Lance Corporal Charles Day.

and capture at Cambrai. He informed them that he was getting better, and that he would appreciate his parents sending food, cigarettes, shaving equipment and a bar of soap, admitting, 'I have not had a wash with soap since I was captured.' Then it was learned that Lieutenant Barlow Woollcombe Smythe had won the Military Cross for bravery some six months earlier at Gaza, when the 5th Bedfords raided Umbrella Hill. Barlow Smythe had dashed across open ground, leading his men, and they had nullified a number of Turkish machine-gun positions, ensuring that the enemy could not fire on the rest of the advancing Bedfords. Barlow Smythe went on to survive the war and perhaps the award of the Military Cross was some consolation to his mother Fanny, who lived on the Green at Eaton Ford, for the death of Rudolph, her other son, at Gallipoli in 1915.

In St Neots, another military concert was held in early February and Barrett's Store started another War Savings Scheme. The St Neots Volunteers, a kind of First World War Dad's Army, were also pleased to receive their first Khaki uniforms and now looked more the part. However, a tragic event was about to unfold half a mile north of St Neots railway station on 13 February, as a troop train was making its way south from Gateshead to London. Aboard was Bernard Harrison, a Private with the 3rd Dublin Fusiliers who had enlisted under the alias of Bernard McElroy and had fought in France during the first month of the war. He was under arrest for desertion and, as the train passed through St Neots, he took drastic action by opening his carriage door and jumping out. His injuries were severe and doctors at the VAD Hospital could not save him. Witnesses told how he was not handcuffed as he had agreed to go back to France, but the carriage he was in was very smoky and he had stood up to open a window to let in fresh air. However, he pushed the carriage door open and, despite the efforts of the others in the carriage, he jumped, even though the train was travelling at 35 to 40 mph. An inquest reached a verdict of accidental death and his body was returned to his native Dublin for burial.

On 8 February, Private Arthur William Childs was in action with the 10th Royal Warwicks and was badly wounded when he was hit by a bullet on the inner right thigh. The wound did not heal and he became more and more seriously ill over the next four weeks, suffering delirium and further haemorrhaging. His condition deteriorated and he died on 5 March, and was buried close to the hospital in Rouen where he was being treated. His mother, Sarah, had written to the doctors who were tending him and the last she had heard was that, although he was very ill, there was still hope. Those hopes were dashed when official notification of his death reached the Eynesbury home of Arthur and Sarah Childs. Arthur Jnr had joined the Hunts Cyclists in October 1914 and had then gone abroad following his transfer to the Warwicks. He had fought on the Somme and at Arras, and had suffered from trench foot before sustaining the wound that killed him in 1918.

St Neots Local Defence Volunteers.

On 27 February, Private Alfred William Brace of the 15th Sherwood Foresters was helping to unload a wagon containing Stokes mortar bombs at 36th Divisional Salvage Dump at Ypres when one of the bombs was dropped. The explosion killed two soldiers immediately and injured six others, including thirty-five-year-old Alfred Brace. His wounds were so extensive that he died later that day and was buried close to Duhallow Dressing Station, north of Ypres. Alfred Brace had lived and worked in Eaton Ford for some time before he married and moved to Dover. The chaplain of the Sherwood Foresters wrote to his wife Alice: 'He was very badly wounded and died an hour or two after. We buried him in a nice grave, with a wooden Cross.' His sister Jessie Coleman, who lived locally, heard of his death during March.

The effects of rationing were hitting hard in these first few weeks of 1918 with meat, butter and margarine all added to the list of rationed items. Indeed, butchers in St Neots ran out of meat during the third week of February, and 'Sold out' signs appeared in their windows. Matters did not improve and most of these shops were unable to provide meat as the new week started, and they remained closed on Monday 18th and Tuesday 19th. The Ministry of Munitions advised people not to throw away old bones, but to sell them back to butchers so grease could be extracted. In Germany, a whole host of foodstuffs and raw materials were in short supply as the Royal Navy's blockade of German ports took hold, seriously affecting both their war effort and the morale of citizens. *Ersatz*, a German word meaning substitute, was in common usage as coffee was made from acorns, and tea from raspberry leaves. The only food that was in plentiful supply was the turnip but familiarity brought contempt, for there were only so many ways that this root vegetable could be cooked. Germans referred to the winter of 1917/1918 as 'the turnip winter'. Perhaps it was the thought of such deprivation that led to a German civilian, who had been interned in Britain at the start of the conflict, committing suicide as he was being repatriated in early 1918. The man in question cut his own throat on board a ship sailing from Boston, Lincolnshire to Holland on 9 January. Boston was the designated port for prisoner exchanges, and three trainloads of Germans had embarked for Rotterdam in return for an equivalent number of British trawlermen over the age of forty-five, captured at sea since 1914.

At the start of February, the *St Neots Advertiser* started a list of all of the local men entitled to the Mons Star Medal and Riband. Over the course of the next few months this register grew, providing information of how long these men had served, if they had been wounded or were indeed still alive. Those soldiers still active would have been pleased to receive the Mons Star, but a less than happy soldier was Private John Haigh of Russell Street, who wrote to the

Advertiser vehemently denying that he had joined up to get away from his wife, or that he had beaten her when last on leave and that he was glad to get back to France.

The war certainly occupied minds and thoughts during those dark winter days and, at the beginning of March, St Neots Council approved a scheme to raise £10,000 to pay for four aircraft. The first week of the month was designated 'Aeroplanes Week' and within five days £15,000 had been raised by the purchase of War Bonds and War Savings Certificates. Undoubtedly, the visit of a squadron of planes that dropped leaflets over the town in support of the scheme helped. In a less generous mood was the Bench at St Neots Petty Sessions that sat on 7 March and fined Lieutenant Reginald Pratt of the Royal Engineers 6s for cycling along the pavement in Cambridge Street. Special Constable Norman was the arresting officer and he had failed to be impressed when Lieutenant Pratt asked him to be a sport and say nothing!

March 1918 saw Germany's final attempt to win the war or secure a favourable peace. By this time, the Germany that Britain had gone to war against in 1914 had changed greatly, being now very similar to the military dictatorship associated with Hitler. Power within Germany now lay with General Erich Ludendorff, with the military controlling both civil and military life. The terms imposed upon a beaten Russia showed that this new Germany was intent upon creating a sizeable empire in the east, and Ludendorff was now the true master, with the Kaiser simply a figurehead.

Ludendorff could now call upon hundreds of thousands of battle-hardened veterans from the Eastern Front, and thus easily outnumbered the combined French and British Armies on the Western Front. The key, as he saw it, was to break these original foes before the full impact of America's intervention could be realised. Millions of American Doughboys were reaching Europe but, as yet, they were not battle ready, and Ludendorff gambled all on breaking the British and French, and securing a favourable peace before the Americans could make an impact. His key card was the use of tactics he believed would bring mobility to the war and would drive a decisive wedge between the British and their French allies. If he could break the Allies' line where the two armies met, then he was convinced that the British would be forced to retreat northwards towards the Channel and the French would see surrender as their only option as they fell back towards Paris.

Storm troopers – men chosen especially for their aggression and trained to move quickly, independently and to achieve maximum infiltration – were the key to success. If they met serious resistance they were instructed to bypass it, leaving it to be mopped up by following, slower troops. Short, hurricane bombardments, so favoured by the British and French, were used, with a proliferation of gas shells, but no tanks featured. The attack's focus was St Quentin, and the troops that bore the brunt of the German offensive were the BEF of Gough's 5th Army.

For the past three years the BEF had been used to taking the offensive, and there was a lack of experience or familiarity in the use of defensive tactics. Gough's 5th Army, on 21 March, was also seriously depleted and had just extended the front that it covered, taking over a considerable section from the French. Actual numbers of men were also reduced, as five divisions had been sent to support the Italians, and the 5th Army at St Quentin was certainly below strength. Soldiers later told that they had company strength to cover an area that previously would have been covered by a battalion. British soldiers were also unfamiliar with the concept of elastic defence, which saw the battlefield divided into zones, notably a forward zone and a battle zone. The forward zone contained a series of redoubts connected by trenches. These were not supposed to be held indefinitely, but rather to inflict damage on the advancing enemy, and then the troops were to pull back to the battle zone, where the real fighting was to occur. It would be something of an understatement to say that the BEF at St Quentin did not fully comprehend this, for many of the 5th Army fought to the bitter end on 21 March, or until surrender.

At 4.40 on the morning of 21 March, almost 6,500 guns opened up, supported by around 3,500 trench mortars, and the storm troopers attacked. The combination of such a bombardment and early morning mist worked very well for the Germans, and their storm troopers overran or slipped by the redoubts. The fog hindered British artillery, which couldn't home in on the advancing German soldiers entering the battle zone. German artillery methodically shelled the British rear areas, causing serious problems for communication and counter-battery fire.

Unsurprisingly, the 5th Army fell back and by the end of the day the Germans had advanced significantly, taking around 100 square miles of the British front, and the static warfare of the last four years was broken. The BEF suffered greatly, with 7,500 killed, over 10,000 wounded and almost 20,000 captured. However, the Germans had suffered around 40,000 casualties, with most coming from their elite storm troopers. Significantly, although the British had been pushed back and severely stretched, they had not broken here or at Arras where Byng's 3rd Army was holding firm. Over the next few weeks the battle raged, and the Germans advanced around 40 miles, crossing the old Somme battlefields and nearing Amiens. However, Amiens did not fall and this was crucial to British resistance. On 11 April, during the BEF's and Haig's darkest hour, the commander-in-chief issued a special Order of the Day that was almost Churchillian in both message and style:

> There is no course open to us but to fight it out. Every position must be held to the last man: there must be no retirement. With our backs to the wall and believing in the justice of our cause each one of us must fight on to the end.

During April, May, June and July, Ludendorff desperately changed the focus of his attack, trying to make the crucial break that would divide the French and the British, but eventually the initiative shifted. On 14 April, the Allies agreed that Foch should be made General-in-Chief of the Allied armies and immediately the effects of this were seen, as Foch rotated troops from the front line, giving besieged British soldiers relief, and also moving French troops to take over sections of the front under attack. What was also noticeable was increasing indiscipline within the ranks of the advancing Germans when they captured Allied supply dumps and found them full of food and drink. This contradicted all they had been told about Allied troops suffering the same shortages that they did. Unsurprisingly, they looted these, and the impetus of their attacks suffered. There was also the problem of supplying troops who had advanced so far. The Allies, having taken and absorbed the blow, were now ready for the counter-attack and this came on 8 August, and was the start of the 100 Days that brought the war to an end.

Men from the St Neots area felt the full fury of the German assault and there were casualties, as the *Advertiser* seemed to indicate on 29 March under the heading: 'The Gigantic Battle in France'. Over the next few weeks, a column in the paper entitled 'News of our soldiers and sailors' expanded considerably as reports of the fate of local men reached the town. The 2nd Battalion, Durham Light Infantry were right in the firing line and at 5 a.m. on 21 March they were hit by a tremendous artillery barrage of high explosive and gas shells that continued for the next five hours. The Durhams' front line was wiped out and by 10.30 a.m. the Germans reached battalion HQ, but here they were halted and driven back 150 yards. By mid-afternoon, however, the situation became critical as the battalion was almost surrounded, yet they kept fighting and held the Germans at bay until orders were received to withdraw. Of the battalion that held the line that day, only three officers and 128 other ranks answered the roll call that night; 121 were dead. Among the dead was Private Donald Chadwick of St Neots, who had originally been with the Army Service Corps but was with the 2nd Durham Light Infantry in 1918. He was buried and has a grave at Vaulx Hill Cemetery near Bapaume.

Also killed on the 21st when the Germans attacked at Gauche Wood, near Cambrai, was twenty-year-old William Smith of the Machine Gun Corps. He had enlisted in 1915, had gone overseas with the Bedfords in July 1916, and had fought at Arras, Ypres and Cambrai; on one occasion he was gassed, when a German bullet broke his gas mask. His mother heard of his death when she received a letter from Lieutenant Darling of the MGC, telling:

> He was one of the gun team situated in the front line at Gauche Wood on the 21/3/18. That morning the enemy captured Gauche Wood, since when no news of any of the team has been received … I think all of the men in the team preferred death to surrender.

The men of the MGC referred to themselves as the 'Suicide Club' as they were targeted by enemy artillery for their killing power and any machine-gunner was usually dispatched quickly, if taken.

Five days later, the 7th Northants came under fierce attack near the village of Meharicourt, on the Somme, and had to fall back as the Germans attacked in force, just before midday. Within their ranks was twenty-nine-year-old Private William Gray, a Peterborough man who had moved to St Neots where he joined up in 1915 under the Derby Scheme. Initially he was reported as missing, but that changed five months later when it was confirmed that he had been killed. On the following day, Guardsman Harry Sharman's war ended when he was killed close to Arras, at the northern end of the German attack. Harry Sharman had volunteered in September 1914 at Stockton-on-Tees, where he was working as a tram conductor. He had been on the Western Front since 1915 and had certainly seen plenty of action, having fought at Loos, the Somme, Arras and Cambrai. Indeed, he was wounded in September 1916 at Guillemont and it was not until 1917 that he returned to the front. In April, at their Eynesbury home, his parents received unwelcome news from Chaplain Lyttelton informing them that their son was dead and buried. That grave was subsequently lost and today he is commemorated on the Arras Memorial.

On the last day of March, the 1st Royal Fusiliers were defending the line north of Gommecourt, between the Somme and Arras, when they came under attack. Company Sergeant Major Alfred Smith, DCM, had only just returned to the ranks after recovering from wounds and now he was killed instantly, as the Fusiliers resisted the German attack. Thirty-seven-year-old Alfred Smith was one of six brothers serving; his wife Sarah heard of his death during early April, at their East Street home. Alfred Smith was a Territorial before the war and, following mobilisation, became an instructor for the New Armies until late 1916. He had won the DCM, an award second only to the Victoria Cross, and had been wounded in the chest and arm at Arras in 1917. Now he was killed on Easter Sunday 1918 and sadly his grave was never relocated. Today he is commemorated on the Arras Memorial.

As April began, the intensity of the German attack increased and Gough's 5th Army came under increasing pressure. As they retreated it became difficult to keep track of what was happening to individual soldiers, for the German advance was rapid and men lost contact with their battalions as they retreated. Most soldiers simply had to walk to escape the advancing Germans, as Private Fred Collins of Eynesbury told in a letter home in early April: 'We have been marching since Sunday night, so you can tell how I feel. We are out of the way of the Germans now.' At least the family of Fred Collins knew he was alive. For other worried relatives these were very difficult times, not knowing what had happened to their menfolk, and it sometimes took months for their actual fate to be discovered. Private Alfred Huckle of Eaton Ford was missing, reported wounded, as was Private Frank Cook of St Neots, but their whereabouts could not be traced.

One person fighting for his life during these first days of April was twenty-nine-year-old Gunner Charles Hawkins from Eaton Socon. He was badly wounded on 21 March close to St Quentin, the heart of the German attack, as the Royal Garrison Artillery were targeted by enemy guns. Charles Hawkins lost that fight on 9 April, dying of his wounds and leaving a wife, May, and five children. Later, his wife received a letter from his officer, Lieutenant Edward Whinfawes, telling how Charles Hawkins had died:

He was killed by a very large German shell which fell in the battery about 5 o'clock on the morning of the 9th. It may be a comfort to you to know that he was killed instantaneously and suffered no pain.

Lieutenant Whinfawes went on to say that the men of the battery would like to send her a small sum of money, for they knew there were five children and they hoped that this would help with bills. The tragedy did not end here, for just over five months later May Hawkins died in Irthlingborough, where they had lived before the war.

On 9 April, the Germans changed the emphasis of the attack and Ypres now became their focal point. For the next three weeks, the British 1st Army faced the onslaught, and five days into the Lys Offensive, as the attack was known, thirty-two-year-old Jack Haynes of Eaton Socon was shot dead as the British defended Nieppe Forest against overwhelming numbers of Germans. The fighting here was called the Battle of Hazebrouck and Jack Haynes was with the 14th Royal Warwicks, working as a stretcher bearer, for which role he had won the Military Medal in 1917. Exactly what happened to him was revealed when his friend, George Bailey, wrote to Jack's parents:

Gunner Charles Hawkins.

It is with great sorrow that I have to write to tell you that dear Jack was shot by a sniper on the Sunday morning, 14th April, and he passed away almost immediately afterwards. I think I am right in saying that he suffered no pain in those few brief moments, which I shall never forget, losing one of the best friends I have ever had. Jack was always very popular in the Company, bright and cheerful everywhere, and we will miss him very much. He was buried close to where he fell.

Jack Haynes was killed by a German marksman who was firing at the British from a house within the forest that the Germans had presumably occupied as they advanced. His grave was lost as the Germans continued their assault and today he is commemorated on the Ploegsteert Memorial. Also killed on 14 April was Private Geoffrey Wagstaffe, born in Eynesbury but living with his parents in South Africa in 1905. He was killed in action with the South African Brigade, fighting at Bailleul, close to the Belgian border.

These worrying days of April brought more news of local men, and Military Medal winner, Frank Cook of Eaton Ford, had been wounded in the right arm. From St Neots, Private Herbert Smith was also wounded and Lance Corporal Bert Cambers had been captured by the enemy. Other POWs included Private William Usher of Eaton Ford and Trooper Sidney Fisher of St Neots, who was not a prisoner in Germany but incarcerated thousands of miles away by the Turks in Palestine.

By the third week of April, the Germans were pressing the BEF hard along much of the Western Front and were advancing towards the old Somme battlefields, where so many thousands of both British and German soldiers had died in 1916. The ground was still marked by old trench lines and shell holes and the BEF fought desperately to hold the enemy back. The town of Albert that had been the operational centre for the BEF throughout 1916 fell to the Germans in April and the Golden Virgin that sat on top of the Basilica finally fell. The statue was visible for miles

Private Jack Haynes MM.

Private Jack Haynes MM later in the war.

around and, when German gunfire had caused it to lean precariously in 1915, it had been shored up with steel wires to prevent it falling, as the story was that if it fell, the war would end. The French engineers who secured it in January 1915 did not want this as Germany still occupied much of Northern France then. By 1916 the legend had grown that the side that brought it down would lose the war. Now, in April 1918, the statue was brought down by British artillery after Albert was lost, for they feared the Germans would use it as an observation tower. Both stories proved to be untrue, for the war did not end and the British did not lose.

As the Germans advanced on Albert, thirty-four-year-old Private Sidney Harris was with the 10th Sherwood Foresters at Mesnil, close to the town, when they came under severe enemy shell-fire. The barrage was so great that all communication was lost between the front-line Foresters and battalion HQ, and the fate of men became hard to ascertain. What was certain was that Sidney Harris had gone missing in action on 21 April and it was not confirmed that he was dead until after the end of the war. Sidney Harris had joined the 7th Bedfords in late 1915, going over to France the following year, and was seriously wounded in 1917. After recovering, he returned as one of those who 'topped up' battalions that were short of men, and he was sent to the 10th Sherwood Foresters, with whom he died on that third Sunday of April. He has no known grave and this Eaton Socon man is commemorated on the Pozieres Memorial, near Albert.

As the fighting raged, news of more men reached St Neots, revealing that six others had been killed by the end of April, and another had died in altogether different circumstances. On 24 April, Privates William Chamberlain, Albert Cross and George Jackson were killed in action; William and Albert with the 7th Bedfords and George with the Royal Fusiliers. The Bedfords had gone into action south of Albert, at Villers Bretonneux; the BEF and the Australians stood their ground, since the fall of this town would be likely to lead to the capture of Amiens by the Germans and this would be catastrophic for the Allies. The Germans attacked, using tanks for the first time, and Villers Bretonneux fell, but a counter-attack was ordered and at 10 p.m. British and Australian troops went forward. In the darkness confusion reigned and the Germans broke so that Villers Bretonneux was recaptured. The Bedfords suffered sixteen dead, 108 wounded and seventy missing. William Chamberlain of Eynesbury and Albert Cross of Eaton Socon were listed among the missing, but that was later changed to killed in action. William Chamberlain's body was recovered and rests today at Villers Bretonneux, but twenty-year-old Albert Cross has no known grave and is commemorated at Pozieres. The 7th Bedfords were part of the 18th Division that attacked that day. The other British division was the 58th and in its ranks was Private George Jackson of St Neots, who was serving with the 1st Royal Fusiliers after being transferred from the Hunts Cyclists. He too was killed in action but, unlike William Chamberlain, his body was never found and his name is yet another inscribed at Pozieres on the Somme.

Much further north, close to Arras, the British 3rd Army continued to resist the German onslaught and, on the day before Villers Bretonneux, twenty-three-year-old Andrew Trapp, a lieutenant with the Royal Field Artillery, was killed in action. Andrew Trapp was the son of Revd Charles Trapp, vicar of Thurleigh, and had been born in Moscow before Charles and his wife Olga moved back to Britain and set up home in Bushmead, close to St Neots. Andrew was commissioned just a year before he was killed and had made a very positive impression since then. His commanding officer wrote to his parents telling them that 'his death is a very keen blow to every officer, n.c.o. and man in the battery'. He is buried at Anzin-St Aubin British Cemetery at Arras.

A fifth local man was killed on 24 April, not on the Western Front but at Belper in Derbyshire. Graham Achurch had been in the Far East at the start of the war with the Singapore Volunteer Artillery but he had returned home in 1916 and had been commissioned in the Royal Flying Corps. While training as a pilot, he was killed when his aircraft crashed at night. His body was brought back to St Neots, where his brothers and sisters still lived, and was buried in the town's cemetery.

Plaque to Lieutenant Andrew Trapp in Thurleigh church.

The last local man to die during April was also far away from the Western Front, for Sergeant Walter Matthews was with the 13th Hussars in Mesopotamia when killed in action on the 28th. Walter Matthews was a professional soldier who had seen service in India for ten years before 1914, then fighting in France during 1914 and 1915, and finally heading to Mesopotamia, where he won the Military Medal. Shortly after the award he contracted smallpox and had only just returned to action when he was killed. News of his death reached his parents' home in Bedford Street, St Neots during May.

In June 1915, the Byatt family of Little Barford Road, Eynesbury had lost the first of their serving sons when Martin died of his wounds. Now a second son, nineteen-year-old Harry, was killed close to the Belgian border. Harry had joined the Hunts Cyclists when under age in June 1915, following his brother's death. He had gone overseas with the 1st Bedfords, had been wounded in France and had served in Italy. On 4 May he was out with a wiring party near Nieppe Forest when the enemy began to shell No Man's Land. Eight of the Bedfords were injured and Martin died. His parents heard this when they received a letter from the Bedfords' chaplain, telling that Harry 'was out with a wiring party when he was badly wounded by a shell late on the evening of the 4th, and died of wounds on the 5th'. He was buried behind the lines, resting today in Tannoy British Cemetery.

Back in Britain, the list of which cuts of meat could be bought without meat coupons changed and now included all sorts of cuts which today many would find unpalatable but in 1918 would have made tasty meals. St Neotians could now enjoy tripe, lights (lungs), calves' heads and feet, pigs' feet, chitterlings (intestines), sheep heads, ox heels, cow heels and sheep feet. If these meats were now available other foodstuffs were about to be rationed, with lard added to the list in July.

By 1918 the condition known today as shellshock had been recognised by the British Military, and even if there was treatment, the men who suffered from it were not always viewed with sympathy, for soldiers were often advised to deal with it in a 'manly way'. The condition affected thousands of men, and not all of them were new to the horrors of war. Alfred Chapman, a veteran of seventeen/eighteen years, had fought in the Boer War and had not been slow in joining up when war broke out in 1914. He was readily accepted and served on the Western Front with the Royal Engineers before being traumatised badly in 1916 when he was buried alive after an enemy shell exploded. Although he was dug out, he was deeply distressed, and shellshock was diagnosed, causing paralysis of the brain. When brought back to Britain, he was initially treated at the First Eastern Hospital in Cambridge, and then six months later he was transferred to Fulbourn Asylum which had started to look after shellshock cases. He died there and was buried in St John's churchyard, Moggerhanger. This forty-eight-year-old left a wife and seven children. As if to recognise the financial hardship being experienced by both widows and disabled soldiers, the Hunts War Pensions Committee implemented new improved rates from 1 May.

In France and Flanders, the German attack continued to affect serving St Neotians. Sidney Haynes was badly wounded by shrapnel in his back, Bertie Tassell was missing in action and Jonathan Darrington of Wyboston was wounded and a POW. News that Privates Frank Murfin, Thomas Thody, Arthur Cannon, Clarence Searle and John Hawkins were also POWs brought

Lance Corporal Albert Watts.

some relief to their worried families. Better news concerned Private John Sandever of Eaton Ford, who won the MM for his work as a stretcher bearer, bringing in men under shellfire for a period of over eight hours.

On 25 May, north of Albert, the 4th Bedfords attacked at Forceville, taking the offensive when a raiding party went out to German lines. Three officers and six other ranks were killed, with eleven missing and thirty-four wounded. Among the dead was Private Bertie Watts of Eaton Socon who had been on the Western Front for almost three years, initially with the 7th Bedfords and then with the 4th. During that time he was wounded and gassed, and had shown bravery at Ypres in December 1915, when he was commended by the Brigadier General of the 18th Division, of which the Bedfords were a part. On that day, the Bedfords were entrenched close to a mine that was being dug under the German line and they were hit by rifle grenades and 'whizz bangs'. The Bedfords responded in kind, and their artillery hit the Germans hard. It was during this exchange that Bertie Watts distinguished himself. In the summer of 1916 he received a certificate from Winston Churchill, Secretary for War in which he was mentioned 'in dispatches' by the Commander-in-Chief of the BEF, Douglas Haig, 'for gallant and distinguished service in the Field'. Now his war ended, as his father read in the letter from the Bedfords' chaplain, H.G. Smith: 'Your son … was killed by machine-gun fire, death being instantaneous.' Sadly, Bertie Watts' grave was lost during the continuing fighting and today he is commemorated at Pozieres.

During the spring of 1918, an even deadlier foe than the Germans and their allies made its first appearance, going on to kill more people than the combined totals of all of the combatants in the Great War. The first cases of La Grippe, or Spanish flu, were seen in March 1918 and it had killed 25-50 million people by the time it abated in 1919. Unusually for flu it struck the young harder than the elderly, and by June 1918 it was having a devastating effect on Allied and Axis soldiers alike.

On 9 June, twenty-one-year-old Trooper Frank Adams from Eaton Ford became the second of four serving brothers to die, when he passed away at Boulogne Hospital. The official cause of death was pleurisy and tuberculosis of the lungs, but it seems likely that La Grippe had struck. Frank Adams had enlisted in 1915 and had been in France for two years when he died. He is buried in Wimereux Military Cemetery close to Boulogne.

On the following day, twenty-year-old Corporal Reginald Gentle died of pleurisy in hospital in Carlisle, after returning from Italy where he had been taken ill. His parents lived in Basmead near Eaton Socon and they rushed to Carlisle as his condition worsened, arriving just days before he died. Reginald Gentle had joined up in 1915 and was with the 1st Norfolks, supporting the Italians, when he became ill. His body was brought back to Eaton Socon and he was buried there with full military honours in St Mary's churchyard.

Also serving in Italy was Lance Corporal Charles Jones, who was with the 11th Sherwood Foresters when the Austrians attacked on 15 June in what became known as the Battle of Asiago. Initially this attack drove the Allies back before they recovered. Charles Jones was killed on the first day of the Austrian attack and his parents heard their son had died shortly afterwards. Twice before they had received news that their son was wounded, but now he was dead and twenty-eight-year-old Charles, who had played for Eynesbury Rovers, was buried in Granezza British Cemetery. Nine days later another Eynesbury family was grief-stricken when Gunner Frederick Ibbett died in Northumberland Military Hospital, about five weeks after being gassed in France. Fred Ibbett was conscripted in early 1918 and was with the Royal Field Artillery when they came under attack in May 1918. Twenty-eight-year-old Fred was with a comrade in a dugout when it was hit by a mustard gas shell and, unsurprisingly, was badly affected, for mustard gas was the most lethal of all gases used in the Great War, causing eye problems, vomiting, and internal and external bleeding as the gas began to affect the bronchial tubes. Victims usually died a very painful death within five weeks. Vera Brittain – who later gained literary acclaim with her book *Testament of Youth*, which told of her work as a nurse during the war – wrote in her diary how this gas affected soldiers: 'Great mustard-coloured blisters, blind eyes, all sticky and stuck together, always fighting for breath, with voices a mere whisper, saying that their throats are closing and they know they will choke.' Fred Ibbett's wife and mother were with him when he died and he too was brought home and buried in St Neots Cemetery. On 30 June, a memorial service was held in Eynesbury Church for both of these soldiers.

July brought news of more gallantry awards for local men. Regimental Sergeant Major George Flint of Eynesbury won the Military Medal for resisting the German advance during May, whilst Sidney Hoitt's medal was presented publicly to his widow, two years after his death on the Somme. In that part of France, just to the north of Albert, the 2nd Bedfords were entrenched at Bouzincourt and, on the last day of June, had carried out a successful attack, advancing under a smokescreen and a Stokes mortar barrage, taking all their objectives and capturing twenty prisoners and three machine-guns. On 1 July they were counter-attacked by the Germans and were driven out of the captured enemy trenches. The fighting then see-sawed, as the Bedfords launched their own counter-attack which was followed by another German one. The Bedfords hung on, bravely resisting until enemy shellfire drove them out, by which time they had suffered 153 men killed, wounded or missing.

Private Charles Wiles, a twenty-four-year-old from Eaton Socon, was among those killed on 1 July, almost two years after going over to France. Charles Wiles, a married man, initially with the Hunts Cyclists, had fought with the Bedfords during the later stages of the Somme in 1916 where he was wounded in the hand. He returned to duty and fought against the

Private Charles Wiles.

Germans as they advanced close to Ypres and the Aubers Ridge in April and May 1918. Now, near Albert, he had gone missing in action. His wife, Lillian, wrote to his battalion asking for information and received a letter from his platoon commander, Lieutenant Fielden, saying: 'He was killed on 1 July and I regret to say it was impossible to recover his body.' Indeed that remained the case and Charles Wiles is commemorated at Pozieres.

By July, Ludendorff's offensives had run out of steam and the Allies prepared to counter-attack. The German Army was badly affected by Spanish flu and food shortages and, in addition, the American Army was now starting to play a fuller role, for in late June they won their first battle in clearing Belleau Wood. However, their casualties were high, with losses of 11,000, as they attacked with the same kind of bravado, tactical naïvety and enthusiasm shown by Kitchener's Armies on the first day of the Somme. Then, on 4 July, the Australians attacked at Hamel using 'all arms tactics' that saw infantry, aircraft, tanks and artillery all coordinated. It was a resounding success that would be repeated with devastating effect in just over a month at Amiens.

In July in St Neots, a regatta for wounded soldiers was held, and on the 23rd another soldier died of illness rather than on the battlefield, when thirty-year-old Private Charles Conquest passed away at home. Charles Conquest had served with the 3rd Northants, but had been ill for some time when he died of bronchitis, and again it seems likely that Spanish flu played a part. He was buried in St Neots Cemetery on 27 July.

As August began, thoughts in St Neots turned towards bringing in the harvest and German POWs were used to supplement the work force. These POWs were paid and it was agreed that they could use their wages to buy any food that was not rationed, which was a sharp contrast to the case for British POWs in Germany.

In the town, tragedy struck when nineteen-year-old Vera Baylis of Filey, Yorkshire died of diabetic asthma whilst staying with her fiancé's family. Vera was engaged to William Bradford, who she had met when he was stationed on the East Coast in 1916 with the Hunts Cyclists. Meanwhile, in Macedonia, twenty-one-year-old Corporal Norman Seward's war was about to end when he was killed during a training flight whilst acting as an observer in an Armstrong Whitworth FK8. The pilot, Lieutenant Gerald Paxton, was also killed. Norman Seward, the only son of St Neots' businessman William Seward, had fought with the Machine Gun Corps during the East Africa campaign and was then transferred to the RAF after being injured in a motor accident. He was training for a commission when he was killed.

In France, 8 August saw the beginning of the end of the Great War when the Allies launched their counter-attack. On this day, the BEF, together with the Canadian and Australian Corps, began the offensive that lasted exactly 100 days and forced Germany to sue for peace. In these 100 Days, the BEF achieved a series of stunning victories showing how tactically adept they had become in employing artillery, infantry, aircraft and tanks together – the so-called 'all arms attack'.

The offensive began at Amiens, and Ludendorff described 8 August in his memoirs as 'the black day of the German Army in the history of this war'. General Rawlinson, who had led the 4th Army on the Somme in 1916, led it again here and sent in ten Dominion divisions and four British divisions, together with one American division, supported by both cavalry and over 400 tanks, against Ludendorff's 2nd Army. The planning had been meticulous and the counter-battery work was exemplary, for virtually every German gun emplacement was nullified by Allied gunners. British artillery had evolved strongly since 1916, and by 1918 it was proving to be a tool to win the war. Shells now had graze fuses that exploded on impact, and counter-battery work was greatly improved, especially in locating, targeting and destroying enemy guns. Allied artillery now had a definite edge, and attacking Allied troops were now not subjected to the deadly German shelling that had been experienced on 1 July 1916 as they advanced across No Man's Land. Equally significant was the evolution of the creeping barrage and the box barrage. These both offered increased protection in the crossing of No Man's Land and consolidation of captured enemy trenches. It was usual for the creeping barrage to be made up of a third shrapnel, a third high explosive and a third smoke, and when it worked it worked very well indeed. The successful employment of the creeping barrage meant that there was no repetition of the slaughter on the Somme and the BEF could advance in greater safety. If attacks succeeded then a box barrage was laid down which enclosed tired troops behind a protective screen of exploding shells that counter-attacking Germans could not penetrate. Box barrages were also used during assaults by the BEF as a method to isolate sections of the enemy front line, and to prevent any German reinforcements from reaching the area under attack.

Lessons learned over the last two years resulted in much more sophisticated tactics being used at Amiens for, in addition to creeping barrages and box barrages, flash spotting and sound ranging had taken counter-battery work to an entirely different level. Machine-gun barrages were commonplace and the emphasis on the platoon meant that each man knew his job – whether Lewis gunner, bomber or rifle grenadier – and worked as a team. Together with more efficient tanks and more belligerent aircraft, this proved to be a winning combination, allied to the fact that achievable targets were being set by those in charge.

The build-up to Amiens saw Rawlinson cleverly disguise the point of attack, and the Germans were certainly deceived, having no idea that the Canadian Corps, of whom the Germans were decidedly wary, would play a leading part at Amiens. He had let it be seen and known that the Canadians were in Flanders, but then secretly the majority of the Corps were moved south in sealed trains, leaving two battalions behind in Flanders to maintain the subterfuge. When the attack went in at 4.20 a.m. on 8 August, these 'shock troops', as the Canadians have been described, were to the fore, as were the Australians. They were very ably supported by the BEF, but the Canadians were much fresher, having generally been spared from the German spring onslaught. A hurricane bombardment from over 200 guns and a dense morning mist aided the British, Canadians and Australians in overrunning much of the German line, with advances of up to 8 miles being achieved and, significantly, only 9,000 casualties being suffered. In comparison, the Germans lost around 12,000 killed, whilst another 15,000 were prisoners and 400 artillery guns were lost. Ludendorff's words were no exaggeration.

The Great War was primarily an artillery war and the protection given from one's own guns was vital for advancing infantry. In order to maintain that protection, the guns had to be moved forward with the advance. Therefore, although the advance at Amiens was very deep it did not go so far as to be out of the reach of the British guns. Another key tactical improvement saw the use of a series of rolling attacks with limited bite and hold tactics; if resistance was met, the BEF shifted the focal point of attack. When the Germans offered stiff resistance after the initial Amiens attack, Byng's 3rd Army went into action between Arras and the Somme. This tactic prevented the Germans from moving support troops around and they did not know where the next blow would come. During August, the emphasis moved from Amiens to Arras and then back down to Albert, before finally hitting the Germans on the Scarpe.

Along the whole of the Western Front the German Armies began falling back, and by the end of September the BEF had driven them back to the Hindenburg Line – but not without cost, for the British 3rd and 4th Armies suffered casualties on a day-to-day basis that were worse than during the Somme campaign of 1916. When the Hindenburg Line was reached, around 190,000 men from 3rd and 4th Armies had been killed or wounded. The Germans retreated in an organised fashion and their machine-guns exacted a terrible toll from the advancing British, which now included large numbers of conscripted young men with limited experience of fighting. The ages of many of those from St Neots who died in these last 100 Days confirms this.

On 29 September, the British 4th Army took on its most difficult challenge in storming the Hindenburg Line. A four-day bombardment preceding the attack saw almost a quarter of a million shells fall on German positions that were daunting to say the least. Part of the Hindenburg Line assaulted required the BEF having to cross a wide strip of water, the St Quentin Canal, and then scale steep banks up to 60ft high. The storming of the Hindenburg Line was a stunning feat of arms, and the 46th Division's use of boats, floating piers and life jackets from Cross

IN HOT WATER

THE KAISER:- "Boo Hoo! It's too hot!"
MARSHAL FOCH:- "There's more coming. I'm not going to stop until you're properly cleaned up."

Cartoon published following British attack at Amiens, August 1918.

Channel ferries to get across the canal was inspirational. This breach in the Hindenburg Line was followed by further ruptures, and by early October the Line was broken. How the fall of the Hindenburg Line impacted upon German morale is not hard to judge, for if the Allies could break this supposedly impregnable defence, then what would stop them?

Next to fall was Cambrai, followed by serious inroads being made in Flanders. Everywhere the Germans were in full retreat and Ludendorff came under increasing pressure, so by October the only solution was to call for an armistice.

The first two weeks of the Allied Offensive were kind to the men from the St Neots area, for although some were wounded, none were killed, and it was not until 21 August that the first fatality occurred. In those first days, Privates Harry Page of St Neots and Harry Richardson of Eynesbury were both wounded, with Harry Richardson's injury so bad that his left leg was amputated. Also wounded from Eaton Socon was Private Samuel Thornton, who had been at the front for four years and had won the MM and Bar, and Private Arthur Frost, who was hit by shrapnel and was also suffering from pneumonia.

On 21 August, the 1st Bedfords attacked at 4.45 a.m. as the BEF sought to recapture Albert and drive the enemy back towards Bapaume. They met with little opposition in capturing their objective and casualties were light, with just forty-seven men being killed or wounded, but sadly Private Eric Riseley was among the dead. His parents ran a draper's business from Avenue Road and Eric had worked with his father, Frederick, before joining the Hunts Cyclists in June 1915. He had gone overseas with the 1st Bedfords and served with them until he was killed. Private R.R. Lambert wrote to Frederick Riseley: 'Eric was struck on the side of the head by a fragment of gas shell and killed instantaneously, happily suffering no pain.' Twenty-six-year-old Eric Riseley was buried and rests today in Sailly-au-Bois Military Cemetery.

On the same day and as part of the same assault, the 4th Bedfords attacked in foggy conditions and, supported by tanks, they overran the enemy's front line. In doing so, nineteen-year-old Lance Corporal Bernard Brown, an only son from Eynesbury, was killed. His parents, Charles and Esther, received a letter from Captain Winters of the Bedfords telling them that his death was instantaneous and painless, but often this was a euphemism given to spare families details of a gruesome death. What is certain is that his body was lost on the battlefield and today he is commemorated on the Vis-en-Artois Memorial near Arras.

Twenty-four hours later, another local man was killed in the fight to retake Albert. Twenty-six-year-old Ernest George Baxter of the 4th Middlesex was the youngest son of James Baxter, landlord of the Rose and Crown in St Neots. He had enlisted in March 1916, and after training had gone overseas. By 1918 he had been wounded three times and gassed once before he was killed on 22 August. Once again, death was described as being instantaneous in the letter his father received from the battalion chaplain who buried him. Today he rests in Serre Road No. 2 Cemetery on the Somme.

The 1st Hertfordshire Battalion was also engaged in the fight to retake Albert and on the 23rd, the day that Albert returned to Allied hands, they lost twenty-six killed and 140 wounded. Private John Mason of Eaton Socon was wounded and the following day he died of these wounds, bringing to an end his part in the war that had begun way back in August 1914 when he was called up as a Territorial with the 5th Bedfords. He had fought and been wounded at Gallipoli, and then gone to the Western Front after being transferred to the 1st Hertfords, fighting on the Somme, at Ypres, Arras and Cambrai before he fell close to Albert. He was buried and rests in Bagneux Military Cemetery.

After the capture of Albert, the BEF turned its attention to Bapaume, the objective just over two years earlier on the first day of the Somme, and this time it fell into Allied hands when the 17th Division captured it on 27 August. However, the Germans remained a fierce adversary; their retreat was methodical and everything that the BEF had come to expect over four years of fighting, as the 6th Dorsets found when they attacked at Flers on the Bapaume Road on

Sunday 25th. In their ranks was another Eaton Socon man who had fought at Gallipoli with the 5th Bedfords and who again had moved to another regiment, this time after recovering from dysentery. Indeed, Private Fred Markham was so badly affected that he had been told by doctors that he 'must not do any hard work' and it seemed as if his military career was over. However, he recovered and was sent to the Western Front, where he was killed in action on the 25th. In early September his parents, Fred and Mary, heard that he was dead when they received a letter from the battalion's padre, and in October another missive gave further information that his body had been found on the battlefield and had been buried. The second letter from a senior chaplain also told them that a ring had been taken from Fred Markham's body and posted home as 'it would be valued by his next of kin'. Fred Markham was laid to rest in AIF Burial Ground at Flers.

As the BEF moved forward, casualties increased; one of those wounded in early September was Private William Bartlett of St Neots, about whom the early news was that doctors were unable to save his leg and it would have to be amputated. Two weeks later that was changed, for the surgeons had been able to save his limb. Then information reached the Eaton Ford that Private Walter Coleman had died on 3 September after a shell fell among the Lewis gun team he was serving with. Walter Coleman was thirty-nine years old and his mother still resided in Eaton Ford, although he was living in Barnet at the start of the war.

More unwelcome news reached Duloe in the first week of September when Grace Payne heard that her thirty-year-old husband, Job, had died of wounds at Heilly Station Casualty Clearing Station on the Somme, three years after his brother Charlie had died at Ypres. Job Payne had fought in Palestine at Gaza with the 15th Suffolks, a Yeomanry Territorial Battalion, before going with them to France, and, as they advanced on the Somme, he was badly wounded on 2 September. Grace Payne heard from one of the Sisters at Heilly that 'he had very severe wounds of the right and left leg, also shell wound of back. He passed peacefully away, free from pain' at 9.20 a.m. on 3 September. Grace Payne was left with four children to raise, the youngest of whom, Albert Edward, was never seen by his father, for he was born whilst Job was in France. Many years later Albert made the pilgrimage that so many make today to the battlefields and cemeteries of the Western Front, and stood at his father's grave at Heilly Station together with his son, Job's grandson, David.

Just as Job Payne left a young son that he had never seen, the same was almost true for Ben Hartop of Eaton Socon, whose son Edward was just sixteen months old. Ben Hartop was able to see his son when back in Blighty for six months from November 1917, recovering from a wound that had seen him lose a thumb. After being conscripted in January 1917, he joined the 1st Essex Battalion with whom he was wounded in October of that year. The loss of a thumb did not deter him, for he returned to the fray in April 1918, acting as a stretcher bearer for his battalion and winning the Military Medal in August. On 10 September, with the enemy in retreat, the BEF were preparing the attack that would break the Hindenburg Line, and at Havrincourt they attacked a strongly-defended German position. As the 1st Essex advanced they came under enemy fire and Private Ben Hartop was badly wounded in his back, with shrapnel penetrating as far as his spine. His wife, Florence, received two letters from one of the Sisters treating him at a field hospital; the first one told how he had been wounded and that there was little hope, although he was not in pain, probably because he was paralysed by the spinal wound or because he had been given morphine. The second letter told that he had died on the following evening, conscious to the end and not in pain. The Sister also sent Florence Hartop a lock of her husband's hair. Ben Hartop was buried in Euston Road Cemetery on the Somme and sadly his son, Edward Ben, followed in his father's footsteps when he was killed on 11 November 1944 as the Allies drove the Germans from Italy.

On 24 September, thirty-eight-year-old Company Sergeant Major George Oakley died when struck by enemy machine-gun fire as the 2nd Royal Sussex advanced towards the St

Private Job Payne,
standing in centre.

Quentin Canal, that formidable bastion of the Hindenburg Line. George Oakley was a Hastings man who had married Louisa Cousins of Eaton Socon; Louisa was no stranger to the tragedy of the Great War herself, having already lost two brothers, Arthur and Frank. Now she was widowed. George Oakley was buried in Bellicourt British Cemetery.

Other local families were perhaps more fortunate. The Day family of Eaton Socon received confirmation that their son Harry was a POW, but this was tempered by news that another son, stretcher bearer George, had received severe bullet wounds to his arm and leg. Also wounded but alive was Private Arthur George of Eynesbury who had a bullet go through his nose, while Lieutenant Barlow Smythe was in hospital in Egypt, suffering from dysentery. Charlie Quince, a Lance Corporal with the Royal Fusiliers, was wounded in the mouth, whilst Samuel Potter of the Queens received his third wound in the last two years, and although this one was in the chest, he recovered. Both men were from Eaton Socon.

The Gilbert family of Eynesbury had sons Fred of the Grenadier Guards hospitalised in France, Herbert of the RFA injured when he was thrown from his horse and Archie of the Bedfords wounded. Another Eynesbury man wounded was Privates Alfred Childs. Corporal Leslie Gayton, the son of the St Neots station master, was badly gassed, just some months after winning the Military Medal.

As September drew to a close with the Hindenburg Line broken, the Allies continued their remorseless advance. On 28 September the British, French and Belgians attacked at Ypres, pushing the enemy back from the ridges surrounding the town for the next five days. Two local men died and others were wounded. Two days before the Allies attacked, twenty-nine-year-old Harry Harris, who had served right through from 1914 with the Royal Garrison Artillery, was wounded in one of the daily artillery duels, dying of wounds at Duhallow Advanced Dressing Station. On 29 September, twenty-two-year-old Private Albert 'Buller' Thody of the 10th Queens was badly wounded as they attacked close to the river Lys and gained all of their objectives. On the next day he died of those wounds and was buried in Lijssenthoek Military Cemetery. Local wounded included Private George Bettles, now with the Lancashire Fusiliers, who was hit in the left hip while working as a stretcher bearer, and Sergeant Fred Simons of the

Private Albert Thody before
he enlisted.

Liverpool Regiment, who was hit
by enemy bullets in the right knee
and left thigh. Both were from
Eaton Ford.

Away from the Western Front,
on 2 October the Thornhill family
of Cross Hall Lodge lost a second
son when John, a lieutenant colonel
with the Seaforth Highlanders, died.
Thirty-eight-year-old John Evelyn
Thornhill was the elder brother of
George, who was killed near Ypres
in 1914. He had been a professional
soldier before the war, having
attended Sandhurst and fought
during the Boer War. He served on
the Western Front from 1915 but
was invalided home in the summer
of 1916 and then acted as one of the
staff officers for Sir John French, the
newly-appointed Commander-in-
Chief, Home Forces. In 1918 he was
appointed General Staff Officer for the Egyptian Expeditionary Force, and whilst travelling
out was taken ill en route and admitted to hospital in Gibraltar, where he died and was buried.

In France and Flanders casualties mounted as the advance to victory continued. Privates
Albert Franklin and William Chapman, and Trooper John Allen, all from Eynesbury, were
wounded and Private George Bettles of Eaton Socon was gassed. Lieutenant John McNish of
St Neots was missing but was later confirmed as being a POW, as was Private Stanley Emery
of Eynesbury. Towards the end of October it was learned that John McNish had been captured
whilst leading a patrol that had been surrounded by the Germans. Meanwhile, fellow officer
and St Neotian Lieutenant Tom Eayrs was badly wounded when his right leg was fractured
by gunshot; to compound matters, he lay out for seven hours before being found and treated.
Sapper Alf Cole of Cambridge Street, who had served four years and had won the MM earlier
in the war, was badly wounded, losing two fingers and a thumb from his left hand, being
severely bruised on the right hand and having pieces of shrapnel in his left eye. Sergeant James
Coppock of Huntingdon Street was wounded for the third time and was brought home to
hospital in Bristol.

On 9 October, the 6th Queens attacked near Noyelles, north of Arras, at 6 p.m. and came
under enemy machine-gun fire that wounded fifteen and killed four, amongst whom was
twenty-one-year-old Arthur Baldock of St Neots. Arthur Baldock was a Territorial before the
war and had joined up in 1914. Two years later he was sent overseas with the 6th Queens and
fought on the Somme, at Arras, Ypres and Cambrai. He had come through these, but was killed
within sight of the end of the conflict. He was buried in Sucrerie Cemetery close to Arras.

Meanwhile St Neots, like towns and cities throughout Britain, was in the grip of the Spanish
flu pandemic. Virtually every house had one person suffering, but some had as many as three or
four. Doctors and nurses were seriously overworked and a number of people had already died,
including a twenty-one-year-old who was thousands of miles away from his own home. Ronald

Lieutenant-Colonel John Thornhill.

Rankin, a sergeant with the 37th Australian Infantry, had a fortnight's leave, so he came to St Neots with his friend Sergeant Arthur Harding. In June he had been gassed and wounded in both legs and he accepted the invitation to complete his recuperation in St Neots, where Arthur Harding had relatives. Shortly after they arrived, Ronald Rankin started to show signs of La Grippe, passing away on 21 October. The doctor who treated him was of the opinion that Ronald Rankin might have recovered if it had not been for the effects of having been gassed. He was buried in St Neots Cemetery with full military honours.

Just under two weeks later, Eunice Howell, of the Women's Royal Air Force, also died of flu when she came to St Neots to nurse her sister who was suffering from the illness. Eunice Howell was also buried in St Neots Cemetery. A third burial took place in the cemetery at the start of November, when Reginald Wilson was interred with full military honours. Private Wilson had died following an operation at Whipps Cross Hospital in Leytonstone on 28 October, a year after he had been seriously wounded at Passchendaele. Reginald Wilson had joined up in March 1916 and had gone over to France six months later, fighting on the Somme, at Arras and Messines before being wounded at Ypres. He was invalided back to Blighty and had then been posted to the newly-formed RAF after he was deemed fit to return to duty, serving with No. 2 Balloon Section. However, his wound continued to trouble him and the operation to try and resolve it did not succeed, so this twenty-one-year-old son of Frederick and Susan Wilson died.

By 23 October, the BEF had pushed the Germans almost as far back as when they had first encountered them in 1914, and at Beaurain in Northern France the 1st Bedfords kept up the pressure when they attacked at 3.20 a.m. They ran into enemy machine-gun fire which held them up for a while, but succeeded in capturing Beaurain village, although in doing so they lost sixteen killed and 112 wounded. Twenty-five-year-old Lance Sergeant George Bellamy was one of those killed, four years after he had enlisted at a recruiting rally in St Neots with his two brothers; they would both survive. George was buried in Amerval Communal Cemetery.

By the end of the month, two more local men were added to the list of those who would never return home. On 30 October, nineteen-year-old Harry Murkett of the 8th Lancashire Fusiliers died of influenza at the Canadian Stationary Hospital. Harry Murkett had worked as a painter before he was conscripted, and lived with his parents, Harry and Elizabeth, in King's Lane, St Neots. After being called up in 1917, he fought during the Kaiser's Battle and up to the later stages of the 100 Days. In November, a letter from Chaplain Pickup told that: 'Pte Murkett contracted influenza in a very serious form and although everything possible was done for him by doctors and nurses it was impossible to save him.' Harry Murkett was buried in Terlincthun British Cemetery at Boulogne.

On the following day, Private William Coppock, 'Z' Company, 18th Lancashire Fusiliers died of wounds in Flanders. The battalion was pursuing the retreating Germans east of Ypres when nineteen-year-old William Coppock was badly wounded, being hit by enemy bullets just over a year after he had been drafted to the front. He had fought during the later stages of 3rd Ypres, throughout 1918, and now he became the only one of the serving Coppock brothers to be killed: Albert, Arthur, James and Robert all survived.

By the beginning of November, moves to try to bring the war to an end began when a German delegation crossed the front line, meeting with the Allies at Compiègne on the 8th, and discussions began that led to the Armistice. Meanwhile, fighting continued and news of more local casualties reached St Neots. Private Arthur Wilson of the Machine Gun Corps had shrapnel wounds in his legs, whilst Private George Brittain of Eaton Socon was badly wounded in the left thigh. Not wounded, but in hospital, was Private Henry Potter who had fought with distinction at the storming of the Hindenburg Line but who now had trench fever. Not so fortunate was nineteen-year-old Private George Howe of Eynesbury, the last local man to die during the Great War, when he succumbed to the awful wounds he had suffered near Cambrai. He was conscripted in May 1918 and had been overseas since June with the 1st Northants when he was hit in the left shoulder, lung and right leg. He died in hospital on 6 November at Le Havre and was buried in Ste Marie Cemetery. On Sunday, the day before the Armistice, his parents, Arthur and Annie, heard at their Luke Street home that they had lost a second son after the death of Jack in 1916. Perhaps it was some consolation to them that another son, Fred, was with George at his bedside when he died.

On the very next day, at the eleventh hour of the eleventh day of the eleventh month, the guns fell silent. The Great War was over.

EPILOGUE

News of the Armistice reached St Neots at around the same time that the guns fell silent, and the people of the town and surrounding villages initially found it hard to believe. Then, when the realisation dawned, they celebrated; by the evening, the streets were full of people rejoicing, although their joy was tempered by the fact that many men would not be returning. Thanksgiving services were arranged, the bells of the churches in Eynesbury and Eaton Socon were rung and people's thoughts turned to the idea of commemorating the fallen with local war memorials.

During December, POWs began to return to the town. Fred Barringer told of receiving only one letter and parcel in eight months of captivity, while Len Cade wanted to be placed in charge of German POWs to get his own back! Meanwhile, Percy Reynolds, Alfred Huckle, William Usher, George Townsend, Harry Day, Amos Hall, Thomas Thody and Sidney Fisher all returned to their families in the first week of December. Thomas Thody had lost around two and a half stone and George Townsend three stone during seven months of captivity. Many of these returning POWs told of poor treatment and dreadful food, saying that it was only parcels from home that kept them going.

The unveiling of Eaton Socon War Memorial in 1921.

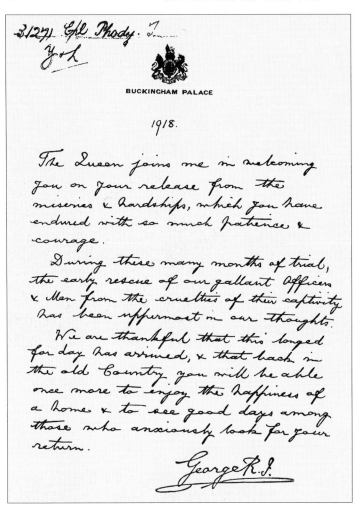

Letter from King George V to Corporal Tom Thody after his release as a POW.

However, the Great War was not yet done with St Neots, Eynesbury and Eaton Socon, for although the fighting had ended, men still died before they were able to return home, mainly as a result of influenza. On 19 January 1919, Private Alfred Walton died at home aged twenty, and then in February two more men died from Spanish flu. Private Sydney Bradshaw had survived the war and was now in 'Civvy Street' when he collapsed in London while finalising his release from the army. This thirty-two-year-old was taken to Eudell Street Military Hospital but died on 2 February of pneumonia and flu. Just over three weeks later, Second Lieutenant William Leonard Knight died of flu while still in France, aged just twenty-three.

Two years later, two more men died; both had Eaton Socon connections and both were buried in the churchyard there. Major Claude Johnson of the Royal Garrison Artillery had served in India during the war. He came home in 1920 and died of pneumonia on 21 March 1921, aged forty-two. Arthur Barnes had fought with the Warwicks on the Somme, but he contracted trench fever and was discharged in 1917. For the next five years he was treated in a number of hospitals, before dying on 11 June 1922, aged twenty-nine.

The thoughts that local people had in November 1918 regarding a lasting memorial to all of the men killed during the Great War became reality in the 1920s, and Eaton Socon, Eynesbury and St Neots all saw memorials unveiled and dedicated. Those memorials remain the focus of Remembrance today on the closest Sunday to Armistice Day, and hopefully the men whose names are inscribed on the memorials will continue to be honoured and 'Not Forgotten'.

Eaton Socon War Memorial photographed in the 1920s.

Eaton Socon War Memorial in 1921 after the unveiling, with all of the wreaths around.

St Neots War Memorial.

Eynesbury War Memorial Names.

INDEX

BATTLES